HarperCollins books may be purchased for educational, business, or sales promotional use. For information, please write: Special Markets Department, HarperCollins Publishers, 10 East 53rd Street, New York, NY 10022.

Produced for HarperCollins by:

HYDRA PUBLISHING
129 MAIN STREET
IRVINGTON, NY 10533
WWW.HYLASPUBLISHING.COM

FIRST EDITION

Library of Congress Cataloging-in-Publication Data has been applied for.

ISBN-10: 0-06-089114-9
ISBN-13: 978-0-06-089114-5

06 07 08 09 10   QW   10 9 8 7 6 5 4 3 2 1

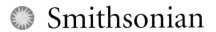

Smithsonian

Q&A

THE ULTIMATE QUESTION
AND ANSWER BOOK

BIRDS

Christina Wilsdon

Collins

An Imprint of HarperCollinsPublishers

BIRDS

Contents

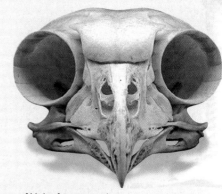

The eyes of birds of prey are set on either side of the head, facing forward, as seen in an owl's skull.

Subdued feather colors, mainly browns, black, and white, are common to many birds of prey, such as the bald eagle.

The sight of soft blue eggs snugly sheltered in their nest is a sure sign of spring.

The sure, automatic grip of a sleeping parrot's feet prevents it from falling from its perch.

THE WONDER AND DIVERSITY OF BIRDS

In June 1833, off the coast of Nova Scotia, the famous avian artist John James Audubon caught his first sight of arctic terns flashing across the sky. Inspired, he immortalized the observation in his journal. "Light as a sylph, the Arctic Tern dances through the air above and around you," he wrote. "The graces, one might imagine, had taught it to perform those beautiful gambols which you see it display."

Although Audubon had seen and recorded hundreds of species of birds by then, they still had the power to startle, even dazzle him with their beauty and their mastery of the air.

Today we share the earth with about 9,600 species of birds. The diversity of these fellow creatures is astonishing: The class Aves includes bee-sized hummingbirds, as well as seven-foot-tall ostriches; birds that have given up flight to specialize in running, diving, and swimming, as well as birds that eat, drink, sleep, and mate on the wing; finches and sparrows garbed in earth tones that elude even experienced birders, as well as birds such as peacocks whose brilliant colors render them iconic.

Left: A flock of white pelicans search pondside for food.

Below: The eggs of the ostrich, the world's largest bird, are also the largest of all eggs, weighing about three pounds. The contents of one ostrich egg are equivalent to two dozen chicken eggs.

This splendid array of bird life perches on one of the same branches of the family tree that humans do. Like us, birds are vertebrates, animals with backbones. Unlike fish, reptiles, and amphibians, however, they are warm-blooded, as mammals are. Unlike mammals, they do not grow hair, not even the tiniest eyelash. When an African ground hornbill bats its eyes, the long lashes curling from its eyelids are modified versions of that uniquely avian invention, the feather. All birds have feathers, which insulate them and enable them to fly.

Flying has allowed birds to make their home in nearly every habitat on every continent, as well as on the vast stretches of ocean between; they live in the heat of deserts and in the bitter chill of Antarctica. Some spend most of their lives soaring over the seas, so at home in their element that they may return to land only to lay eggs.

Over millions of years, as birds moved into habitats around the world, they adapted to their environments—some to a life of wading or swimming, others to filling niches in a tropical rain forest, a woodland, or a coniferous forest. They specialized in preying on mammals, feeding on insects, sipping nectar, or crushing seeds.

The birds that currently share the planet with us continue this process of adaptation and change. Though many species follow in the wing beats of

Even the eyelashes of ground hornbills are really modified feathers.

their ancestors, migrating along ancient pathways, flying achingly long journeys over fields and forests, coastlines and mountains, other species are in the process of blazing new routes. Species continue to move into untried areas, sticking their claws in the water, so to speak, to see if the habitat feels right. If moving in fails, individuals will perish. If the move succeeds, the species expands its range.

Today, however, human activity presses many environmental changes upon birds, and these changes often happen with great suddenness. A change may take the form of an invasive species being released, as in Hawaii, where human colonizers brought pigs, rats, plants, and insects that devastated the islands' bird life and continue to threaten remaining native species. Frequently, changes involve complete alterations of habitats. Wetlands are drained for building and farming. Land is paved. Small farms with their many microhabitats for wildlife give way to huge farms that, for birds, are virtual "green deserts." Waterways are dammed and coastlines developed, shrinking feeding areas for birds and forcing migratory species to fly farther to find rest stops and congregate more tightly once there. Fragmentation of forests has allowed predators and nest parasites, such as cowbirds, to gain access more easily to woodland birds' nests. Conflict between the needs of birds and the desires of humans,

Peregrine falcons have made a remarkable comeback in the wild.

combined with outright overhunting, pesticides, and pollutants, has caused the extinction of some species and threatened others. The dodo, the passenger pigeon, the Carolina parakeet, and many beautiful Hawaiian honeycreepers are among the intriguing animals that have disappeared. The threatened ones currently go about their business, unaware that their species may be living on borrowed time.

And yet, interwoven with the disheartening accounts of disastrous interactions between humans and birds are stories of successes and tidings of joy, tales that bring hope, like the sound of the first birdsong on a cold, gray, late-winter day.

Perhaps one of the best known avian success stories is that of the peregrine falcon. In the 1950s and 1960s, North America's peregrine population plunged; by the mid-1960s, none were to be found in the eastern United States. The decline was attributed to DDT and other pesticides. Adult birds were dying because their prey was laced with pesticides. Pesticide contamination may also have caused eggshell thinning. The eggs peregrines laid broke, their shells too thin to bear the weight of an incubating bird. Peregrines, found on every continent except Antarctica, were suddenly in danger of slipping away.

An unprecedented response involving a program of captive breeding and release of birds, along with laws banning DDT, prevented this swiftest of raptors from becoming extinct. The slim slate-and-cream-colored birds have made a remarkable comeback and in some places exist in even greater numbers than they did before their brush with extinction. Pairs of birds can even be found in some cities, nesting on window ledges of skyscrapers and stooping to catch pigeons.

The existence of birds that have managed to eke out a living in the midst of human activity may sometimes inspire a false sense of security, an impression that the slide has been securely blocked and that all birds' situations must therefore be improving. But the success of these species can also be read as an ode to the persistence and adaptability of birds. Given a little help, some consideration, and a bit of elbow room, birds persevere in the struggle

to survive and to produce young. In making room for the animals that we've long considered our "feathered friends," we simultaneously cultivate a world conducive to our own physical and mental health—and to the survival of our own descendants.

For birds are everywhere humans are; our lives are inextricably bound up with theirs. Like the proverbial canary in the coal mine, they are reliable indicators of the health of the environment. The loss of a species in a particular habitat can signal the presence there of toxins or other pollutants, or the advancing march of an invasive exotic species that may also choke out or harm other living things.

Although we watch birds in this scientific way, we also watch them simply for their sheer beauty. As birdwatcher and writer Simon Barnes notes, birds live, like us, in a world of color, sight, and sound quite different from the scent-based world of other mammals. "We humans," he writes, "can thrill to the song of a nightingale almost as if we were nightingales ourselves."

What the birds make of us is another matter. Certainly many regard us warily, knowing we can be predators, while others consider us with bright eyes, watching us to see if we will leave that picnic basket unguarded on the beach, or if we will kick up some tasty insects with our earthbound feet as we shuffle across a field with our eyes gazing skyward in search of birds.

Many birds are adaptable to changes in their environments, such as the blue tit that has devised ways to exploit humans for food.

CHAPTER 1

THE BIRD'S BODY

If asked to draw a bird, most people will quickly produce a two-legged creature with wings and a beak, the contours of its body indicated by a covering of feathers. These features, shared by all birds, exhibit a stunning variety shaped over eons as birds adapted themselves to life in nearly all of Earth's habitats.

The basic bird that springs to mind is one that can fly. Inside and out, birds are a collection of adaptations that enable them to take to the air and sustain powered flight. The skeleton is strong but light, with arm and hand bones rearranged to form wings and large muscles dedicated to flapping them. A highly efficient respiratory system provides fuel. Bills are devoid of weighty teeth. Feathers—light but strong—are unique to birds and serve many functions, from insulating the bird to advertising its species. Flightless birds retain many of the features of their airborne kin. The rhea, with its small wings and shaggy feathers, would still be identified by even a very young child as a bird. From its beak (long or short) to its toes (which may number two, three, or four), a bird's body is a celebration of form following function.

Above: A greater rhea strides across a Brazilian grassland, eating leaves and snapping up insects. If pursued, the rhea runs a zigzag course, alternately raising and lowering its wings to help it balance.

Left: An African fish-eagle displays the traits common to all birds—feathers, beak, and a pair of legs with scaly skin revealed—as well as the powerful claws that mark it as a bird of prey.

Bones and Muscles

Q: Are birds' bones hollow?

A: The rigors of flight demand that a bird's skeleton be rigid and strong in order to support its muscles without adding excessive weight to its frame. Several adaptations enable the skeleton to meet this twofold demand.

First and foremost, the bones themselves are hollow, making them light, with larger ones strengthened internally by struts. The air-filled spaces inside the bones are linked to the bird's lungs and air sacs and function as part of its respiratory system, a feature known as pneumatization.

Another adaptation, the fusing of various bones, increases strength and rigidity without adding weight. This fusion is most noticeable in the bird's backbone, in which a section between the rib cage and tailbones has fused so completely as to be entirely lacking in individual vertebrae.

Many species, however, exhibit variations on this skeletal theme. Birds that dive deeply in pursuit of prey, such as loons, have skeletons with less pneumatization. Penguins, which cannot fly, have solid bones. In these species, dense bones add weight that is a useful aid to diving. Flightless land birds known as ratites, such as ostriches and rheas, also have solid bones.

Q: Why do most birds have keels and wishbones?

A: The V-shaped structure in a bird's chest, known to anyone who has ever roasted a chicken as the wishbone, is a bird's version of collarbones. This bone, scientifically known as the furcula, is made up of two smaller bones, called clavicles, fused together. Each clavicle is connected to a pair of thick, strong bones called coracoids (which survive only as knobs on mammalian shoulder blades). The coracoids, in turn, are linked at their upper ends to the bird's shoulder blades, or scapulas. Where they meet, they form a pocket into which the upper bone of each wing fits. Together, furcula and coracoids work as struts, bracing the wings when they are held out in flight.

Collectively, the furcula, coracoids, and scapulas form the pectoral girdle, a sturdy, rigid structure that keeps the bird's chest cavity from caving in as it beats the air with its wings. It is also flexible: the furcula spreads wide as the wings move down, then springs back together on the upstroke. Together with the rising and falling of the bird's breastbone, or sternum,

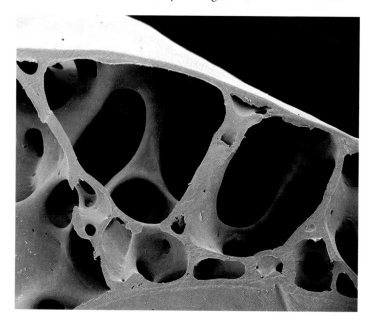

A section of bone from a falcon's skull reveals the system of struts and air spaces that give a bird's larger bones both strength and lightness. Both are adaptations for flying, providing a rigid structure without adding weight to encumber the bird.

this flexibility may help pump air through the bird's extensive respiratory system, giving it an extra boost during flight.

The sternum itself forms the base for another skeletal structure readily visible in a chicken carcass: the plowlike extension called the keel. This large slab of bone is the point of attachment for the large, powerful flight muscles. The size of the keel often provides a clue to a bird's flying power. Hummingbirds, the helicopters of the avian world, have proportionally the largest keel of all birds.

Wishbones and keels, however, are not features shared by all birds. Many small parakeets lack wishbones, retaining only vestiges of clavicles, and some parrots do not even have these; it is thought that this is an adaptation that allows them to clamber more freely about in trees, and maintain their balance. Ostriches, emus, cassowaries, rheas, and kiwis—the flightless ratites—lack both a wishbone and a keel.

Q: How do birds perch and sleep without falling?

A: A bird's ability to grasp a branch with its toes is due to the action of tendons in its leg that are pulled tight when a bird crouches on a perch. The tendons are attached to muscles above the bird's heel—the joint that appears to us as a "backward-bending knee" in the portion of the leg not covered by feathers. These flexor tendons, as they are called, run down the backs of the legs and to the tips of the toes. When the bird sits, the tendons pull on the toes and close them tightly, like a fist. This automatic grip is strong enough to allow the bird to sleep while perching. The same mechanism is at work when a raptor seizes an animal, serving to clench the talons and pierce the prey on impact.

Above: A scarlet macaw dozes peacefully, its feet securely clasped around a branch. It is in no danger of falling thanks to the built-in gripping mechanism in its legs, which automatically clenches the toes when the bird settles on a perch.

Left: A diagram of a typical bird skeleton. The fusion of bones in the spine and pelvis adds strength without extra weight.

Bird Skeleton

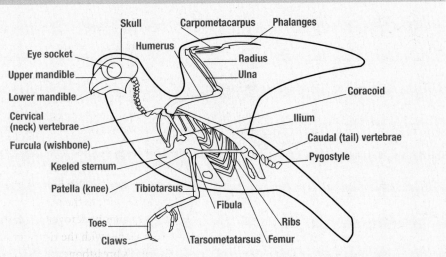

- Skull
- Carpometacarpus
- Phalanges
- Eye socket
- Humerus
- Upper mandible
- Radius
- Lower mandible
- Ulna
- Cervical (neck) vertebrae
- Coracoid
- Furcula (wishbone)
- Ilium
- Keeled sternum
- Caudal (tail) vertebrae
- Patella (knee)
- Pygostyle
- Tibiotarsus
- Toes
- Fibula
- Claws
- Ribs
- Tarsometatarsus
- Femur

The Respiratory System

Q: How does the respiratory system of a bird work?

A: A bird's lungs, like ours, serve as a site for gas exchange, where oxygen is absorbed into the bloodstream and carbon dioxide is released from it. Birds need oxygen, just as we do, to fuel chemical reactions that produce energy. But the structures associated with this gas exchange are strikingly different.

A mammal inhales by contracting muscles in its rib cage and a sheet of muscle in its chest called the diaphragm. A bird lacks a diaphragm, but likewise inhales by contracting muscles in its chest cavity. In a mammal, an indrawn breath goes through a two-step respiratory cycle. The oxygen-rich air enters the lungs, where gas exchange takes place. The oxygen is taken up by the bloodstream. Then the mammal exhales, which gets rid of carbon dioxide, before taking its next breath. It is an in-out system.

In a bird, respiration creates a continuous flow of air through its system instead of an in-out rhythm. A single respiratory cycle in a bird involves two breaths, not one, and four steps instead of just two. It includes not only the lungs but also air sacs located in the bird's chest and abdomen. These air sacs are linked to the many air spaces that run through a bird's skeleton and function as highly efficient bellows to keep air flowing through the respiratory system. First, a breath of air enters the bird's trachea and travels through its main

A continuous flow of fresh air circulates through a bird's respiratory system due to a unique array of bronchial tubes and air sacs that permeate its body and some of its bones. The vessels in the lungs, where gas exchange takes place, are thus constantly bathed in oxygen.

Bird Respiratory System

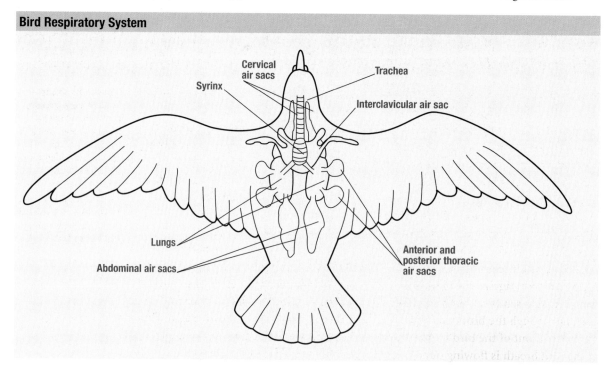

Cervical air sacs

Trachea

Syrinx

Interclavicular air sac

Lungs

Anterior and posterior thoracic air sacs

Abdominal air sacs

bronchial tube in its lungs into the hindmost abdominal air sacs. Then the bird exhales—but exhaling does not send this breath out of its body just yet. Instead, the air sacs contract and push the air into tubes leading back into the lungs.

Inside the lungs, gas exchange occurs in a network of air tubes and tiny blood vessels. This air then flows into the air sacs in the bird's chest while the bird inhales its next breath of air. Finally, the bird exhales again and the air sacs contract. This sends the now-stale air back up through the bronchus and trachea and out of the bird's body—even as the next breath is flowing out of the

abdominal air sacs and into its lungs. This unique system enables a bird to wring every bit of oxygen from a breath of air in a highly efficient way. Because air is continually flowing through the lungs, the blood is being continually replenished with oxygen without the brief downtime caused by a less efficient "breathe in, breathe out" respiratory system.

A bird's respiratory system not only allows it to sustain high-energy functions such as flight but also serves as an interior cooling system. Muscles produce heat as they flap, and the air flowing through the air sacs helps remove excess heat and stabilize the bird's body temperature.

Flight, as demonstrated by these white pelicans, is a taxing activity that requires a great deal of energy. The bird's respiratory system has adapted to meet the demands of flight. Even the act of flapping, and the forces it exerts on the bird's thorax and abdomen, assists in maintaining airflow.

Eating and Excreting

Q: What is the function of the crop?

A: Eating poses a conundrum for birds: food provides energy, yet a bird in flight can't afford to tote excess weight in the form of body fat or a full belly. As a result, birds have evolved a highly efficient digestive system that processes food quickly as well as adaptations for storing and transporting food.

A bird's crop may be as simple as a bulge in the esophagus that is useful for transporting food to chicks or as elaborate as that of the hoatzin, which functions as a fermentation chamber for the tough leaves it ingests. A hoatzin's full crop bulges prominently and can make flying awkward.

One adaptation that many birds possess is a crop—a pocket that protrudes from the esophagus. Chickens, turkeys, quail, pheasants, pigeons, and doves all have well-developed crops. These birds eat seed and grain, nutritious foods that are time-consuming to digest. By storing food in their crops, they can feed quickly and prodigiously while out in the open, and then retire to a place of safety to digest it later. The crop can hold a remarkable amount of food. Wild turkeys, for example, have been found carrying up to a pound of seeds and nuts in their crops. A very large and muscular crop is found in the hoatzin, a leaf-eating bird of South American tropical forests. The crop grinds the tough, thick leaves while bacteria start digesting them, working in a manner similar to a cow's rumen.

In many species, the esophagus is elastic enough to function as a crop when the bird needs to store or carry food. A cormorant, for example, can carry a fish back to its young in its esophagus.

The crops of pigeons and doves perform the most remarkable function of all: They produce "crop milk," a thick, nutritious fluid that is fed to nestlings.

Q: What is a gizzard?

A: The gizzard is the second digestive adaptation found in most birds. The gizzard has thick, muscular walls and a strong, rough lining. Its job is to crush food much in the way food is ground inside the mouths of toothed animals. This kind of gizzard exists in many plant- and seed-eating birds, such as turkeys, ducks, and finches, as well as in shorebirds. These birds may also swallow sand, gravel, and other grit to further grind their meals. Their powerful gizzards can crush items as hard as whole nuts and mussel shells.

Hawks, owls, and many insect-eating songbirds have thinner gizzards for collecting indigestible parts of their prey, such as bones, exoskeletons, and claws. These items wad together to form a pellet, which is later coughed up.

Turkeys, chickens, quail, and pheasants feed heavily on seeds, grains, and nuts and store them in their crops. Later, the foods are ground up in the strong-walled gizzard with the help of ingested grit.

Q: Can birds store food as fat?

A: Although keeping weight down is important for flight, birds do store some food as fat. A bird preparing for a long migration may stuff itself until it is carrying 30 to 50 percent of its body weight as fat. It is quickly burned off by the rigors of flight. A study of migrating blackpoll warblers found that the birds lost about half of their body weight during migration.

Birds also store some body fat to survive cold weather. Penguins have a thick layer of body fat. Small songbirds that spend winter in cold regions need enough fat to survive long winter nights, when they may lose up to 10 percent of their body weight by morning.

Q: Do birds produce urine?

A: Birds, with the exception of the ostrich, do not have bladders; they do, however, produce urine.

A bird's body produces uric acid, a highly concentrated waste that does not require transport by a large quantity of water (unlike the urea produced by a mammal's excretory system, which does require a great deal of water to flush from the body). Any water involved in this process is reabsorbed into the bird's body in the intestines. At the end of the intestine, the waste enters the cloaca, where it mixes with feces and is then excreted as a white paste out the bird's vent.

Although most birds carry little body fat that would weigh them down during flight, penguins, such as this rockhopper, store a thick layer that helps protect them from the frigid temperatures of their Antarctic habitat.

Birds as Warm-Blooded Animals

Q: **How do birds control body temperature?**

A: A bird is warm-blooded, just as mammals are. Typical bird body temperatures range from 99.9°F (37.7°C) to 112.3°F (44.6°C) depending on the species. As in other animals, activity as well as external conditions can raise or lower a bird's body temperature.

Birds employ a variety of behaviors to maintain a constant temperature. On cold days, for example, a bird may tuck up one of its legs or find a sheltered spot. Its metabolism can also kick into high gear to create greater body heat, and shivering also raises its temperature. Some species, such as bluebirds, may huddle together for warmth. Ptarmigans dive into snowbanks, and then nap in the relative warmth of a pocket insulated by fluffy snow. A chilly songbird fluffs its feathers. The fluffed feathers trap air, forming a layer of insulation and slowing the loss of body heat.

A bird trying to cool off will do the opposite. It slicks down its feathers to eliminate heat-trapping air pockets, retreats to a shady spot, and raises its wings to catch cooling breezes. It may open its beak and pants like a dog, losing body heat as water evaporates from its throat and mouth. Some birds, such as pelicans, also flutter thin tissues in their throats to increase the effectiveness of their panting.

The roadrunner of southwestern deserts must, like many birds worldwide, cope with both heat and cold. After a chilly night, the bird greets the morning by spreading its wings with its back to the sun, soaking up warmth via a patch of exposed black skin. It then hunts for food before retiring to the shade to ride out the blistering heat of midday.

Q: **What features of a bird's circulatory system help maintain its body temperature?**

A: It is hard to imagine how a web-footed gull or duck can endure paddling in frigid water or standing on ice. The secret lies in a cluster of veins and arteries that redirects blood flow so as

A boreal chickadee raises its feathers on a chilly day. Fluffed feathers hold pockets of air and form a ball of insulation around it, slowing the loss of body heat. If the weather is warm, a bird can flatten its feathers to lessen their insulating effect.

to reduce heat loss. This cluster is often referred to as a "heat exchanger." Warm blood flowing through arteries would normally flow into the bird's legs before returning to the heart via veins. When the legs are exposed to cold, however, the artery in each upper leg constricts and forces blood to flow through the heat exchanger. In the heat exchanger, the blood vessels intertwine. Warm arterial blood flows in the opposite direction to the colder blood flowing through veins from the bird's leg. The two streams of blood thus "rub up" against each other. In the process, the colder venous blood is heated by the warm arterial blood, resulting in a "countercurrent" exchange of heat. Thus, the arterial blood is cooler when it flows into the legs, with little body heat to lose to the environment but just enough warmth to keep the feet from freezing. Meanwhile, the venous blood is heated nearly to body temperature as it flows back toward the heart.

Q: Do birds hibernate?

A: The Hopi Indians of the southwestern United States knew of a hibernating bird long before science did. They named it *Hölchoko*, "the sleeping one." This species, the common poorwill, responds to cold temperatures and a lack of food by drifting into a state called torpor. During torpor, its temperature may drop up to 40 degrees lower than normal. Its heartbeat and breathing are nearly undetectable, and it is completely unresponsive to touch or sound. When

temperatures rise and food is available again, the bird slowly emerges from torpor and resumes its normal activities. Other birds, such as hummingbirds, may also go into torpor overnight to conserve energy. Many birds, such as roadrunners and turkey vultures, experience a drop of body temperature overnight, saving energy but not going into actual torpor.

The greater roadrunner, a desert dweller, outwits the sun's burning rays by hunting during the coolest parts of the day. After a chilly desert night, however, it seeks out warm spots to sunbathe and raise its temperature.

The Bird's Senses

Q: How well do birds see?

A: We use the term "eagle-eyed" to describe a person with keen eyesight, but even the sharpest human eyes cannot match the visual acuity of a raptor's. A golden eagle, for example, can spot potential prey, such as a rabbit, from a distance of a mile. At closer range, the eagle perceives much greater detail than a human observer can.

The eagle's superior vision is largely due to its retina, the screen at the back of each eye. A bird's retina is thicker than a mammal's and more densely covered with cells called cones that are light-sensitive and detect color. Most day-active birds have from two to five times the number of cones packed into a tiny section of the retina

A red-tailed hawk, with its large eyes and beetling brows, boasts the keen vision typical of birds. The forward placement of its eyes, like those of a cat, provides binocular vision crucial for determining distance and depth. The jutting brows shade the eyes and also protect them from struggling prey.

than a human eye does. Droplets of red, orange, and yellow oil in the eye appear to aid in perceiving color and may also, in some species, reduce glare.

Like the human eye, a bird's eye has a spot on the retina called the fovea, where cones are especially close-packed. The fovea enhances focusing. A songbird, for example, relies on the fovea to help it find and feed on tiny insects. Many birds also have a second fovea that is used to track actively moving prey.

A bird's eye, moreover, can detect ultraviolet light. Studies show that in certain species of birds, their plumage patterns look different under UV light. Eurasian kestrels apparently use UV light while hunting mice; urine trails left by mice appear black under UV light and point the way to the prey.

Nocturnal birds rely on retinal cells called rods, which are sensitive to levels of light. These are the cells that enable humans to see in the dark, too.

Q: How well do birds hear?

A: Birds lack the prominent external ears of mammals, but their hearing is no less acute for that. Their ears consist of small openings that are covered with special feathers that keep out debris while funneling in sound waves. Collectively, birds' hearing spans a wider range than human hearing does. Different species, however, have hearing attuned to just a portion of this wide range, so an individual bird does not experience the same range as a person.

An owl that hunts at night has particularly keen hearing. Its ears are also set asymmetrically in its head, which helps it judge a sound's source. A barn owl can catch a tiny mouse in pitch darkness by relying on its hearing

foraging over vast waters more efficient and also makes nighttime foraging possible. Tubenoses that nest in burrows use smell to help them find their "address," too.

On land, turkey vultures and king vultures locate carrion by smell. In New Zealand, the flightless, nocturnal kiwi pokes in the soil with its bill, sniffing out earthworms with a pair of nostrils perched at its tip.

The kiwi's long slender bill sports nostrils at its lower end. Using its excellent sense of smell and flexible bill, the kiwi pokes the earth in search of worms, berries, and seeds to supplement its diet.

Q: Can birds detect tastes?

A: Birds appear to have little sense of taste, judging by the scant number of taste buds they possess. A human has more than 10,000 taste buds. A mallard or parrot has no more than 400. A chicken has but 24. Yet studies show that birds learn to shun bad tastes, so perhaps the few buds they have are enough to keep them from swallowing something unpleasant.

Q: Can birds detect smells?

A: The vast majority of birds appear to have a poor sense of smell, but a few species have sensitive "noses" and depend on smell to find food.

Among these species are seabirds known as "tubenoses," named for the tubular nostrils on their beaks. This group includes albatrosses, shearwaters, fulmars, and petrels. Petrels are particularly adept at sniffing out patches of potential food floating on the ocean. Having a keen sense of smell makes

The turkey vulture of North America forages by soaring over areas, relying on its highly developed sense of smell to help it find dead animals. Other vultures may keep their eyes on turkey vultures, using them as indicators for the location of carrion.

The Bird's Beak

Q: What accounts for the diversity of birds' beaks?

A: Birds have evolved a wide variety of beaks to feed on an equally wide variety of food. Their beaks also enable them to pick up, carry, and otherwise manipulate objects, such as nesting materials. The shape of a bird's beak tells you a great deal about how that bird lives its life.

Many birds have a basic "garden variety" beak that can handle an array of typical tasks. A crow's strong, general-purpose beak, for example, in the words of scientist John M. Marzluff, is like a Swiss Army knife because it can "cut, tear, crush, gape, probe, rip, and open just about anything."

A bird's beak exerts its greatest force at its base, so the stout, short beak of a finch is perfect for crushing seed shells. Some finches can even crack open cherry stones! The finches of the Galapagos

The aptly named long-billed curlew has a curved bill that is nearly nine inches long in the female, who is larger than her mate. This largest of North American shorebirds eats a wide variety of invertebrates on grasslands during breeding season, including earthworms. On its wintering grounds, its bill proves adept at catching crabs and shrimps found in deep burrows on tidal mudflats.

A yellow-throated toucan's large bill, used to pluck fruit, is lightweight due to air pockets inside it. Its color is thought to aid in species recognition and may have a startling, deterrent effect on hawks and other predators.

Islands, made famous by Charles Darwin, include birds with thin, pointed beaks for eating insects; finches with beaks for eating either small or large seeds; and finches with beaks for eating fruit and leaves or digging insects out of bark.

Other seed- and insect-eaters have also evolved specialized bills. A grackle has a sharp ridge inside its upper bill that works as a nutcracker. Woodpeckers have sharp, stout beaks as well as tongue and skull adaptations that enable them to hammer wood, and then probe deeply for insects. Crossbills of coniferous forests have curved upper and lower mandibles that cross at the tip. This unusual bill works like pliers to pry apart scales of cones so that seeds can be extracted with the tongue.

The beaks of hummingbirds and many Hawaiian honeycreepers are long and slender, perfectly adapted for dipping into flowers and sipping nectar. In tropical areas, hummingbirds' bills seem to match specific flowers, evidence that these birds and blossoms may have formed evolutionary partnerships.

Long bills also suit the feeding habits of waders and shorebirds. Their length allows for probing into mud and sand to find prey or to grab fish from the water. Different species exhibit variations on this common theme: A curlew's extraordinarily long bill can reach into mud and wet sand to extract worms and clams that other birds cannot. An oystercatcher's long bill is extra narrow for wedging into shells and prying them open. An avocet's bill curves upward at its tip, and the bird feeds by sweeping its bill back and forth in the water to stir up tiny plants and animals from the bottom.

Some of the bird world's most specialized beaks belong to fish-eaters. A pelican has a pouch under its bill for scooping its catch. A puffin has ridges in its beak to help it grip prey. A black skimmer's lower bill is longer than its upper one; to feed, the bird flies low over the water, slicing the water with its bladelike lower bill until it detects a fish, and then slams its beak shut.

Ducks called mergansers, which dive after fish, have long, thin bills with spikes that work like teeth to hang onto prey. Other ducks have wide, flat bills for grubbing up roots and skimming food from the water's surface. None of these beaks fit the bill for a bird of prey; eagles, hawks, owls, and their raptor kin have sharp, hooked beaks for tearing apart their catches.

Yet within this extraordinary diversity of beak form there is always room for one more oddity, such as the flamingo's beak. Its large, bent bill is made for filtering minute creatures from mud and shallow water while the bird's head is upside down, sucking in mud and water and then pressing it out with its tongue.

Left: Small, spiny projections on the roof of an Atlantic puffin's upper mandible enable it to grip and carry up to 30 small fish at one time and carry them to its young. The fish are held crosswise and pressed tightly into place by the puffin's equally spiny tongue.

A white pelican's pouch is extremely flexible and expands as it scoops up fish. Contrary to popular belief, they do not carry fish in their pouches; they swallow them, then regurgitate the food for their young.

The Bird's Feet

Q: What accounts for the diversity of birds' feet?

A: All birds have two legs, but, compared to humans, walk on tiptoe. The portion of a bird's leg that we call its foot is really its toes, and the long "leg" that protrudes from its feathered belly is actually the rest of its foot. But no matter how its legs are labeled, a bird's limbs are ideally suited to its habitat and way of life. Like beaks, birds' feet and legs come in many forms.

Perhaps the most familiar feet are those of the perching birds. Sparrows, robins, and other familiar birds have such feet, with three toes in front and a long hind toe, perfect for grasping a twig.

Birds of prey such as hawks and owls also have feet with three forward-pointing toes and one hind toe. Their toes, however, are tipped with long, curved talons for grasping prey and, in some species, killing it. An osprey's toes feature spiky scales that help grip fish; the bird can also rotate one forward-facing toe backward to better clutch its slippery, struggling meal. Owls can also rotate their toes in this way and often perch with two toes facing forward, two back.

Most other birds have four toes, too, though the hindmost toe is often reduced in size and doesn't touch the ground, as in pheasants. In some birds, not one but two toes face backward, the other two forward. Such feet are typical of woodpeckers and parrots, which use them to grip tree trunks (though in some species of woodpecker, the fourth toe has disappeared).

Birds that wade and feed along the shore typically have long, skinny legs. Long-legged wading birds can stride into deep water without soaking their feathers. Shorebirds such as sandpipers have long toes

All four toes of a blue-footed booby's foot are webbed, making it a highly efficient paddle for this swimming, diving bird. The colorful feet figure prominently in the birds' courtship, which includes high-stepping prancing. Boobies also keep their eggs warm with their feet.

Two toes point forward, two backward on the foot of a parrot. Parrots are one of the few birds that use their feet for lifting food to their beaks.

that help them walk on wet mud and sand. The little northern jacana boasts toes that are four inches long, which helps to spread its weight so evenly that it can trot across floating lily pads.

Some waders and shorebirds have varying amounts of webbing between their toes to make walking on wet ground easier. But the best-known webbed feet belong to the ducks and geese. In these birds, webbing links the three front toes, turning the foot into a paddle for swimming. Gulls and other waterbirds have webbed feet, too. Some species have flaps of flesh on their toes instead. These are known as lobed feet and are found in such birds as coots and grebes. The lobes open wide to form a paddle as the bird's foot

pushes back, and then fold up tightly as the foot moves forward. A pelican offers yet another variation: Its webbing extends to all four of its toes, front and back.

Swimming birds also have legs placed to maximize efficiency in the water. Diving ducks, such as mergansers, have legs placed far back on the body. In some birds, such as loons, the legs are so far back that the birds can only creep on land. Swifts, which spend much of their life on the wing, have small, weak legs that are useless for walking, but their feet have four forward-facing toes equipped with strong claws well suited for clinging to rock walls.

Unique among birds is the two-toed foot of the ostrich, an adaptation to its life as a flightless bird that runs swiftly to escape danger. Its foot, with one large toe and one small, puts one in mind of the stages in the evolution of hooves in speedy mammals such as horses and gazelles.

A glossy starling of Africa exhibits the four-toed foot typical of most birds: three toes point forward and one extends backward. The rear-facing toe is called the hallux. Other configurations in some species involve a rearrangement of the toes. Toes are tipped with claws, and both legs and feet are covered in tough, scaly skin.

Hormones at Work

Q: How do hormones influence bird behavior?

A: Hormones are chemicals secreted by glands that exert control over bodily functions. Many of a bird's hormones perform the same functions as their counterparts in mammals. The pancreas,

A western meadowlark sings his flutelike song from atop a fence wire, declaring his ownership of a patch of prairie. The onset of breeding season unleashes a cascade of hormones in birds that stimulate courtship, breeding, nesting, and parenting behavior in cooperation with cues from the environment.

for example, secretes insulin and other hormones that control blood-sugar levels. Adrenal glands produce hormones that spur a fight-or-flight response as well as hormones that urge the development of secondary sexual characteristics. Hormones also control bodily processes such as molting, egg laying, and growth.

But behavior, too, can be influenced by hormones. Anybody who has witnessed a male robin fighting with its reflection in a window has seen hormones in action. The bird, under the influence of testosterone, is goaded to attack intruders on its territory—even if the intruder is just a mirror image. When the same bird sings sweetly from a perch, he is likewise encouraged by a surge of breeding-season hormones.

Female birds are also influenced by hormones. Estrogen and progesterone, secreted by the ovaries, work in concert with prolactin, secreted by the pituitary gland, to induce nesting and brooding behavior. High levels of prolactin are also present in males of species in which the father helps feed the young.

Hormone production, in turn, is influenced by other factors. A primary stimulus for the production of sex hormones, for example, is increasing day length. An important stimulus for the production of hormones that inspire broodiness is pressure on a female bird's brood patches, such as she might feel when sitting in a nest.

The annual cycle of migration is a complex drama in which hormones, inheritance, and external stimuli all play important roles. The ancient urge to migrate, and in some cases the routes themselves, are encoded in the bird's brain, but hormones and the environment are vital for initiating this behavior. Various hormones first compel a bird to feed heavily and gain weight. Then the amount of daylight stimulates the secretion of hormones that add to its inborn, seasonal sense of restlessness, its desire to be on its way.

Q: What role do hormones play in seasonal changes in the bird's body?

A: As in migration, length of day is a primary agent in activating a cascade of hormonal changes. It affects the pituitary gland, located in the bird's brain, which controls the activity of other glands, including the gonads (the primary producers of sex hormones such as testosterone and estrogen).

A bird's sex hormones, in turn, influence the development of what are called "secondary sexual characteristics." Some, such as basic plumage, may be permanent developments. Other characteristics appear only during the breeding season. Puffins, for example, sport vividly colored beaks during their summer breeding season. Great and snowy egrets grow graceful white plumes. Cattle egrets grow buffy ones, and their black legs turn orange. Male scarlet tanagers wear stunning red plumage. European starlings boast bright yellow bills. Peacocks flaunt colorful trains. Female phalaropes, which court males, develop bright colors. Later in the season, hormones will likewise play a role in molting. Another seasonal body change orchestrated by

Male and female snowy egrets sport graceful plumes on their neck, chest, and back during the breeding season.

Spurred by hormones and lengthening daylight, summer tanagers leave their Central American wintering grounds and migrate north. They arrive in the United States from late March into early May. The adult males, which are rosy red year-round, sing to attract females and defend their territories. The song of another male spurs aggressive behavior, including the chasing of intruders.

hormones in response to various environmental cues is the development of brood patches. These are blood-vessel rich patches of bare skin on birds' bellies. Incubating birds nestle their eggs close to these patches to keep them warm. The hormone prolactin stimulates this change and also causes pigeons to produce "crop milk" for their young. High prolactin levels also cause gonads to shrink. A European starling's testes, for example, are almost five times heavier in the breeding season than in the nonbreeding season, thus keeping it focused on raising one clutch before trying to start another.

> "Those little nimble musicians of the air, that warble forth their curious ditties, with which nature hath furnished them to the shame of art."
> —IZAAK WALTON

CHAPTER 2

FEATHERS: FORM AND FUNCTION

Birds are the only animals with feathers. Made of keratin, feathers are lightweight, strong, sturdy, and flexible, and provide birds with the lift and stream-lining that enables them to fly. The waterproofing and insulating properties of feathers allow birds to thrive in nearly all of the world's habitats. The adaptability of feathers shows in their many forms and the many functions they serve. They range in size from tiny, bristly eyelash feathers to long, frilly plumes. The colors and patterns of feathers give birds their often astonishing beauty. Some birds, such as potoos and woodcocks, wear earth tones, the better to blend in with sand, rocks, branches, and leaf litter. Even bright green parrots can disappear in leafy treetops. Some birds, such as inky black crows and white snowy owls, are striking because they are monochromatic. Other birds are avian fireworks, bursting with color. In many species, it's the male who is boldly marked, his colors an advertisement to females and a warning to other males. The orange and black feathers of the hooded pitohui of New Guinea may be a warning to all: Its feathers are poisonous!

Above: The bald head and neck of the California condor is an adaptation for feeding on carrion. Heavy feathering on these parts would pose a hygiene problem for these birds.

Left: A greater flamingo preens. Its pink color comes from its diet of algae, crustaceans, and other items rich in caratenoids. In zoos, carrot juice mixed in with feed keeps captive birds in the pink.

A Feather Close Up

Q: **What are the parts of a feather?**

A: The structure of a feather is easily seen in a typical wing or tail feather. The stiff central portion is the shaft. Its lower, hollow portion, called the calamus, is the part hidden from view in the skin. The upper portion of the shaft is called the rachis.

Along both sides of the rachis are rows of fine, parallel filaments called barbs. Each barb, in turn, has rows of parallel barbules growing from its sides. The barbules are lined with hooks that catch other barbules, working in a manner similar to Velcro. By meshing together in this way, they form the

Right: Barbules in a feather work rather like Velcro, with the hooked tip of one barbule latching into the channel of another. The barbules can also slide along these channels, allowing the feather to flex without coming "unzipped."

Below: The shaft of a feather is like the stiff trunk of a tree, with the barbs of the vane coming off it like branches. Each barb is lined with barbules that hook to those of a neighboring barb.

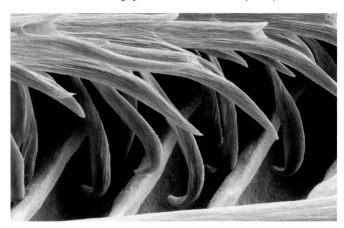

smooth, flexible, seemingly solid surfaces of the feather's vanes.

The vanes of a feather can be easily pulled apart so that the feather looks like a gap-toothed comb. They are just as easily repaired by smoothing them together again. When you see a bird preening, it is combing its feathers to zip them together to keep them in top-notch flying condition. Well-groomed feathers can also serve as waterproof raincoats in most species.

Q: **How many feathers does a bird have?**

A: Feather counts done over the past 200 years have tallied numbers of contour feathers on different species. These feathers are the body, wing, and tail feathers visible when glancing at a bird. These painstaking efforts have yielded the following figures: The tundra swan boasts 25,216 feathers, with 20,177 of them cloaking just its head and long neck. A ruby-throated hummingbird, with its low

Features of a Flight Feather

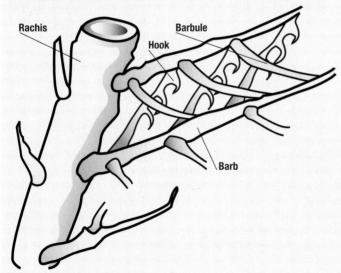

Rachis

Barbule

Hook

Barb

count of 940 feathers, would cover just a tiny patch on a swan.

Other plucky researchers have counted contour feathers and come up with figures in between these extremes. In general, most perching birds have between 1,500 and 4,000 feathers. Not surprisingly, birds often sport more feathers in winter than in summer if they live in cold climates. White-throated sparrows, for example, nearly double their feather counts in winter. Birds that are residents of hot climates often have fewer feathers, which may also have fewer barbs.

In general, larger birds have more feathers than small birds—by virtue of their greater size—but small birds tend to have more feathers relative to their size than large ones do. Small birds have a greater surface area in relation to their body core, and so they lose heat more easily, hence they need a greater volume of feathers in order to keep warm.

Although we often use the phrase "light as a feather" to describe feather-weight objects, many a bird's plumage actually outweighs its skeleton—a testament to how exquisitely birds' bones are adapted for flight. A bald eagle that weighed 9 pounds (4.1 kg) was found, upon dissection and weighing, to have a skeleton that weighed 9 ounces (272 g). Its 7,182 feathers combined with innumerable down feathers added up to 23 ounces (677 g) of plumage. This was not only more than double the skeleton's weight, but also about one-sixth of the bird's total weight.

More than 25,000 feathers cover a tundra swan, with the majority of them growing on its head and neck. This swan's feathers are heavily coated in mud picked up while grubbing for food.

Kinds of Feathers

Q: **What sort of feathers form a bird's plumage?**

A: A bird's plumage is made up of several different kinds of feathers, each serving a different purpose. The strong, stiff, but flexible feathers of the wing are used for flying. Called remiges, these feathers provide lift during flight. Remiges are closely attached along the wing bones, giving these feathers extra support for flight. Tail feathers, called rectrices, also aid flight. They function like the tails of squirrels and cats, helping a bird keep itself balanced while flying, and are also used in changing direction and braking.

Smaller feathers, called coverts, grow above and below the wing and tail feathers. Feathers also cover the head, neck, back, and front of a bird. These feathers cushion and insulate it. Muscles in the skin control the feathers, enabling the bird to fluff its feathers to increase its insulation or sleek them down to keep cool. All of these body feathers, collectively known as contour feathers, are also waterproof in most birds. Rain literally rolls off them like water off a duck's back.

Hidden from view are other feathers tucked beneath the contour feathers. These soft, fuzzy feathers—called down—are the same insulating material used by humans to stuff jackets, comforters, and pillows. Unlike the contour feathers, down feathers do not have the hooklike tips on the barbules to zip them together—so the barbs move freely. They also lack a central rachis like the contour feathers; all of the barbs attach at the feathers' bases. The result is a fluffy "pom-pom" close to the bird's body.

Semiplumes are another insulating type of feather found along the dividing lines between sections of the bird's

A bird's feathers grow from specific sections of its skin called tracts. Muscles in the skin are used to move the feathers. The terms used to identify different feathers frequently appear in field-guide descriptions as aids to identification.

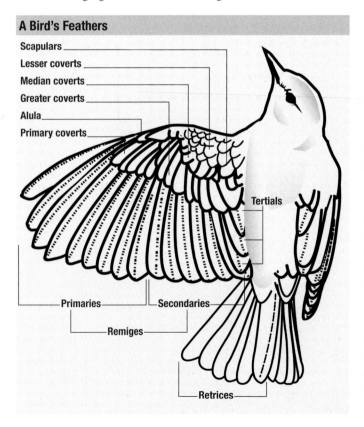

A Bird's Feathers

Scapulars
Lesser coverts
Median coverts
Greater coverts
Alula
Primary coverts

Tertials

Primaries
Secondaries
Remiges

Retrices

base of their beaks. The bristles are also whiskerlike in function, providing birds with extra protection of the face as well as adding tactile and sensory information.

From these basic feathers spring the array of specialized feathers that distinguish so many species. A woodpecker's retrices, for example, are stiff enough for the bird to use as a brace. It props its tail against a tree trunk as it chisels with its beak, the pointed, spiky tips of the feathers helping it grip. The central two feathers in its tail are so essential to this stance that a woodpecker does not molt them until brand-new tail feathers on either side have already grown in. Chimney swifts also have stiff tail feathers that prop them up as they cling to sheer walls. A number of species have retrices or tail coverts that form splendid plumes during the breeding season.

Wing feathers have also been modified in some species. Owls, for example, have evolved specialized flight feathers to muffle the sound of their flight as they pursue prey. Instead of a sharp, crisp edge, some of its leading-edge remiges are fringed, buffering its attack on the air. Most owls also have a velvety texture to their wing feathers that also helps mute the sound of flight.

Powder-down feathers, found in herons, bitterns, pigeons, cockatoos, and a few other species, exist only to self-destruct. These fluffy feathers crumble into powder at their tips. The powder dusts the bird's plumage and can even make black birds appear gray. In herons, the powder may help the bird sop up oils from its fishy meals. Its purpose in other species is still being studied.

A pileated woodpecker braces itself with its stiff, pointed tail feathers, using them as a prop as it clings to a tree. A woodpecker always has some tail feathers to depend on: It does not molt the middle pair of retrices until the others have already been molted and regrown.

plumage. Like the down, they lack the Velcro-like quality of the contour feathers. Semiplumes do, however, have a central shaft to which the fluffy barbs attach. Birds may also have hairlike feathers called filoplumes tucked among the plumage of the head, neck, and wings that seem to function much like whiskers, keeping them informed about the positions of their feathers and the touch of breezes.

Some birds also grow stiff, hairlike feathers called rictal bristles. Nightjars, poorwills, swallows, and other flying insect catchers sprout rictal bristles at the

Preening and Cleaning

Q: Why do birds run their beaks through their feathers?

A: A dirty bird is a vulnerable bird. Birds need to keep their feathers clean or else their plumage will lose its insulating and waterproofing qualities, and parasites will run rampant on them. Unkempt wing and tail feathers will likewise compromise flying.

When a bird runs its beak through its feathers, it is cleaning them, or preening. A bird uses two preening techniques. It may pull the feathers through its beak in one sustained motion, "zipping" together barbs and barbules that have come undone and smoothing them out. Or it may run the feathers through its beak slowly while nibbling them from base to tip, cleaning off dirt and picking out mites and other parasites.

A heron scratches its head with its long toes. Herons possess a serrated claw on the middle forward-facing toe, known as a feather comb, used in grooming. Herons also have areas of powder-down feathers on their breasts and rumps that provide a built-in supply of dusty powder that may help in removing excess oil.

A young white ibis rummages among its feathers with its long bill, nibbling and preening. Its long, flexible neck enables it to reach nearly every part of its body.

Q: Do birds have any specialized body parts to aid in grooming?

A: Many species of birds have an oil gland at the base of the tail. This oil is spread on the bill and distributed on feathers while preening. It may act as a moisturizer and is thought to have antibacterial and antifungal properties. Nightjars and some herons have a toothed middle claw, called a feather comb, that may help rake out parasites. All birds benefit from having flexible necks that can twist and stretch to reach nearly all parts of the body.

Q: How do birds use their environment in their grooming?

A: Water, dust, and sunlight (as well as a few rather surprising items in their habitats) are all exploited by birds in their efforts to keep clean. Water is almost universally enjoyed among birds for bathing. A songbird in a puddle or birdbath goes through a specific sequence of motions to splash water all over its body, its feathers ruffled to benefit from every drop. If a bird cannot find a puddle, it will bathe in the film of water on a leaf or the dew beaded on grass. Many birds will also, seemingly gleefully, spread their wings and flutter in rainfall or dart through the spray of a sprinkler. Swallows, swifts, hummingbirds, and other frequent fliers have been seen bathing in this way as well as diving to take quick dips in puddles without landing.

Many birds bathe just before preening, and it is thought that water assists in spreading oil from the oil gland through the feathers. It may also wash out some dirt and parasites and help in keeping the bird cool in hot weather.

Chickens, turkeys, house sparrows, and some other species indulge in dust bathing, just as some mammals do. Belly-down on the ground, the birds scrape with their feet, flap their wings, and ruffle their feathers to sift dust onto themselves. The dust may help dislodge parasites, remove old oil, and shake out and rearrange clumped feathers, thereby improving their insulating ability in much the same way that shaking a down comforter redistributes its filling.

A sunbathing bird, flopped on the ground with wings outspread, is a startling sight—the bird appears to be near death, until one steps close to rescue it and receives a seemingly dirty look from the bird before it flaps away. Birds may also sunbathe while perching with wings spread wide, as eagles, storks, and turkey vultures do. This behavior is sometimes used simply to warm up, but may also help keep feathers limber and drive out hidden parasites, making it easier to remove them while preening. But the strangest behavior of all is

anting. More than 200 species of birds worldwide have been observed rubbing ants into their plumage or flinging themselves onto anthills and allowing the insects to swarm through their feathers. It is thought that the formic acid produced by the angry ants may kill parasites or soothe skin vexed by mites or molting. Birds have also been recorded using other irritants while anting. The list includes coffee, bits of lemon, orange juice, beetles, vinegar, hot cigarette butts, berries, and mothball. An emu was even seen tucking live bees into its plumage.

Birds go through a ritualized series of motions when they bathe in water, turning themselves into a flurry of ruffled feathers and activity. Droplets of water flung among the feathers cleanse them without soaking them. Even waterbirds, such as this redhead duck, take time to bathe.

How Feathers Grow

Q: How does a feather grow from a bird's skin?

A: Although a bird appears to be encased in a seamless cloak of feathers, in most species its plumage actually grows from specific patches on its skin. These patches are clearly visible on a plucked bird and are known as feather tracts. Individual feather follicles stipple the tracts. In between tracts are bare patches where feathers do not grow.

The vibrant feathers of a parrot flaunt a portion of the rainbow of colors that adorn birds. Native peoples of Central and South America have traditionally used parrot feathers for ceremonial clothing such as headdresses.

As a feather forms in a follicle, it is nourished by a blood supply and painted with pigments. A sheath surrounds the developing feather. This sheath protrudes visibly from the skin and is often called a pinfeather. The feather, furled neatly inside the sheath, slowly fans out when it emerges from the sheath's broken tip, like paper roses bursting from a magician's wand.

Inside the follicle, blood vessels are reabsorbed into the body when they are no longer needed for growth. This is why the calamus (the lower portion of a feather's central shaft) is hollow. The feathers that give so much beauty to a bird are, like our hair, made up of dead cells.

Q: What kinds of feathers does a newly hatched bird have?

A: Some baby birds have no feathers at all upon hatching. Baby robins, for example, tumble out of their sky-blue shells looking like pink baby mice, their bulging eyes sealed shut. They depend on their parents to keep them warm until their own feathers appear.

Down quickly grows and within a few days pinfeathers appear on the nestlings' wings, heads, and backs. Now it will not be long until they are completely feathered. Blue tits, for example, sport their first plumage by the time they are just two weeks old. Pelicans are also naked upon hatching, but soon sprout white down. This fluffy natal down will not be replaced until the chick is about one month old and on its way to being independent.

Bald eagle chicks possess the same glowering features as their parents but are clad in fluffy white down instead of feathers. The eaglets' natal down insulates them and will be shed and replaced with juvenal plumage. It will be several years before they share their parents' adult plumage.

Other hatchlings emerge already equipped with down. A duckling, for example, clambers out of its shell in a slicker of wet down, which quickly dries and fluffs up to keep it warm. Some species, such as snowy and barn owls, hatch with scanty down coats, then grow a new set of down feathers.

Q: When does a baby bird acquire adult plumage?

A: The young of some species hang on to their fluffy coats of baby down longer than other species. A golden eagle chick is still clad in white down at six weeks of age; it will not leave the nest until it is about two to three months old. An emperor penguin chick snuggles inside a thick coat of gray down until it is from six to eight weeks old, well insulated against antarctic cold. Hatchlings' down feathers perch on the tips of new feathers growing behind them and are eventually shoved out of the follicle as juvenal feathers emerge.

A baby bird's first set of plumage—its juvenal plumage—may or may not resemble the parents' plumage. The emperor penguin chick, for example, replaces its down with the black, yellow, and white plumage of an adult. An immature snowy owl is mostly brown, which helps camouflage it during its first summer. Large gulls take up to four years to mature, and so must progress not only through juvenal plumage but several summer and winter plumages before acquiring full-fledged adult plumage.

A double-wattled cassowary chick displays patterning that is also exhibited by the young of many other ground-dwelling species. Blotchy or stripy coloration camouflages a chick by breaking up its shape and helping it blend in with shadows and sunny spots.

Molting Feathers

Q: Why do birds molt?

A: A bird's feathers take a beating. They scrape against twigs, branches, bark, leaves, and grass during daily activities. As the bird flies, they are beset by all kinds of weather. They brush up against the nest and nestlings and are abraded by sand and dirt if the bird lives in a burrow. If the bird is a predator, its feathers may be disheveled by struggling prey. If the bird is prey, its feathers may be damaged while making an escape.

Because feathers, like hair, are made up of dead materials, wear and tear cannot be repaired (though if a feather falls out, it is quickly replaced by a new one). A bird must therefore molt its old feathers and grow replacements.

Most birds molt at least once a year. Some grassland sparrows and wrens in North America and larks in African deserts molt twice a year because their environments are particularly tough on feathers. Ptarmigans, which live in the arctic and high on mountainsides, grow three sets of plumage: brown, then white and brown, and then white, which keeps them camouflaged in summer, winter, and in between.

In many species, there is a second, partial molt in springtime that doesn't involve flight feathers. This molt reveals a bird's breeding finery. Some species, however, appear freshly clad in springtime without going through a partial molt. Instead, they wear off the tips of the previous year's fresh feathers to achieve their breeding

A male cardinal, fondly known as a redbird in part of its range, owes its vivid vermilion to carotenoids it consumes during its molting period. The new feathers have gray tips, which wear off by abrasion in time for the spring breeding season. Studies indicate that brightness of color correlates with improved breeding success of males.

colors. European starlings, for example, molt during late summer into feathers spangled with stars. By spring, the stars have faded and the feathers are glossy black. Male house sparrows' black bibs, male cardinals' red bodies, and male bobo-links' black and white patterns are similarly revealed in springtime by abrasion.

Q: What happens during the process of molting?

A: Typically, a bird molts feathers section by section. These sections, called tracts, are visible on plucked birds as distinct areas dotted with feather follicles. Depending on the species, the bird molts just one tract at a time or may molt several tracts at once. Molting usually washes over the bird from front to back. The old feathers are pushed out by the new feathers growing in.

Q: Are some birds unable to fly while molting?

A: Most birds lose their flight feathers in a symmetrical pattern—a single feather drops off the right wing at the same time as its counterpart on the left.

Although flying with fewer feathers is more laborious, this symmetrical molting does not unbalance the bird.

A surprising number of species, however, are rendered flightless by molting. This is true of many waterbirds. Ducks, geese, swans, grebes, loons, flamingoes, and anhingas lose all their flight feathers simultaneously. This molt occurs after the breeding season but before migration begins. While they are flightless, these birds are doubly wary and rely on water as a place of safety.

Female hornbills of Asia and Africa that reside in sealed nest holes while incubating and caring for young, exploit their captivity by molting all their feathers at once. The flightless females are fed by the males during this time. The males also molt in a more leisurely fashion during this time, when food is plentiful and easy to catch, and energy used for growing new feathers is quickly renewed.

Above: A male black-necked swan gives a lift to his downy chick. The chick will molt into juvenal plumage and acquire darker neck feathers by the time it is three months old. Its parents will undergo their annual molt and, like ducks, be flight-less during that time.

Left: Most ducks, such as the wood duck shown here, undergo a complete molt in between the breeding season and migration. While females are incubating and caring for young, males molt their breeding plumage into drab "eclipse" plum-age. They are unable to fly at this time. Females likewise molt after they have finished nesting.

The Color of Feathers

Q: What colors are produced by pigments?

A: Pigments are colored materials that give paints, leaves, and birds many of their colors, whether they are bold and bright for breeding or more subtle to provide camouflage. Birds utilize three different types of pigments that give color to feathers as well as other body parts.

One of these pigments is melanin, familiar to us as the pigment that colors human skin. Melanin produces colors that range from yellow to reddish brown to black. Just as a concentration of melanin in our skin produces lighter or darker shades, so too does melanin concentration vary in birds' feathers and skins to create a range of hues. Scientists have found that feathers high in melanin are physically stronger than lighter feathers, which is one reason why many white or pale seabirds have wings tipped or barred with black. Dark

wing tips may also help birds recognize their species in flight and aid in flocking. Porphyrins are another group of pigments produced in a bird's body. They give rise to various red and brown hues, and increase their palette by mixing with melanins. One group of vivid African birds, the forest-dwelling turacos, possesses a green and a red porphyrin pigment found in no other birds.

Pigments called carotenoids give birds bright yellow, orange, and red colors. Carotenoids are produced by plants and give color to such things as autumn leaves, carrots, pumpkins, and marigolds. By eating plant parts or animals, such as insects, that have dined on plants, a bird can incorporate these colors into its body.

Sometimes, pigmentation goes awry. Genetic mutations may deprive a bird of melanin, producing an albino bird. Such a bird may be white, but it may also have colors produced by other pigments. A lack of other pigments may result in birds with dilute coloration. An overload of melanin produces darker-than-normal plumage.

Q: What colors are produced by a feather's structure?

A: Hummingbirds, quetzals, blue jays, peacocks, bluebirds, and parrots are among the brilliantly colored birds that owe their vivid hues to the structure of their feathers.

The blue of a blue jay is produced by air pockets encased in the layer of material that forms the outermost layer of the feather, which is actually dark brown with

A barred owl's feathers are a subtle tapestry of browns, whites, and grays. Pigments produced by the bird's body create these colors and are likewise responsible for black and brown hues of mammals. The pigment melanin also adds strength: darker portions of feathers are stronger than pale ones.

kaleidoscope of flashing colors that shift and change depending on the point of view of the observer.

Q: Does a bird's diet contribute to the color of its plumage?

A: As noted above, some reds, oranges, and yellows in birds are produced by plant pigments, which can only be obtained by eating plants or plant-eating animals. Even the yellow bill of a male European blackbird will grow brighter when he gets enough carotenoids in his diet.

Flamingoes and roseate spoonbills' pink plumage also comes to them courtesy of their diet. They obtain their rosy pigments from the crustaceans they eat. A captive flamingo deprived of these foods will eventually fade.

Some birds' feathers are colored not by their ingestion of food, but by their pursuit of it. Cranes, swans, and geese often have heads, necks, and chests stained red-brown by minerals in their muddy, watery habitats.

Left: A blue jay's color is conjured up by a trick much like the one that creates the sky-blue of the heavens. Light is scattered by air pockets that cover brownish feathers, producing blue.

Below: The rosy hue of a greater flamingo is a product of its diet. Carotenoids in its food are incorporated into its feathers.

melanin. (This material, keratin, is the same substance that forms fingernails.) The air pockets scatter the light that strikes them, particularly the wavelengths of blue, indigo, and violet. Thus, the feather appears to be blue. This process also creates purple hues when the feather contains reddish brown melanin. In parrots, a yellow-tinted sheet over the air pocket cells turns the blue to green.

The ever-changing rainbow sheen of a soap bubble or an oil slick on a puddle is an example of iridescence, and some birds' feathers have structures that make them glimmer, too. Layers of keratin streaked with melanin granules and air pockets reflect and bend light to create a

> **When nature made the blue-bird she wished to propitiate both the sky and the earth, so she gave him the color of the one on his back and the hue of the other on his breast.** —*JOHN BURROUGHS*

CHAPTER 3

BIRDS IN MOTION

In 1851, marveling at the graceful motion of a circling hawk, Henry David Thoreau wrote in his journal: "What made the hawk mount? Did you perceive the maneuver? Did he fill himself with air? Before you were aware of it, he had mounted by his spiral path into the heavens."

The power, beauty, and seemingly effortless nature of bird flight have long carried the human imagination aloft. Birds soar and sail in myth and poetry and across the canvases of artists. Aviators too, have studied birds on the wing to better understand the dynamics of flight, and then applied their observations to devise their own flying machines.

Although in many people's minds the essence of birds is flight, birds get around in other ways, too: They run, they hop, they dive, and they swim. There are even birds that have given up flying altogether. For some flightless species, this means they have only given up flying in air—penguins, for example, have simply adapted to flying underwater.

Above: The bodies of penguins are designed for gliding in the cold waters that surround their Antarctic habitat.

Left: Hawks soar in thermals—spiraling, rising currents of warm air. They hop from one to another, gliding within each thermal until they reach the next one.

How a Bird Flies

Q: Do birds fly in the same way that aircraft do?

A: The same aerodynamic principles that lift and support a 747 jumbo jet are at work when a bird takes to the air. Nonetheless, the bird's wing—with its 50 muscles, 9 to 12 primary flight feathers, and 8 to 32 secondary flight feathers—is more efficient and adjustable than any manufactured wing. A bird's wing, like an airplane's, is what is known as an airfoil. An airfoil naturally rises when it moves through air, an effect caused by its asymmetrical yet streamlined shape. An airfoil's front edge, called the leading edge, is wide. The part behind the leading edge, known as the trailing edge, is narrow. The bottom curves downward; the top is rounded. This particular configuration produces the force known as lift when the airfoil is in moving air. This moving air is called an airstream.

As a bird glides or flies, each of its wings slice through the airstream— forcing part of the air to flow over the top of the wing and the rest to flow under the wing. This flowing air behaves much like a fluid due to what is called the Bernoulli principle. The airfoil shape of the wing ensures that, as air moves over the more curved top surface, it speeds up. This faster speed makes the air pressure above the wing lower than the air pressure under it. The higher pressure underneath, in effect, pushes upward, creating lift that lofts both bird and plane into the air and keeps them there.

Both birds and planes also need another force, called thrust, to keep them flying. Propellers or jet engines provide an airplane's thrust. A bird's thrust is produced by flapping. Flapping is not a simple up-and-down motion that rows the bird through the air.

Historical artwork of birds in flight drawn by the Italian artist and scientist Leonardo da Vinci (1452–1519). The patterns of the birds' flight can be seen together with his notes. His interest in bird flight influenced some of his designs for flying machines.

A bird's wings and flight feathers describe a complex series of motions as they flap, motions that continue to be studied and analyzed by scientists and engineers.

Slow-motion photography shows that a bird's inner wing mainly moves up and down, while the outer wing basically draws a figure eight in the air with each flap. The outer wing dips down and forward, and then moves up and back. This outer-wing motion, accompanied by a twisting of its primary feathers, works rather like a propeller and produces the thrust that pushes the bird forward. The figure-eight shape is more pronounced when a bird is taking off than when it is in sustained flight.

A bird can also manipulate its wings and feathers, spread and twist its tail, and change the position of its body to speed up, slow down, change direction, and land, just as an airplane's wings and tail retract or extend various flaps to alter speed and position. Watch a swan land on water, and you will see it extend its neck, tilt its body, spread its tail, extend its legs forward, and flap its wings to create reverse thrust, for all the world like a jumbo jet coming in for a landing.

Hummingbirds, with their ability to hover, fly backward, and take off vertically, have more in common with helicopters than airplanes. Their wings, like a helicopter's rotors, are airfoils. Like other birds and like airplanes, hummingbirds can fly forward; unlike them, they can switch to an extreme figure-eight motion, with the wings rotating at the shoulder and the lower surfaces twisting to face upward. This unique flapping produces continuous lift, enabling a hummingbird to hover in front of a flower while sipping nectar.

Above: The turtle dove's inner wings flap up, down, and then up again. Its outer wings form a figure-eight shape as it flies, which is not visible in this still photograph. The figure eights push the air behind the wings to propel the bird forward.

Below: A whooper swan prepares to land on water, with neck extended and legs pushed forward.

Have you ever observed a humming-bird moving about in an aerial dance among the flowers—a living prismatic gem . . . it is a creature of such fairy-like loveliness as to mock all description.

—W. H. HUDSON, GREEN MANSIONS

Wing Structure

Q: How is a wing's bone structure adapted for flight?

A: A bird's wing contains very little muscle: It is made up mainly of skin, bones, and feathers. It contains many of the same bones found in the human arm, but the bones that correspond to our wrist and hand bones differ. Some bones are fused together, while some "fingers" are completely lacking. Fusion means fewer joints, which means less range of motion and greater rigidity, but this trade-off makes the wing strong enough to endure the stresses exerted by flight.

The outer wing is the bird's "hand" and is part of the wing where the primary flight feathers attach—providing thrust for the bird to fly. A set of fused "fingers" make up the outermost section. One of these bones, called the alula, resembles a thumb and can move independently of the other bones. The largest

bone in the outer wing is called the carpometacarpus. This bone is actually fused hand bones and is the connection to the birds "wrist" and inner wing.

The inner part of a bird's wing is similar to a mammal's arm. The ulna bone, found in the lower part of the arm, provides the connection for the secondary flight feathers—giving the wing the consistent lift needed for flight. Like the bones, the joints in the wing are also adapted to assist in flight. The "elbow," where the upper and lower arm bones join, cannot bend forward. This "locking" gives the joint strength during the stress of flight without requiring extra muscle to hold its position.

The bird's upper-arm bone, the humerus, is analogous to a human's, but its top is broader, with pronounced bumps for the attachment of the powerful flight muscles found in the chest. The joint where the upper arm bone meets the pectoral girdle, or shoulder girdle, is likewise configured so that it naturally holds the inner wing at the most effective angle for flight.

The hummingbird, not surprisingly, puts its own spin on wing skeletal structure. The tiny avian helicopter's arm

Above right: Although a hummingbird cannot glide, its specialized wings enable it to hover as it delves into flowers, searching for nectar.

Below: General skeleton of a bird in flight, showing wing and body bone anatomy. The insets show a cross section of hollow bone and microscopic feather structure.

Skeletal Anatomy of Bird in Flight

bones are greatly reduced in size. The joint that links them to the pectoral girdle has evolved so that the hummingbird can freely rotate its wings at the shoulder. The "elbow" and "wrist" are less flexible, more "locked" in place than those of other birds, with most of the wing consisting of the "hand" bones that serve as propellers. These specialized wings do not permit a hummingbird to glide or soar, but give it an unmatched ability to maneuver.

Q: **How do wing feathers aid in flight?**

A: Wing feathers are what make a wing an airfoil. Soft feathers, called marginal and lesser coverts, line the leading edge of the wing, cloaking the bases of the flight feathers. They overlap the slightly larger main coverts behind them. Together, the coverts create a smooth, curved surface, the essential form of an airfoil. The greater coverts, in turn, overlap the flight feathers, which give the bird both lift and thrust.

Each flight feather itself is a miniature airfoil, with a leading edge and a trailing edge. The primary feathers—those on the "hand" part of the wing—twist as the bird flaps so that they overlap on the downstroke to produce a solid surface, maximizing thrust and lift. Each feather's barbules have hooks that link barb to barb to create a feather's surface. These slide to and fro as the feather twists, maintaining its smoothness. During the upstroke, the feathers twist so that slots appear between them, which lets air flow through freely and makes it easier

to raise the wing. Protruding from the "wrist" of most birds is the bony, feathered alula. A bird can move its alula to control airflow over its wings. This control is especially useful to prevent stalling at slow speeds and when the bird is hovering or landing. Raising the alula creates a thin slot. By being forced through this narrow space, the airstream moves faster, which restores lift and keeps the bird from dropping. The bird can also adjust other flight feathers to control airflow, just as an airplane's wings utilize slots and flaps for the same purpose.

Left: Overlapping feathers, shown close-up. The three layers of a bird's wing, including its marginal and lesser coverts, greater coverts, and flight feathers, create a smooth surface that serves as an airfoil.

Below: The steady, buoyant wing beats of the Eurasian jay allow it to glide between trees.

Kinds of Wings

Q: What accounts for the diversity in wing length and shape among birds?

A: The shape of a bird's wings reveals much about where and how it lives, just as its beak, feet, and legs do. Wings, a wondrous adaptation to begin with, have evolved to enable birds to fly in the most energy-efficient and practical manner possible for their species' lifestyles and habitats. Ornithologists group wings into four basic categories based on wing shape and performance, from the long, pointed wings of albatrosses and petrels to the short, wide wings of grouse and crows.

Q: What birds have long, thin wings?

A: Long, thin, pointed wings are typical of seabirds that exploit ocean winds for soaring. Albatrosses, gannets, shearwaters, and petrels glide on very long, narrow wings; gulls glide on modified versions. A hallmark of this type of wing is a very long inner wing. The inner wing provides much of a bird's lift, and this extra-long version generates the most lift of all. A seabird with such wings can soar for hours on ocean winds with hardly a flap, expending only the energy necessary to hold open its wings and adjust them as necessary when air currents shift.

The extremely long, narrow wings of albatrosses have earned them their renown as wandering seafarers. These seabirds cover vast stretches of ocean using a technique called "dynamic soaring." An albatross flying in this manner first soars on the wind at a height above the water, and then glides down toward the surface, picking up speed just as a bicyclist does when rolling downhill. Close to the water, where the wind's speed slows down due to friction with the ocean's surface, the albatross swoops up again, this time facing into the wind while the momentum of its dive carries it upward, the same way a bicyclist can ride the momentum of a downhill plunge partway up the next hill. Once aloft, the albatross can turn again and glide on higher-speed winds before plunging down and up again. This alternation of cross-wind gliding and downwind gliding allows

The long, thin, pointed wings of the northern gannet are representative of many seabirds. Seabirds with these kinds of wings often soar for hours.

the albatross to tack across the ocean rarely flapping its wings—and therefore expending very little energy.

Long, narrow wings, however, are not easy to maneuver and can make takeoff and landing awkward. Many seabirds circumvent this problem by plunging from cliffs to take off. Others, such as albatrosses, run to build up speed. For some of these birds, landing is anything but graceful—the sight of albatrosses tumbling clumsily upon landing no doubt earned them their nickname of "gooney birds."

Q: What birds have long, broad wings?

A: Long, broad wings enable vultures, eagles, storks, pelicans, and hawks to soar on rising currents of air over land. Their wings also possess a feature called slotting—the gapping between primary feathers at the wing tips in flight that makes the birds look as if they are spreading apart "fingers." Slotting increases lift,

as each feather is itself a miniature airfoil. It also reduces the turbulence that normally spills off a bird's wing tips. Slotting, length, and breadth add up to form wings that can be used not only for soaring but also for flying at very low speeds. Low-speed flight is a necessary ability when hunting from the air.

Raptors are particularly adept at riding on spiraling, rising currents of warm air known as thermals. A hawk hitches a ride aloft on a thermal by spreading its wings wide and soaring upward. It can then continue to float lazily in circles, all the while watching the ground for prey while exerting far less energy than it would if it were actively flying. It can also travel by hopping from thermal to thermal. To do this, it rises to a great height, and then glides out of the thermal. Gliding, unlike soaring, causes it to lose altitude, but it glides only until it reaches another thermal. It then rides this thermal aloft and repeats the process. Migrating hawks are often seen in thousands, spiraling in a column known as a kettle.

Left: Royal albatrosses are powerful flyers, but need to run to take off and land in a characteristically awkward tumble.

Right: The outspread wings of the painted storks display "slotting," the gapping between primary feathers that increase these birds' lift.

Q: What birds have broad, rounded wings?

A: Long wings are great for birds that fly in wide-open spaces but would encumber birds that live in tighter places. A bird that lives in brush or among trees needs wings that can help it fly among twigs and branches. This need is ably met by what is known as the elliptical wing—a broad, rounded wing that is neither strikingly long or short and marked by varying degrees of slotting. Elliptical wings allow nimble maneuverability and help many birds burst quickly into flight.

Many of our most familiar birds have elliptical wings: crows, sparrows, finches, pigeons, woodpeckers, and chickadees, for example. Owls and hawks that live and hunt in woodlands have elliptical wings, too. Grouse and pheasants' elliptical wings enable them to spring explosively into flight directly from the ground.

Right: Like other birds with high-speed wings, the American kestrel beats its wings rapidly and then glides. It may also glide through a thermal or hover.

Below: The ring-neck pheasant is an example of a broad, round-winged bird. It flies in a straight line, often with short bursts of stroking and then gliding.

Straight-line flight with varying amounts of flapping is typical of birds with elliptical wings, but many smaller birds also get around by using a variation known as bounding flight. In bounding flight, a bird flaps furiously and then folds up its wings so that it turns into a compact, streamlined missile, describing an arc in the air before unfolding its wings and flapping again. Bounding in this way enables small birds, which do not soar or glide, to save a great deal of energy.

Q: What birds have high-speed wings?

A: Avian speed and endurance records go to fliers in the group possessing the fourth type of wing—the sharply pointed one known as a high-speed wing (though not all birds with this sort of wing are speedsters). This wing allows a bird to achieve and maintain a high speed—with lots of flapping, though, because high-speed wings are not adapted for soaring.

This is the wing you will see on sandpipers, willets, and other shorebirds that leap from the sand and wheel away in fast-flapping flocks when you approach, and on the swallows that dip and dive around you as you stroll across a field, kicking up insects with every step.

Birds such as falcons and the aptly named swifts zoom on high-speed wings, the former as it preys on other birds and the latter as it chases insects. The pointed wings of ducks and geese carry them on migration twice yearly. The Arctic tern, the record-setting migrant that traverses the globe from north to south and back again each year, likewise makes its epic journeys on sharply pointed wings.

Q: How do birds maneuver in flight?

A: No matter how their wings are shaped, birds share various maneuvers that control speed and direction in flight. They bank or partly fold a wing to turn;

they fold in their wings to increase speed in a dive. They may bank so steeply that wings and body are angled entirely sideways, with only the head facing forward, so as to lose altitude before landing. Some species hold their wings in a V-shape to stabilize their flight while gliding. These constant adjustments of wings and tail are what make a bird's flight maneuvers appear to be so effortless.

Above: The Arctic tern flies gracefully, flapping its sharply pointed wings at a nearly even beat. When it spots prey, it hovers before swooping down to the water's surface.

Below: Swallows commonly fly swiftly, alternating short but deep wing lifts with straight glides.

Turning, Twisting Tails

Q: How does a bird use its tail in flight?

A: Tail feathers, or retrices, are grouped with the stiff feathers of the wing as flight feathers. They are attached to the pygostyle, which are the last bones of the bird's spine. The base of the retrices is covered on top by tail coverts. In some birds, such as peacocks, coverts may be so large that they are confused with the actual tail. Retrices serve many purposes. One of their most frequent uses is as a rudder to aid in steering. As a bird banks to turn, its tail twists sideways, too.

Although birds can usually fly just fine without their tails, a long tail can assist in making sharp turns. The Cooper's hawk, for example, has a long tail that helps it flit through the woods in pursuit of small birds. This North American accipiter's

counterparts in Europe, the sparrow-hawks, likewise have long tails that help them maneuver in woodlands. So, too, do African hawk-eagles that hunt in forests.

Tails are useful not only for steering, but also for braking. Many birds lower and fan their tails when they land, increasing the surface area that meets with air resistance to help them slow down.

Birds such as grebes, puffins, and loons, which have very short tails, are not able to make tight turns—a trade-off for avoiding the increased drag caused by a long tail. They compensate by sticking out their wide, webbed feet and spreading them, which turns them into satisfactory rudders and brakes.

The tail's most important function may be to impart lift, particularly when a bird is flying slowly. A snowy owl, for

Below left: Atlantic puffins favor crustaceans and small fish for sustenance. In order to circle down into the sea and retrieve prey, they rely on webbed feet to help them turn, rather than their stubby tails.

Below right: Spreading its tail wide helps the snowy owl alight and assists it while it hovers, adding a lift under the wings and tail to control its speed.

example, spreads its tail wide when it takes off from the ground. A widespread tail provides extra surface area for lift and also appears to affect how air flows over the inner wings by creating a slot between wing and tail. This slot causes the airflow to speed up, which further increases lift. The added lift prevents the bird from stalling as it flies at low speed, much as the alula does.

A widespread tail also provides extra lift to a bird when it hovers. Hummingbirds flare their tails as they hover. Kestrels spread their tails as they hang over a field, facing into the wind with wings held out stiffly, occasionally flapping.

Q: Do some birds have forked tails?

A: Some of the nimblest avian fliers are equipped with forked tails, in which the outermost tail feathers are the longest. A forked tail gives an extra boost to the maneuverability already afforded by a long tail and also supplies extra lift at low speeds. Many aerial acrobats that chase insects, such as scissor-tailed flycatchers and swallows, have forked tails. The swallow-tailed kite not only eats insects midair but also keeps flying as it snatches frogs off trees. Terns, sometimes called "flying scissors," hover and dart over water as they fish. Forked tails also serve as aids that help birds recognize members of their species and attract mates. Female barn swallows, for example, appear to favor males with the longest, most symmetrical forked tails.

Q: What bird is known for having a diminutive tail?

A: One spectacular aerialist has a tail distinctive for being diminutive—the bateleur of Africa's savannah. This eagle's tail is so short that, during flight, it does not extend beyond the feet. The bateleur's bright-red face and stubby tail have earned it the scientific name *Terathopius ecaudatus*, which roughly translates from the Greek into "marvelous face without a tail," while its common name attests to its flying skills: *Bateleur* is French for "acrobat." It soars as much as 300 miles (483 km) each day in search of food, rocking from side to side when it flies. But it is the birds' courtship flights that dazzle. Male and female engage in antics such as diving steeply, rolling upside down, playing follow-the-leader, and even looping the loop in sweeping barrel rolls.

A color engraving adapted from a John James Audubon illustration of the least tern. Terns will dive-bomb human intruders just as they do prey in the water below.

The bateleur, a short-tailed eagle, soars for hundreds of miles every day, searching for prey. It is best known for its frolicking aerial courtship.

Birds on Foot

Q: How do birds move on the ground?

A: Birds hop, walk, and run as they forage or search for nesting material on the ground. Some species use just hopping or walking, while others are adept at both.

Birds that spend most of their time in trees tend to hop, just as they do when they travel from branch to branch. Think of a house sparrow hopping across a sidewalk after bread crumbs. Many small birds are exclusively hoppers.

Hopping is a very energetic activity, however, so birds that spend much time on the ground tend to walk, which is less demanding. Ground-dwelling birds such as grouse and quail walk, as do wading birds and shorebirds.

Starlings, which frequently feed on the ground, also walk, as do pigeons and doves. Crows, ravens, and magpies all walk in a stately fashion; if threatened, they begin to hop, and then shift to an awkward stride midway between hopping

and running as they increase their speed. Roadrunners dispense entirely with hopping and break into the fleet stride that gives them their common name.

Ducks, geese, and swans walk with a distinctive waddle because they have broad bodies and wide-set legs. Hawks, eagles, owls, and other birds of prey also waddle when they walk. Penguins waddle, too, but have the advantage of being able to flop down on snow and ice and slide on their bellies while pushing with their feet and wings—a habit aptly termed "tobogganing."

Some species, particularly those adapted for using their feet to swim and dive, have legs set so far back on their bodies that walking on land is difficult. Loons, for example, can scarcely walk, therefore they often hitch themselves along on their bellies on land. Because they need to patter across water in order to gain lift for flight, most loons cannot take off from

Above right: Penguins often flop onto their bellies and slide along the ice—which can be a far more efficient way of getting around than their distinctive waddle.

Right: The webbed feet of the laughing gull allow it to easily walk along sandy shorelines as it forages.

the ground—a circumstance that strands birds that land on wet parking lots that they have mistaken for lakes. Grebes and diving ducks, such as ruddy ducks and mergansers, are also less than agile walkers.

Birds that spend much of their lives on the wing may also be ill-adapted for hopping or walking. Swifts, for example, have tiny, weak legs that can barely push them back into the air if they become grounded, and that cannot hop or walk.

Q: Are flightless birds strong runners?

A: Included among the flightless birds are penguins, kiwis, and certain species of ducks, pigeons, rails, a cormorant, and even a parrot. Many of these birds evolved on islands largely free of ground-dwelling predators. Yet, none of them can keep pace with the runners of the bird world: the rhea of South America, the cassowaries of Australia and New Guinea, the emu of Australia, and the ostrich of Africa. All are large and flightless. The rhea, emu, and ostrich live in grasslands. All three are formidable runners, with the ostrich taking the lead at 40 miles per hour (64.4 kph), or even faster, according to some sources. It can keep up this pace for about half an hour. The cassowary, which lives in rain forests, can dash at 30 miles per hour (48.4 kph), its head protected from branches by a built-in helmet called a casque.

Q: How do birds cling to trees and vertical surfaces?

A: Woodpeckers, woodcreepers, and treecreepers all hop up the sides of trees in search of insects. Strong leg muscles combined with strong feet tipped with sharp claws enable them to grasp the smallest niches in bark. In addition, stiff, spiny feathers in their tails serve as props to brace them as they cling. Nuthatches lack such tail feathers, depending entirely upon their feet and long claws for clinging. A nuthatch grips with one foot and props itself with the other, an ability that allows it to creep headfirst down a tree as well as climb upward.

Swifts' feet and claws are also adapted for clinging, enabling them to cling to sheer vertical surfaces such as cliffs and the insides of chimneys. Some species also have stiff tail feathers, like a woodpecker's, for propping. Some, such as the chimney swift, have feet with all four toes facing forward to enhance their clinging ability.

The horny outgrowth on the head of a colorful southern cassowary helps this flightless bird push its way through dense vegetation—an important protection for a bird that can dash at speeds of up to 30 miles per hour (48.3 kph).

"Happy being! Equally fitted for travelling through the air and the water, and not altogether denied the pleasure of walking on the shore."

—*John James Audubon*
writing about the common goldeneye duck

Birds in the Water

Q: How do birds swim on the surface of water?

A: Birds whose natural habitat is water have feet adapted for use as paddles while swimming. Many swimming birds have webbed feet, in which thin flaps of skin join the toes. Ducks, geese, loons, gulls, swans, and others have webbing between their three forward-facing toes. Pelicans, gannets, and cormorants have webbing between all four toes. Grebes and coots have toes that are individually lined with flaps of flesh to form what are known as lobed feet.

To swim, a bird pushes back first with one foot, and then the other. When the foot moves back, the toes spread apart and the webbing opens. The wide surface area thus created pushes back on the water to propel the bird forward. When the bird pulls its foot forward again, its toes draw together and the webbing folds up. This decreases the surface area and reduces resistance. A coot's lobed foot works similarly, with the toes and lobes folding up on the forward stroke.

Swimming birds also have wide bodies, like rowboats, which help them float. Air held within their dense plumage, as well as the air sacs in their bodies, enhances their buoyancy. The anhinga, a waterbird of the southeastern United States, swims just under the water's surface instead of atop it, with only its long neck and bill showing. Its feathers soak up water, which lowers their buoyancy and enables it to swim low and dive quickly. The anhinga's appearance in the water has earned it the nickname "snake bird."

Q: What birds dive?

A: Many swimming birds also dive in pursuit of fish or to forage underwater, and many species boast specific adaptations that suit them for this task. The duck family, for example, includes species known as "diving ducks." This group includes mergansers, sea ducks (such as buffleheads), bay ducks (such as canvasbacks), and ruddy ducks. Diving ducks have legs far back on their bodies to aid in swimming underwater. On land, this

Above: Mallards are well adapted to life on water, with webbed feet that serve as flippers and naturally oiled feathers that repel water.

Right: Dabbling ducks tip bottoms-up and then bob vertically as they forage underwater.

by air sacs in the head, neck, and chest that cushion the blow. This spearlike descent can carry the birds down to 30 feet (9 m) underwater. Brown pelicans dive into water from a height headfirst, too, but they submerge only their heads and land with a huge splash. The kingfisher, which is not adapted for life in water, nonetheless plunge-dives expertly for fish, quickly returning to its perch to eat its prey.

From high in the air, brown pelicans can spot fish swimming on the surface of the sea. They plunge downward and grab the prey, submerging only their heads.

leg position causes a diving duck's stance to be more vertical than that of a dabbling duck, which feeds at or just below the water's surface. Loons, cormorants, grebes, and anhingas also have legs set back on their bodies.

A diving bird on the water's surface typically dives by rearing slightly back, rising while arching its body, and then slipping underwater. A pied-billed grebe uses a different technique: It forces air out of its air sacs and feathers to sink rapidly when frightened. Other diving birds also force out air to decrease their buoyancy and make it easier to hunt underwater. Loons and grebes have bones that are more solid than other birds' skeletons, which further aid them in sinking.

Plunging into water from high in the air is a method employed by other diving birds. Boobies and gannets are particularly renowned for their high-diving acts. From heights up to 300 feet (90 m), these birds sight fish underwater and then plunge steeply, holding their wings tightly to their sides so that they are completely streamlined by the time they knife into the water. The force of impact is lessened

Q: How do birds swim underwater?

A: Birds use either their legs and feet, or their wings, or a combination to swim underwater. Penguins actually "fly" underwater with flipperlike wings. Members of the auk family, such as puffins and murres, also fly underwater. Feet help push the birds when diving from the surface and are also used for steering. Cormorants, anhingas, loons, coots, and grebes use mainly their feet for propulsion, pushing both of them back simultaneously. Mergansers typically use both wings and feet.

Magellanic penguins appear to fly underwater, skimming through the undersea currents propelled by their flipperlike wings.

CHAPTER 4

FINDING FOOD

Hang a bird feeder, and they will come: finches to crack open seeds, bushtits to hang upside down from a suet basket, chickadees to nab a seed and then dart away, juncos to feed on the ground below. A hawk may even visit to snatch an unwary diner. One's backyard birds, as are birds everywhere, are endlessly engaged in a search for food. Some, birds, such as crows and gulls, are generalists who will not turn up their beaks at any even remotely edible offering. Other birds have more specialized diets—limiting their menu to mainly one type of food. These other special diets can range from seeds, insects, fruit, or fish to nectar, sap, and even plankton. Birds' bodies feature adaptations that maximize their ability to get the particular food they need. Birds also display remarkable cunning when it comes to feeding and foraging. Gulls drop shellfish onto rocks to break them open. Egyptian vultures fling rocks at ostrich eggs to smash them. Some finches use twigs to probe in bark for insects. Birds have also figured out how to exploit humans for food—and their ingenuity goes far beyond frequenting bird feeders. In England, for example, blue tits learned to peck through the foil lids of milk bottles to sip the top layer of cream.

Above: British blue tits have developed a clever method of retrieving food: They sip the layer of cream on the top of milk bottles left at back doors.

Left: A hanging bird-feeder offers backyard birds, such as these American goldfinches, ample nourishment during the winter months.

Food as Fuel

Q: **How much food does a bird need to eat each day?**

A: Birds need to stoke the furnace of their metabolisms with a food intake that is comparatively higher than that of mammals and other vertebrates. The energy demands of flight create this high avian metabolic rate.

Small birds have proportionately larger surfaces (through which heat is lost) in relation to their mass of metabolizing tissue than do large birds, so they need to feed more frequently and eat relatively greater amounts of food. A tiny chickadee, for example, may need to eat 35 percent of its weight in a day, while the larger raven requires meals that total just 4 percent of its weight. Hummingbirds, with their tiny bodies and high activity levels, have the highest metabolic rates of any bird.

Q: **Why do some birds feed in flocks?**

A: A bird gains two advantages by feeding in a flock: The combined efforts of many birds seeking food gives individuals a better chance of finding a meal. Individuals also benefit

from having many eyes and ears on the alert for danger. These advantages outweigh the cost of sharing the spoils.

The various species of waxwings travel in flocks as they seek fruit, the mainstay of their diet, thus maximizing their efficiency in finding this clustered resource. Gulls and terns are also adept at exploiting the efforts of their fellows in foraging. When they see other birds diving or flocking in one place, they quickly join the throng. Vultures likewise keep an eye on the behavior of other vultures.

Some birds band together to cooperate in catching prey. For example, a few species of cormorants form a slowly swimming armada, frequently poking their heads underwater; when one bird finds a fish and dives, the others follow suit. Any alarmed fish not caught by the early diver may be grabbed by another. White pelicans form a semicircle and actually herd fish together, making it easier for each bird to scoop them up.

Some birds join mixed flocks made up of several species. Relatively smaller downy and hairy woodpeckers, for

Above right: A flock of gulls searches for food. Group foraging offers each individual bird a greater chance of finding nourishment, and provides the protection of its flockmates.

Below: Compared to smaller birds, the hefty ravens, such as the Australian raven shown here, eat less food proportionate to their size and weight.

example, tag after pileated woodpeckers, letting the bigger birds yank bark off trees, and then eat the insects the bigger woodpeckers overlook. Downy woodpeckers also utilize vigilant chickadees and titmice as alarm systems. In Australia, yellow robins follow brush turkeys, eating insects turned up by the turkeys as they scratch in leaf litter.

Mixed flocks of songbirds commonly form after the breeding season. Flocks of creepers, warblers, and tits flit through northern forests in fall and winter in search of insects. Studies show, however, that in time of prey abundance birds are less likely to form mixed-species flocks.

Q: Do birds change their diets from season to season?

A: Birds employ a variety of strategies to cope with seasonal fluctuations in food availability. Seedeaters, for example, eat different kinds of seeds as they become available throughout the year. Certain species also store seeds to eat in the off-season. Seedeaters also catch insects during the breeding season to feed to their young and may switch to insects when seeds are unavailable. The African queleas, for example, are seedeaters that will switch to termites when seeds are in short supply. Many tundra-nesting shorebirds feed their young insects in summer, eat berries to prepare for migration, and then dine on shellfish all winter.

Many species alter their diets so drastically that their digestive systems actually change to meet the challenge. Starlings, dunnocks, and bearded tits, which feed heavily on insects in summer, develop longer intestines and more muscular gizzards to cope with a winter diet of seeds.

Birds may also add unique items to their diet for part of the year. Sandpipers on the tundra eat small bones picked from owl pellets and small animal carcasses to get the calcium they need for egg laying. Female ostriches likewise eat broken eggshells to replenish their calcium supplies. Marabou storks and bateleur eagles in Africa supplement their usual scavenging ways with hunting small prey in order to supply their offspring with calcium-rich bones.

Migrating is another way to cope with seasonal food shortages. Recent studies, however, indicate that many migrant birds do not simply swap one locale for another—they also change their diets. Half of the species that migrate from North America to the tropics, for example, do not feed solely on insects upon arrival but also eat a great deal of fruit.

The Marabou stork is found throughout most of tropical Africa on dry, open savannahs near large lakes or rivers. It alters its diet when feeding its young by adding the calcium-rich bones of small prey.

Feeding on Plants

Q: Can birds eat leaves and grass?

A: Seeds, fruits, nectar, and starchy food-storage components such as bulbs are the most nutritious parts of plants, but some birds have adapted to feeding primarily on the tougher, less nutritious leaves, buds, flowers, and twigs. Among these birds are geese, grouse, swans, and a few ducks.

Leaves contain cellulose, which is an indigestible fiber. Extracting their nutritious sap is a demanding digestive process, as evidenced by the complicated four-chambered stomach and slow, cud-chewing behavior of ruminants such as cattle. Some birds emulate ruminants by relying on bacteria that can digest cellulose. Grouse, which eat buds and shoots, harbor such bacteria in a pair of intestinal outgrowths called caeca. Each caecum serves as a fermentation chamber, where partly digested food is further broken down by the bacteria, and then returned to the intestines for nutrient absorption. Bacteria also help digest leaves in the outsized crop of the hoatzin of South America; the strong odor of the fermenting food has earned the hoatzin the nickname of "stinking turkey."

Grazing geese feed heavily and frequently, digesting their food quickly in their tough, muscular gizzards. Great quantities of grass race through a goose's system in two hours or less. The kakapo, a flightless parrot of New Zealand, bypasses the burden of a bellyful of grass by grinding unplucked blades in its beak and sucking out the sap.

Q: What plants do waterfowl eat?

A: Geese and swans consume, in addition to grass and grain, the roots and starchy tubers of plants that grow in water, using their bills and tongues to pull them up. A dabbling duck often feeds in shallow water by plunging its head and neck below the surface, with its tail pointed up and legs paddling to keep it in place—a stance known as "tipping up." Dabblers also feed from the water's surface, skimming off small plants such as duckweed. Plantlike organisms called algae are eaten, too. Brant also feed on algae in the form of seaweed.

The toothlike spikes around the edges of its bill work like strainers as an Egyptian goose grazes in shallow water in search of water plants.

Q: What birds feed on nectar?

A: About one-fifth of the world's approximately 9,600 species of birds include nectar in their diets. Among these species are birds specially adapted for drinking nectar, some of which have names that reflect their feeding habits.

The honeyeaters of Australia and New Guinea possess long, grooved tongues with brushy tips for reaching into flowers and lapping up nectar. The sweet liquid flows down a honeyeater's throat and straight to its intestines, skipping processing in the stomach. Sunbirds of Africa, Asia, and Australia have tubular tongues with forked tips for lapping nectar. Their

neighbors, the white-eyes, roll their brushy tongues into tubes. Hawaiian honeycreepers are famed for the extraordinary diversity of their bills. Little parrots called lorikeets feed primarily on the nectar of Australian trees and bushes.

Hummingbirds, however, steal the show when it comes to nectar feeding. Their long, thin bills enclose a tubular tongue, split at the end, adapted for probing deeply into flowers and sipping nectar. Their ability to hover in front of blossoms is also an adaptation to their diet. Hummingbirds often travel a regular route while foraging that gives flowers time to refill their nectaries, a strategy known as traplining. The jewel-like birds, like many nectar feeders, "repay" the flowers by aiding in pollination.

Other species of birds have figured out ways to simply swipe nectar without repaying the flower. Purple finches and grosbeaks may nip flowers off a tree and squeeze them to extract nectar. The glossy flower-piercer of the Andes, as its name implies, uses its recurved beak to pierce the base of a flower.

The red-legged honeycreeper of Central and South America is one of the many bird species that include nectar in its diet.

Although evening grosbeaks are primarily seedeaters, they will sometimes squeeze the nectar out of flowers that they have removed from a tree.

Fruits, Seeds, and Nuts

Q: **How do birds extract seeds and nuts from shells?**

A: Many birds eat seeds and nuts as part of their diets. Those that feed primarily on seeds are, logically enough, referred to as seedeaters, a group that includes the finches.

Finches, like other birds that feed on seeds and nuts, have beaks, bodies, and behaviors adapted for feeding on these highly nutritious, energy-rich foods that often come enclosed in difficult packaging. Many finches have thick, conical bills with enough crushing power to crack open seed coats. The hawfinch of Europe can even crack open cherry stones. A finch's beak has a sharp edge on the lower bill and a notch on the upper bill. By turning a seed with its tongue, the finch wedges the seed into the notch and aligns its seams with the lower bill's cutting edge. It cracks the seed and then uses its lower bill and tongue to turn the seed and remove the husk.

The Cassin's finch feeds on primarily buds and seeds, especially those from conifers, and fruit. The finch supplements its diet with insects during the summer.

Watch a house finch at a bird feeder opening up a sunflower seed and you will see this process in action.

Finches with more slender bills shun large seeds to focus on smaller ones ignored by birds with bigger beaks. Redpolls cling to birch twigs to pick tiny seeds from the catkins. Goldfinches dangle from thistles as they pluck small seeds. Crossbills are finches named for their unique beaks in which the upper and lower mandibles overlap. With this beak, a crossbill can pry open a scale on a cone and twist it, and then wriggle its tongue into the gap to extract the seed. The size of the beak is a clue to what kinds of cones the crossbill seeks: White-winged crossbills and red crossbills with smaller beaks feed on larch, hemlock, spruce, and fir cones, while big-billed red crossbills take on the bigger, harder pinecones.

The hard shells of nuts foil many birds, but others are quite up to the challenge of breaking them. Parrots, with their stout bills formed like pliers, easily crack open nuts by squeezing them against a hard section of the upper jaw. The palm cockatoo can even crack open palm nuts. The birds' tongues and pointed bills then deftly pick out the edible portion of the nuts. Other birds, lacking nutcracker bills, still manage to open nuts. A European nuthatch wedges a nut into a chink in a branch and then hammers at it with its beak. A crow likewise hammers at a nut, holding it in place with one foot, or carries it high and then drops it on a hard surface, such as a paved road.

Q: What fruits do birds eat?

A: Fruits enjoyed by humans are also on the menu for birds, as anyone who has witnessed birds bingeing in a cherry tree knows. But birds also dine on many fruits humans do not eat, such as mountain ash berries. These berries are favorites of both cedar and Bohemian waxwings, which feed primarily on fruit for more than half the year. In fall and winter, they feast not only on mountain ash berries but also on the fruits of such plants as vibernum, dogwood, and juniper. Summer's bounty of fruit offers them strawberries, blueberries, cherries, serviceberries, and other crops both wild and farmed.

Berries of the tree-dwelling desert mistletoe sustain phainopepla species of the southwestern United States and Central America. A phainopepla eats about 250 mistletoe berries a day and even feeds them to its young. The berries move quickly through the bird's short, efficient digestive tract. The sticky waste, full of seeds, is excreted on a branch. Thus, the bird "plants" its own food source by distributing its seeds. Offering birds fruit in exchange for seed distribution is a strategy employed by many other plants, too.

Birds in the tropics are especially avid consumers of fruit. Hornbills of African and Southeast Asian forests eat figs and other fruits. Toucans in Central and South America's forests pluck nutmegs, figs, and more than 100 other fruits with their long, colorful beaks. Nocturnal oilbirds in South America rely on their sense of smell to find palm fruits in the dark. Quetzals in Costa Rica and elsewhere feed heavily on wild avocados.

Above left: The previous autumn's crab apples are delicious to a Bohemian waxwing but unappetizing to humans.

Below: The toco toucan eats mainly fruit and uses its huge, but light, bill as a tool for picking it. It also feeds on seeds, spiders, insects, eggs, and an occasional lizard or bird.

> I value my garden more for being full of blackbirds than of cherries, and very frankly give them fruit for their songs.
>
> —JOSEPH ADDISON

Dining on Invertebrates

Q: What invertebrates do birds eat?

A: Insects rank as the most important food source for birds. Many songbirds feed primarily on insects and feed them to their young. Birds that eat plants will also snap up insects; even hummingbirds pluck insects from plants in order to obtain protein not supplied by nectar.

Birds also eat many noninsect invertebrates. On land, they snap up spiders, pillbugs and sowbugs, snails, slugs, millipedes, centipedes, and the like. At the beach, gulls happily eat sea stars, while small birds pick along the wrack line for tiny crabs and sandhoppers. Shorebirds probe in mudflats and on beaches for clams and other buried treasure. They also feed on mussels and other bivalves that cling to rocks. Many seabirds skim small crustaceans called krill from the ocean's upper layers. Krill also sustains many penguin species, although king penguins have a fondness for squid.

But birds are most often linked in people's minds with worms, which do indeed nourish many species. The nocturnal kiwi of New Zealand specializes in feeding on them, and shorebirds relish the ones they find in mud, sand, and soil.

Q: What birds have body parts that aid them in catching insects?

A: Most birds catch insects quite easily with the all-purpose bill of the generalist. A starling, for example, uses its beak as a wedge to pry apart soil in search of larvae. Even ducks with their specialized bills take insects; shovel-billed mallards readily eat mosquitoes and their larvae.

Other birds have beaks especially adapted for concentrating on insect prey. Woodpeckers, for example, have sharp, stout beaks for drilling into bark and a skull that can withstand the force of their drumming. They have also developed an extra-long hyoid: a "tongue bone" that wraps around the skull and supports a long tongue with a stiff, sticky, bristly tip for extracting insects. One woodpecker, the wryneck, has a sticky tongue that measures two-thirds of its body length. It plunges its tongue into ant nests, in a manner similar to an anteater, to snare ants. Warblers and titmice have short, thin beaks for daintily picking insects off twigs and leaves. Bee-eaters of Africa and jacamars of Central and South America have long, sharply pointed bills for grabbing insects while flying.

A roseate spoonbill sweeps its bill underwater in a semicircular motion, until its prey is captured within the whirlpool and brought to its open mouth.

them to cram up to 2,000 insects into their throats, an ability that has earned some species the name "frogmouth." One nightjar, the chuck-will's-widow, can even scoop up small birds.

Q: How do birds avoid being stung or otherwise harmed by insect prey?

A: Birds have ways of coping with difficult insect prey. For example, they quickly learn to avoid bad-tasting, poisonous insects. Studies show that chickadees will avoid such unpalatable fare nearly a year after first sampling them.

Stinging, biting insects are also a concern, but some species specialize in eating them. Bee-eaters handle such prey by disarming them. They carry bees back to a perch, where they squeeze them and rub them against the perch to get rid of their venom. Bee-eaters can apparently distinguish which bees are harmless drones lacking venom and dispense with this procedure when they catch them. Swallow-tailed kites also eat wasps and will even bring whole wasp nests back to their nests. A scientist discovered another kite with a bellyful of fire ants. The thick, spongy stomach lining of this species may help protect it from such irritable snacks.

Tyrant flycatchers that glean small insects from leaves and branches have warblerlike bills, but flycatchers that take off from perches to catch insects—a technique known as "hawking"—have long, broad, flattened beaks with hooked tips for nabbing bees and other insects in midair. The base of hawking flycatchers' beaks is tufted with hairlike feathers called rictal bristles, which may act as windscreens protecting the birds' eyes.

Rictal bristles also sprout on the faces of some flying insectivores such as swallows and some nightjars. A swallow has a short beak, but the span of its mouth, called a gape, is wide. Swallows fly with beak open wide and scoop insects out of the air. A swift's short beak also has a wide gape and is held open in flight to sweep up small insects in its path. After dusk, nightjars take over this niche. The extraordinary gape of these birds allows

Above left: The hairy woodpecker finds its insect prey by feeling the vibrations they make moving about in wood. It then extracts the insects from holes with its barbed tongue.

Below: Bee-eaters get their names from their preferred food. They squeeze the venom out of a bee prior to eating it.

The Predators

Q: What are raptors?

A: Although many birds are predators, only the ones with taloned feet are known as the birds of prey, or raptors—a word derived from the Latin *rapere*, meaning "to seize and carry away." This group includes diurnal hunters such as falcons, hawks, eagles, and ospreys (as well as secretary birds and the scavenging vultures) and their nocturnal counterparts, owls. Raptors all use their feet to catch prey, unlike other predatory birds, which use their beaks.

Prey taken by these birds ranges from small animals such as insects, frogs, lizards, fish, small mammals, and birds to large ones such as monkeys and monitor lizards. One raptor, the bearded vulture of southern Europe and Africa, even breaks open large bones by dropping them onto rocks, and then scoops out the marrow with its tongue. Many raptors, particularly falcons, eat other birds. Some falcons catch prey in flight, flying high above it

and then diving, striking the other bird with the feet. The impact of this forceful blow stuns the prey, which is then seized and killed. Larger falcons, such as the gyrfalcon, catch birds the size of ducks; smaller falcons, such as the peregrine, can go after pigeon-sized prey.

Mammals are food for a number of raptors. Lemmings, mice, voles, rabbits, and other small mammals end up in the relentless grasping feet of many kinds of hawks, eagles, and owls. Some very large raptors do not hesitate to seize bigger mammals: The martial eagle of Africa routinely kills antelope calves, and the great Philippine eagle hunts flying lemurs, squirrels, bats, monkeys, and even small deer. Harpy eagles attack sloths and monkeys in South American rain forests. Snakes and other reptiles are eaten by the

Above right: When prey is sighted, an osprey dives steeply, its talons outspread, and splashes into the water. After quickly resurfacing it flies off, adjusting the fish in its claws so that the head is pointed forward.

Below: Raptors, such as the barn owl, capture prey with their feet rather than their beaks.

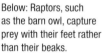

secretary bird of Africa; it kicks and stomps on them and then delivers a killing bite. The crested-serpent eagle of Asia goes after tree snakes, swallowing them headfirst. The white-bellied sea eagle eats water snakes as well as fish. Other eagles, such as the bald eagle, also rely on fish. The osprey is exclusively a fish hunter.

Certain raptors have very specific dietary needs. The snail kite of Florida, for example, is named for its dependence on a diet of snails. Snails also are food for the hook-billed kite of South America, which hunts them on the ground and in trees and will even hang upside down from a branch to seize them.

Q: How do birds catch fish in water?

A: Raptors such as eagles and ospreys snatch fish from the water with their feet. Kingfishers perch or hover above the water and then dive to grab fish. A white pelican swims along the surface, often in the company of other pelicans, and scoops up fish with its pouched beak. Cormorants dive and seize fish with their pointed bills, while mergansers grasp their slippery prey with serrated bills. Anhingas spear fish with their open, knife-like beaks. Other birds that dive to catch fish include penguins, puffins, loons, and grebes. Gannets and boobies are famous for their spectacular plunge-diving, in

which they shoot into the water from on high.

Long-legged wading birds stalk the margins of bodies of water. Herons, storks, and cranes quickly snap their long necks and bills into the water to grab fish. The black heron spreads its wings over its head to shade the water, a tactic that may reduce sun glare on the water and also lure fish that seek out shade. The snowy egret often stirs up the water and mud with one foot to scare fish into revealing themselves. Green herons use bait to lure fish. They drop feathers or bits of leaves on the water's surface. A heron in captivity even used pellets of fish food to attract fish.

Left: The snail kite has a curved beak especially designed to extract snails from their shells.

Below: The grey heron stalks slowly through the shallows, quickly snapping its narrow neck and beak to catch fish.

Eating Leftovers

Q: Do birds store food for the winter?

A: Species of jays, titmice, nuthatches, woodpeckers, and chickadees worldwide cache (hide in a secure place of storage) food for winter use. Thick-billed nut-crackers in Europe and Asia plant pine seeds in soil in summer and fall, and then recover up to 70 percent of them in winter, even though most of the seeds are buried under snow. In North America, blue jays tuck nuts and seeds into the ground under a cover of leaves. Gray jays shove seeds and even insects into bark crevices, gluing them in place with sticky saliva.

Woodpeckers also diligently fill larders. In North America, Lewis's and red-headed woodpeckers stuff nuts, seeds, and corn into crevices of trees, utility poles, and even fence posts. Colonies of acorn woodpeckers work together to chisel row after row of holes in pines and firs and then jam the holes full of acorns, wedging them in so tightly that even a greedy

Black-capped chickadees stuff seeds into bark for winters in Alaska and other cold climates.

Acorn woodpeckers work together to prepare for the barren months ahead by wedging thousands of nuts into holes they have pecked into fir and pine trees.

squirrel cannot winkle them out. One tree was found to contain 50,000 acorns.

Many species of chickadees are just as diligent. Black-capped chickadees in Alaska and other cold places cache thousands of seeds in bark. Boreal chickadees stuff spruce seeds into lichen. They also store insect larvae under loose bark and press wads of aphids among spruce needles. Bits of bark and lichen strung together with saliva and cobwebs serve as tiny "blankets" to hide some foods. In Europe, the Siberian tit may cache nearly half a million seeds and other items annually.

Recent studies of chickadees have revealed that a part of the brain devoted to memory (the hippocampus) actually grows in size when it begins storing food, and then shrinks in the spring when food is abundant, which may explain how they remember the locations of their caches.

What birds are full-time scavengers and specialize in feeding on carrion?

A: Birds are opportunists, always seeking ways to save energy while foraging for food. A dead animal is a bonanza that many species eagerly exploit. Certain species of birds, however, are specially adapted for scavenging. The best-known full-time scavengers are vultures.

Vultures typically have strong beaks that enable them to pierce a carcass's hide and tear it open (although if the hide is very thick, smaller vultures may wait for another scavenger to do the job). Their long necks easily snake into a carcass. The head and neck of vultures are either bare or covered with down; feathers would only become filthy with gore. Vultures also have long, broad wings for soaring. As they soar, they scan the landscape with sharp eyes (although the turkey vulture of North America uses its sense of smell). In Africa, they track their fellow scavengers, the hyenas. Vultures also watch each other. If a far-off vulture suddenly descends, other vultures home in from miles around to see what it has found.

A group of vultures feeding on a carcass looks like a melee, but there is a hierarchy in the mass of squabbling birds. In the grasslands of East Africa, a definite pecking order exists. The first to dine are big, aggressive lappet-faced vultures that can tear open the toughest hides and pull meat from bones. They are closely attended by white-headed vultures, and then are soon joined by higher-flying vultures that spied their descent: white-backed vultures and Rüppell's griffons. These two species thrust their heads into the carcass to rasp meat from the bones with rough tongues. Next in line are the small hooded and Egyptian vultures, which eat the leftovers. Last of all come the bearded vultures to eat small bones and smash open large ones by dropping them on rocks to expose the edible marrow.

Scavengers fill an important ecological niche by cleaning up waste in the environment. Just how vital their sanitation services are has been dramatized in India, where vulture populations have declined drastically since the mid-1990s, and one species is near extinction. As a result of their decline, animal carcasses rotted outside villages, attracting rabies-ridden packs of dogs. The vultures' die-off was caused by veterinary painkillers in the flesh of dead cattle they ate. The painkillers' use has now been banned.

Lappet-faced vultures are the first in line when a carcass has been spotted. Their task is tearing the hide from the animal and the meat off the bones.

CHAPTER 5

HOW BIRDS COMMUNICATE

In Percy Bysshe Shelley's ode "To a Skylark," the poet marvels at this high-flying bird's liquid notes: "All that ever was/Joyous and clear and fresh, thy music doth surpass." For the skylark, however, singing is serious business—an intense activity performed to win a mate and defend territory. The beautiful and sometimes bizarre movements of birds are likewise adaptations for communicating with each other. A bird-of-paradise's topsy-turvy acrobatics, a crane's ballet, and an albatross's heads-up display are all designed to send messages to

potential mates. Although the birds are "speaking" with each other, their conversations have the power to inspire human eavesdroppers—and even our own music. Mozart is said to have been inspired by the singing of his pet starling. Some birds, in turn, are excellent mimics who augment their songs with sounds borrowed from humans. If Mozart's starling were alive today, he might have followed the lead of other starlings and embroidered his songs with sounds such as a sheep's bleating, a bus's rumbling, a woodpecker's drumming, and a telephone's ringing, as well as the voices of other birds.

Above: Because the skylark lives in open grassland habitat with few lofty vantage points, it often soars high into the air to deliver its warbling song.

Left: The song of the field sparrow is an unusually clear, plaintive whistle, often sung at sundown and in the early twilight.

How Birds Vocalize

Q: What is a syrinx?

A: A person who sings well is often said to sing like a bird. But even the best human singer cannot hope to match the performance of a songbird, let alone sing a duet on his or her own. The human larynx, a single-chamber organ containing vocal cords, is simply not equipped to function like a bird's "voice box," the syrinx. The syrinx is located along a bird's windpipe at the point where it divides into two bronchial tubes leading into the lungs. It is made up of two chambers that have thin membranes in their walls. The entire structure is surrounded by an air sac. The continuous flow of air circulating through a bird's highly efficient respiratory system courses through the syrinx, too. Exhalation of air also pumps up the pressure in the air sac around the syrinx, which then presses on the membranes

and makes them bulge into the air flowing through the syrinx. All this activity sets the membranes vibrating.

Moreover, pairs of muscles attached to the syrinx change the tension of the membranes. A songbird has from five to eight pairs of these muscles. In addition, each of the two chambers in the syrinx can be controlled independently. Thus, a bird can make two sounds at once, one in each chamber, in effect duetting with itself.

This complex structure is operated by a song control center in the brain. Researchers have found that songbirds with large repertoires have correspondingly larger song control centers. Birds that do not learn their songs but are born with them instead have differently structured brains. Research has also revealed that a bird's song control center waxes and wanes in response to sex hormones. It is larger in the breeding season when birds are

The syrinx of a bird is shaped like an upside-down, hollow Y. To sing or squawk, a bird tightens up its syrinx muscles so that air moving through the syrinx is compressed. This causes a membrane inside the syrinx to vibrate, making a sound. A bird can control its syrinx muscles to produce a variety of sounds.

The Bird's Syrinx

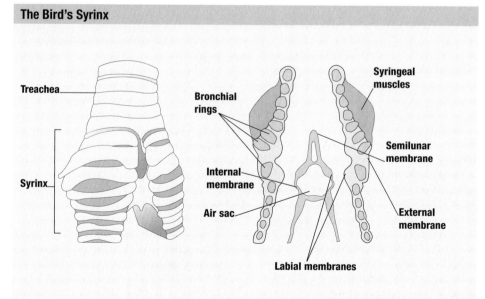

actively singing and shrinks in the nonbreeding season. Some species, such as turkey vultures and storks, lack the muscles to control a syrinx. Though they have no voice, these birds can hiss and make other sounds.

Q: Which species of birds use air sacs to make sounds?

A: Every bird can be said to use air sacs to vocalize because the syrinx is surrounded by a sac that, if punctured, silences it. Some birds, however, use air sacs in special ways to produce sounds. These sacs are part of the bird's esophagus, not its respiratory system. The sounds they produce are most often associated with breeding.

Sage-grouses of North America, for example, court females by rapidly inflating and deflating esophageal pouches. This action produces a loud popping noise and also reveals large yellow-green bare patches of skin on the neck. Greater prairie-chickens likewise inflate orange sacs to make a moaning sound. Kakapos in New Zealand inflate air sacs to send out booming cries that carry for up to four miles. Capuchinbirds in South American rain forests use air sacs to make loud mooing sounds. American bitterns, secretive denizens of marshes, distend the esophagus to make an eerie pumping sound. The bittern's call has earned it nicknames such as thunder pumper, stake driver, and water belcher. The male frigatebird inflates a red throat pouch called the gular sac as part of its courtship display. He rattles his bill against this enormous scarlet balloon and calls loudly when a female flies by, vying with other displaying males for her attention.

A sage-grouse usually make a coarse *kak, kak, kak* call. During courtship, however, it expels air through esophageal pouches to produce loud pops.

Although the mating ritual of the reclusive American bittern is rarely seen by humans, the resounding boom of the courting male carries far across his wetland home.

Birdsong

Q: Why do birds sing?

A: Birdsong brings out the poet in humans, but in birds singing is a serious, practical business. Male birds sing in order to claim and defend territory and attract mates, and some female birds sing to back up territorial claims and reinforce bonds with males.

In many songbird species, singing gets under way in temperate zones when birds migrate north to breeding grounds in spring (although nonmigratory birds that defend territory year-round, such as European robins, sing in all seasons). Males, whose testosterone levels rise in response to increasing daylight, establish themselves in territories. Frequently, they sing from a prominent perch. For a bird to announce his presence in this way signals that something other than high spirits is urging him on. His posture and song are warnings to other males of his species. If an intruder enters his territory, he gives chase. Scientists have found that males will even attack loudspeakers that play recordings of other males singing. Males also listen carefully to the songs of their neighbors to keep tabs on their activities. They can tell their neighbors' voices apart from those of strange males, who may warrant closer monitoring.

These songs also play a role in courtship. By singing, a male announces that he and his territory are available. Females may judge a male by the quality or endurance of his singing: A robust male with a large repertoire of songs who can spend time singing

Above right: The loud, cheerful song of the western meadowlark is a series of flute-like gurgling notes that go down the scale.

Below: The pugnacious little European robin sings a fluting, warbling song in the breeding season and a more plaintive version during the winter.

instead of foraging or repelling intruders may be an extremely fit fellow with an extra fine territory.

A male's song may also prime the female for mating and egg-laying. Playing a recording of a male canary singing stimulates a female canary to nest and lay eggs. If the male's repertoire is expansive, she responds even more strongly and lays a greater number of eggs. Studies of western meadowlarks have also shown that males with large repertoires are more attractive to females than males of less virtuosity.

Scientists admit, however, that they still have much to learn about birdsong. Research has explored the behavior of only about 300 songbirds out of the approximately 4,600 species of songbirds that exist, with most of the attention focused on just a few of those species (such as black-capped chickadees and white-crowned sparrows). The sounds and songs of perching birds not classified as songbirds remain even more of a mystery—barely a dozen of these species have been studied.

Q: Why are some birds called songbirds and not others?

A: About 4,600 of the world's 9,600 bird species are songbirds. They are all in the order known as passerines, or perching birds. Scientists split passerines into two groups: the oscines, or songbirds, and the suboscines.

Songbirds typically share certain characteristics, such as the structure of their sound-producing organ, the syrinx. A greater number of muscles are associated with the syrinx in an oscine than in a suboscine. Songbirds must also learn to sing. Although a songbird nestling is born with an ability to make certain sounds and a latent template for recognizing its species' songs, it will not sing properly as an adult if it does not have an opportunity to hear adults singing when it is young.

Suboscines, on the other hand, generally do not have to learn their songs. Their music is already encoded in their brains. Researchers have recently found, however, that a species of suboscines called bellbirds seem to include some learning in acquiring their noisy songs. Parrots and many hummingbirds, which are not passerines, also learn their songs.

Moreover, not all songbirds sing. Cedar waxwings, for example, call but do not sing. And not every songbird's song sounds like music to human ears: The harsh song of the largest songbird, the raven, is not extolled by poets.

Ravens are considered songbirds, but their drawling croaks can be unpleasant to human ears.

"The birds pour forth their souls in notes/Of rapture from a thousand throats."
—WILLIAM WORDSWORTH

Learning to Sing

Q: **Is a songbird born knowing how to sing?**

A: Learning to sing is one of the distinguishing features of songbirds. How much a nestling must learn and when it must learn it depends on its species, but lab and field research on birdsong in the past four decades has provided insight into the learning process. The results indicate that songbirds are born with a "talent" for their species' song and an ability to recognize it. The hearts of song sparrow nestlings even beat faster when they hear a song sparrow's song for the first time.

Some studies have focused on what happens to a songbird chick raised without any opportunities to hear adults of its species sing. White-crowned sparrows growing up in this deprived atmosphere sang very odd versions of the adult song. Nestlings allowed to hear white-crowned sparrow songs, however, readily learned to sing properly. Nestlings exposed to recordings of other sparrow species "reject" them. If a live sparrow of another species is their sole source of music, however, they may acquire its song. Deaf nestlings also sing abnormally; baby songbirds need to hear themselves practice in order to acquire the right songs.

Just as human children acquire language more easily before they reach their teens, so too do young songbirds appear to have a critical span of time in which to learn to sing properly. Scientists call this span a sensitive period. For many species, this period occurs between the ages of 15 to 50 days. After that, learning becomes more difficult. Certain species, however,

Above right: The male northern mockingbird sings a medley of songs including those of other species, repeating each phrase several times before moving on to the next.

Below: A male song sparrow performs from about six to more than twenty different melodies.

Although young canaries learn their songs by closely copying a nearby adult, they will eagerly pick up songs that sound nothing like their species' melodies.

learn new songs throughout their lives. Mockingbirds and thrashers, for example, constantly add to their repertoires and are not above swiping melodies from other songbirds. Catbirds' singing is not hampered by lack of opportunity to hear their species' songs as nestlings. Sedge wrens learn some songs but also spin dozens of tunes of their own devising. Canaries, whose owners may even buy recordings of birdsong to inspire their pets to sing, surprised researchers in recent studies by eagerly learning computer-generated songs. When they experienced their first wave of reproductive hormones, however, they reverted to time-tested canary standards.

Q: What is a subsong?

A: A subsong is a fledgling's muted, jumbled version of its species' song or songs. In many songbird species, young birds begin crooning subsongs shortly after leaving the nest. Typically, a young bird singing a subsong perches quietly, often with its eyes closed and head tilted to one side. Its throat pulses faintly as it warbles in a whisper, its voice barely audible even to someone standing quite close. Researchers often describe the bird's attitude as trancelike.

The subsong itself is likened to a baby's babbling. It includes random snatches of the proper songs that the youngster will sing as an adult, interspersed with quiet call notes. If the young bird is interrupted, it immediately stops singing and snaps to attention, fully alert, almost as if saying, "Who, me? Singing? Never!" Over time, the young bird's subsong grows louder, as if with practice comes growing confidence.

Adult songbirds are known to sing quietly to themselves, too. These songs are called whisper songs and, like a youngster's subsong, can be heard only at very close range. Unlike a youngster's subsong, it is a quiet version of the species' repertoire, though sometimes a few new notes are tossed in. Whisper songs are typically lisped by birds in hiding or on the nest, and in some species both sexes sing them.

A fledgling warbler emits a quiet subsong, which is often a jumbled version of the adult song of his species, as he masters its complexities.

Duets and Dialects

Q: What is duetting?

A: Duetting occurs when a mated pair of birds sings together. Sometimes the two sing in unison, harmonizing so well that the song sounds as if it is pouring from the throat of just one bird. Other pairs take turns singing so skillfully that they achieve the same effect.

Certain species of birds, such as the northern cardinal, sing complicated duets.

Both forms of duetting are particularly prominent among tropical species of birds, which make up most of the 200-odd species that sing duets. These tropical duettists remain in mated pairs throughout the year, and some also defend territories year-round. Duetting may keep their pair bond strong as well as help them stay in touch in thick tropical vegetation.

Among the best known duettists are Australian whipbirds. The male sings a song that concludes with a resounding crack and is promptly answered by a snatch of song from his mate. In East Africa, red-and-yellow barbets sit side by side and burst into song together, with each bird singing different notes. The smaller D'Arnaud's barbets also sing such duets as the rest of their flock listens in silence; if the dominant male vanishes,

Individual male marsh wrens deliver their reedy warbles and dry trills in varying song patterns, ranging from about 40 in eastern populations to nearly 150 in some western regions.

another male steps into his place and expertly sings his part of the song. A female black-headed gonolek of Africa sings clicking notes a split second after her mate's song stops, as if applying a period to the end of his sentence.

A few species of birds outside the tropics sing duets, too. For example, a female red-winged blackbird's brief song overlaps the final trill of her mate's. Female Carolina wrens do likewise. Swans, which mate for life, greet each other with loud honking duets. Female cardinals sing in response to their mates' song. Even the unmusical ravens sing duets.

Q: Do all birds of the same species sing the same song across the species' range?

A: The songs of many songbirds vary from location to location. These variations are called dialects. Fledglings learning to sing pick up the dialects of their parents and neighbors. In many species, male songbirds that disperse also match their songs to those of neighboring males, thus perpetuating a local dialect.

Sometimes, dialects are so distinct that birds of the same species will not interbreed. Marsh wrens

As do other warblers, the male Kentucky warbler sings a single, relatively simple song to females. Unlike many other warblers, however, he does not use dialects during squabbles with competing males.

of the eastern and western United States, for example, sing differently from each other and do not breed with each other, even though they are capable of learning each other's songs. Researchers are currently studying if dialects can inhibit the dispersal of birds and if they played a role in the evolution of songbird species.

Most suboscines, whose songs appear to be genetically wired into their brains and do not need to be learned, sing the same songs across their ranges. Studies of alder flycatchers in North America reveal the same song being sung on both coasts.

Recent studies of tropical bellbirds, however, have shown that these suboscines appear to have dialects and can learn their neighbors' sounds. Ongoing research into birdsong and dialects

continues to tantalize ornithologists with new discoveries and exceptions that challenge generalizations. The blue-winged warbler, for example, sings the same song to females across its range, as does the chestnut-sided warbler. Both birds, however, use local dialects for the songs they sing at dawn and in altercations with other males. Scientists theorize that being able to speak to any female that happens by is of benefit to a male. Using dialect to speak to male neighbors might be in keeping with the behavior of many songbirds, which engage in countersinging. Countersinging is a sort of "dueling banjos" session between male birds defending their territory, in which they match each other's songs one for one as if holding an old-time cowboy "cussing contest."

Calls and Warnings

Q: What is the difference between a song and a call?

A: Ultimately, a bird's song is not defined by its musicality but rather by its delivery and purpose. A song is sung loudly, often from a highly visible location such as a fence post or high branch. Its primary aim is to defend territory and attract a mate. It may be simple or complex; it may or may not be musical; and it is often seasonal. If the singer is a songbird, some learning went into its acquisition. A call, on the other hand, is produced any time of the year, by both sexes. It is usually an inborn behavior, not one that must be learned (though researchers have found that adult American goldfinches and other species can learn to adapt their calls to match their mates'). Birds use contact calls to keep in touch while feeding and to find each other in breeding colonies. Other calls signal fear and warn of danger. These calls are often recognizable to birds of other species as well as many mammals.

Birds also have calls they use to threaten other birds and intruders of other species. Young birds who have left the nest call to let their parents know where they are.

Q: Why do baby birds peep?

A: A songbird with a beakful of insects is confronted by a crowd of gaping mouths when it returns to the nest, as well as a frenzy of peeping. "Feed me!" each nestling seems to cry—and that is exactly what it is saying. A peep is a begging call, the first of many calls it will learn to make.

Nestlings that are helpless upon hatching, such as songbirds, do not peep right away. At first, the parent bird must urge them to eat; a black-capped chickadee, for example, uses a particular squawking sound to encourage its babies to open their beaks. Nestlings also possess a reflex reaction that causes them to open wide when the fleshy corners of their beaks are touched. But typically, within a day or two, they begin to peep—at first softly, and then in loud, demanding voices. Birds that are well developed and active shortly after hatching, such as ducklings, do not beg for food. Instead, they peep to keep in touch with the parent caring for them, who also vocalizes to let the young know where he or she is. This is the dialogue one hears as a mother duck waddles at the head of a line of peeping ducklings, quacking softly.

Ducklings and other baby birds that hatch ready to walk and feed themselves are termed precocial. Researchers have found that precocial baby birds start

The nightingale sings its melodious song at night, often from high on a tree branch, from where the song carries a long way. One male nightingale may have as many as 300 love songs in his repertoire, as well as songs that lay claim to his territory.

A mother duck quacks softly and her trailing ducklings peep in order to keep track of one another.

peeping while still inside their eggs. A few days before they are ready to hatch, they begin to make clicking and cheeping sounds. Vibrations also pass between the eggs, which are tucked closely together inside the nest. This contact appears to synchronize the hatching so that all the youngsters are ready to leave the nest at the same time with their parent. Studies of young bobwhite quail show that the babies even learn to recognize their mother's call before hatching.

Q: What vocalizations do birds use to warn one another of danger?

A: Cries given by birds when they spy a predator are known as alarm calls. An alarm call is often a high-pitched sound that warns of danger without precisely revealing the location of the caller. This sound is very different from the loud, noisy calls that the same birds may give as they band together to harass a predator. Some birds, such as Florida scrub-jays, even relay just how dire the threat is by the intensity of their calls.

A bird's alarm call is recognized not only by its mate, young, and fellow species members but also by birds of other species. In mixed flocks, some species that are particularly adept at spotting danger function as sentinels. Some sentinels, however, have learned to use alarm calls to trick other birds. In the Amazonian rain forest, the white-winged shrike-tanager will sound an alarm, and then help itself to insects while the other birds flee. The thick-billed euphonia, a blue-and-yellow tropical bird, cries out the alarm calls of other species to get them to mob a predator that has spied her nest.

A Florida scrub-jay can modulate the intensity of its call to convey to other jays the severity of a potential threat.

Drumming, Flapping, and Snapping

The long tapered wing tips on the male broad-tailed hummingbird produce a trilling sound during flight, especially during mating or aggressive encounters.

Q: What birds communicate with sounds made by their wings and tails?

A: According to an old joke, hummingbirds hum because they do not know the words of songs. Actually, the hum is the sound of their rapidly beating wings, and most of the time is nothing more than the sound of flight. There are times, however, when hummingbirds purposely use their wings and tails to make sounds for communicating with other hummingbirds.

A Lucifer's hummingbird puts on a performance that includes noises made by its wings and tail that are frequently likened to the sound of a deck of cards being shuffled. A male broad-tailed hummingbird's wing tips are modified so that they make a loud trilling noise during aggressive encounters.

Many other birds use aerial displays combined with feather-produced sounds in their courtship and territorial activities. The American woodcock patrols the skies at dawn and dusk. As it spirals upward, three thin, stiff primary feathers

on each wing tip vibrate as air rushes through them to produce a twittering sound. The Wilson's snipes likewise soar, and then dive while making a choppy whistling noise known as winnowing. The sound is produced by two stiff feathers, one on either side of the tail, as they vibrate in the air. Nighthawks and the African flappet lark also make distinct sounds with their wings during courtship displays.

Other birds utilize wings and tails to make sounds while on the ground. The ruffed grouse of North America beats its wings in front of its chest at a rate of up to 20 flaps per second. This action

A ruffed grouse alights on a drumming log. These drumming logs are used by males in the spring to attract a mate.

compresses the air in front of it and produces a thundering noise. By standing on a hollow log, it further amplifies its drumming. The resulting sound can be heard a quarter of a mile away.

In the forests of Central and South America, colorful manakins perform vigorous courtship displays that include loud snapping and ripping sounds made with their wings. Researchers recently discovered that one species, the club-winged manakin, makes violinlike sounds with a pair of wing feathers. One feather is shaped like a hollow club. A bent feather next to it brushes against it when the manakin hits its wings together over its back. The male of another tropical species, the Montezuma oropendola, has special long, twisted wingtip feathers that make a deep rushing sound employed in courtship as well as in aggressive encounters with other males.

Q: How do birds use their beaks to make sounds?

A: Birds drum, clap, click, and snap with their beaks to communicate with each other. The song of a woodpecker, for example, takes the form of drumming. A feeding woodpecker makes tapping noises as it searches for insects, but a woodpecker seeking a mate or announcing its territorial claims actively and rapidly drums with its beak. The rate of drumming is astounding—the great spotted woodpecker of Eurasia and northern Africa, for example, may pound 25 times per second.

The male lesser adjutant stork performs an array of ritualistic displays to attract a mate. As well as preening and flying about, he will snap his bill open and shut in his attempt to draw a female's attention.

Both male and female woodpeckers drum, and the sound travels far. The woodpecker ensures that the sound will be loud by selecting a dead tree, stovepipe, gutter, metal flashing, or even a garbage can as its "drum." Its thick skull has strong muscles that absorb the shock of drumming. The skull serves the bird so well that it has even been studied in order to produce more effective football helmets.

Other birds use the bill alone to produce sounds. Mated pairs of storks rapidly snap their beaks open and shut when they greet each other, a behavior known as clattering. A pair of tricolored herons will make rattling sounds while nibbling at each other. Black-footed and wandering albatrosses rapidly clap and click their bills during courtship. Angry owls click their beaks when threatened. Bill clicking and snapping is used to indicate irritation in a variety of other birds.

Body Language

To ward off a threat a red-winged blackbird will seek a high perch, such as this cattail, and call loudly, as well as point its beak skyward.

Q: What role do postures and gestures play in bird communication?

A: Body language is an extremely important part of communication among birds. It figures largely in their efforts to protect their nests and territories, fend off aggressors or appease them, and win and keep a mate.

Watch a group of herring or western gulls feeding, and you are likely to see a typical display of aggression. As do many species, gulls take on threatening stances that intimidate other birds. An aggressive gull will stretch its head and neck forward and hold out its wings as it advances on another bird. The attitude clearly indicates that pecking may follow if the threat is not taken seriously. Geese and boobies likewise snake their heads forward. Many songbirds, such as black-capped chickadees and red-winged blackbirds, point their bills skyward. The great blue heron fluffs up its head and neck plumes and then stretches its long bill skyward before stabbing it forward. Pelicans also ward off other birds with a raised bill.

Each of these actions includes a presentation of the bird's main weapon: its

beak. It is similar to the showing of teeth by a dog or the lowering of the head by an animal with horns or antlers.

A threat display may also involve actions that make a bird look larger. A great horned owl puffs up its feathers and raises its wings, which makes it appear twice its size. A parrot may erect its head feathers. A European robin tilts its head back to display its red breast to the best advantage. The sunbittern of Central and South America, normally secretive and well camouflaged, erupts into a beautiful sunset display when it spreads its wings and tail wide as a threat. Such displays are not directed toward birds only; they are also used to ward off predators, including humans, or animals that may

A Brant goose in the typical defensive posture with neck stretched far forward.

step on nests, such as cattle. By threatening rather than actually attacking, a bird lessens its risk of getting injured in a fight. The threatened bird can likewise avoid injury by respecting the threat. It can flee or offer an appeasement display to mollify the aggressive bird. An appeasement display typically conceals the bird's weapons and makes it look smaller. A goose, for example, curls its long neck and tucks down its head. Sleeking the feathers, turning the head to point the beak away, crouching,

breeding plumage, such as the flashes of color on a mandarin duck or the magnificent tail of a peacock. Male Victoria crowned-pigeons bow to prospective partners, drawing attention to their lacy crests. Grouse inflate their air sacs, raise feathers on their heads, and reveal vividly colored wattles. Birds of paradise flaunt spectacular plumes and may even hang upside down. Ducks and other waterbirds engage in ritualized motions that range from head bobbing to elaborate "dancing."

and folding the wings also serve to curb a threat. Young crows lean away from a threatening adult and may even roll over on their backs, indicating submission just as a puppy does.

Appeasement displays are also an important part of maintaining a pair bond between mates and harmony in the nest. Birds such as albatrosses and boobies engage in mutual displays that help defuse any aggressive tendencies.

The body language of birds reaches its height in courtship displays. The variety of actions exhibited by courting birds rivals the diversity of bird species itself. Many displays involve showing off

Left: A group of mockingbirds display characteristic defense postures, including spreading wings and tail feathers to appear larger to an opposing bird.

Below: During courtship displays, the spectacular Victoria crowned-pigeon can raise its large crest of lacy head feathers.

CHAPTER 6

SEEKING A MATE

The mating behavior of birds is rarely secretive. Male birds sing, croak, squawk, screech, and moo to lure females and ward off rivals. They inflate strange air sacs and build elaborate bowers and avenues. Pairs of birds dance and display. Many exchange gifts. Snowy owls, for example, present females with rodents. Bohemian waxwings woo with gifts of fruit; two birds may perch together and pass the same berry back and forth up to 14 times.

It is small wonder, then, that humans have long associated their own courtship behavior with that of birds. We speak of lovebirds who fondly bill and coo. In medieval times, it was believed that birds found mates on February 14, a heritage that influenced future celebrations of the feast day of Saint Valentine. Humans have particular admiration for monogamous birds, which are often portrayed as emblems of true love. Images of doves, for example, abound on Valentine cards, and the red-crowned crane is revered in Korea and Japan as a symbol of love and fidelity. Recent studies, however, show that the bird world is rife with divorce and infidelity, even among monogamous species.

Above: It may be because these petite parrots develop a fierce loyalty to their mates that lovebirds, such as the green masked lovebird, became a symbol of true love.

Left: During the fall, a Bohemian waxwing plucks a bright rowanberry. Come spring, he will court a potential mate with offerings of fruit, such as berries.

Sexual Dimorphism

Q: Why do males and females of many species look different from each other?

A: When a male and female of the same species differ in size or appearance, they are said to exhibit sexual dimorphism. Sexual dimorphism is very common in birds. A difference in plumage is one of its most prevalent forms.

A field guide to backyard birds readily yields examples of plumage differences between males and females. The male American robin sports a russet breast, while his mate's is paler. Male cardinals are bright red; females are duller. Worldwide, numerous species are marked by males boasting an array of secondary sexual characteristics such as long plumes, colorful wattles, and inflatable air sacs.

In many species, a difference in color is striking in the breeding season but less so in the nonbreeding season. Males may even molt into plumage much like the females'. A male scarlet tanager, for example, is bright red with black wings in the breeding season. In late August, however, he molts into an olive-colored plumage with black wings, similar to his mate's yellow-green feathering with dark gray wings. The males and females of other species, such as crows, black-capped chickadees, European robins, jays, and magpies, resemble each other all year long.

Certainly, drab colors befit a female, who can only benefit from camouflage as she incubates her eggs and broods nestlings. The male's eye-catching plumage would only draw attention to the nest. Dramatic male ornamentation occurs most frequently in species where the male either does not incubate the eggs or is not involved in raising young at all. Although brightly colored males of many bird species may not incubate eggs, they are often actively involved in feeding the voracious young.

Researchers speculate that in sexually dimorphic species a male's plumage is an identity badge that signals his species, ensuring that a female of his same species will pair up with him. Courtship displays with ritualized behavior also help the

Right: The scarlet tanager is named for the striking breeding plumage of the male. After the breeding season draws to a close, he molts into olive-green plumage that resembles a female scarlet tanager's coloring.

Below: The plumage of both black ducks and mallards exhibit limited sexual dimorphism, as this comparison demonstrates.

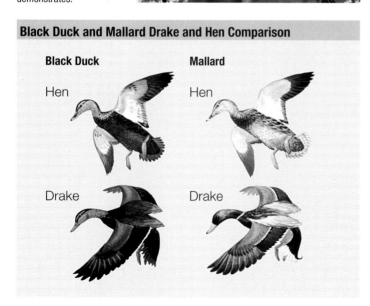

Black Duck and Mallard Drake and Hen Comparison

Black Duck

Hen

Drake

Mallard

Hen

Drake

right birds meet. Birdsong is also a species clue, one that is particularly useful when two species look almost alike. Even birders often distinguish similar species by listening for markedly different songs.

In some species, sexual dimorphism is flipped around. Female phalaropes, which court males and do not tend offspring, are more vividly patterned than their mates. Many female birds of prey, such as eagles and owls, are larger than males. It is thought that this size difference stems from interfemale rivalry for territory that will provide for their young. Evolutionary forces have selected for large, strong females but have left males untouched.

Q: What are some of the more spectacular adornments displayed by males?

A: Males of many species are adorned with little more than a bold patch on the back of the head or a bib under the throat. Others appear to be decked out for a costume party. The three-wattled bellbird of Central America has a face draped with black, wormlike wattles. A long, feathered wattle dangles from the throat of the male Amazonian umbrellabird. Frigatebirds inflate enormous red sacs under their throats to impress the larger females.

Outrageous tails are frequently flaunted. Male birds-of-paradise flare stunningly colored tails, which are often displayed as the birds hang upside down from a branch. Peacocks raise and rattle huge colorful tail coverts to impress drab peahens. Studies show that peacocks with plentiful eyespots on their tails experience greater breeding success, which supports the idea that these incredible adornments have evolved due to sexual selection. Females may select males with superior ornamentation because they may be a sign that the male is fit, healthy, able to intimidate rivals, and possesses genes she would prefer to pass along to her offspring.

Left: Male peacocks display ostentatious plumage that attracts females. Peahens choose mates by brightness and number of eyespots on the feathers.

Below: During courtship displays, the male frigatebird forces air into the cervical air sac, inflating it into a startling red balloon. He then sits quietly in a group with other males. When a female flies overhead, he waggles his head from side to side, shakes his wings, and calls. If the display is attractive enough, the female will land beside him.

Courtship Displays

Q: What courtship displays involve dancing or other elaborate movements?

A: Many birds use song and other sounds in their courtship and territorial displays. Many species also augment sound with actions. These actions may be as simple as the flaring of a red-winged blackbird's crimson epaulets or a mockingbird doing an energetic flip. Many birds also engage in courtship displays that are highly acrobatic and even, to the human eye, artistic.

Cranes have long been admired for their dancing. Pairs of whooping cranes perform an ecstatic ballet that includes leaping three feet off the ground, flapping, and throwing the head up and down. The male sometimes leaps right over the female. Crowned cranes in Africa jump and circle each other. Blue cranes of southern Africa may dance for as long as four hours. Young cranes forming new pairs dance the most, older pairs less. Because cranes mate for life, however, the exuberant dances also help maintain pair bonds.

Birds-of-paradise in Australia and New Guinea also perform spectacularly during courtship. In most of these species, males compete to mate with as many females as possible and are not involved in rearing young. They entice females with dazzling plumes, loud calls, and bizarre maneuvers. The blue bird-of-paradise, for example, flares body feathers to form a vivid azure fan, and then hangs upside down and vibrates.

Seabirds, shorebirds, and waterfowl also engage in ritualized motions while courting. Mallard drakes dip their heads

Right: Blue-footed boobies mate according to an elaborate ritual in which the male raises his feet and struts, both sexes point their bills skyward, and the male whistles.

Below: Believed to mate for life, during spring, young pairs of the stately, forty-four-inch-high common cranes celebrate their bond with exuberant courtship dances.

and raise and lower their bodies while swimming to attract females, a performance sometimes likened to a "solemn quadrille." Blue-footed boobies prance to show off their blue feet. Grebes lift themselves up in the water and, paddling their feet, race across the surface side by side. Some dancers waltz demurely: Australian masked plovers may circle each other, stand side by side, and bob their heads for more than an hour.

Other dancers include the many species of grouse. These birds erect feathers and leap, flap, and stamp to impress females. In East Africa, the male Jackson's widow-bird employs similar theatrics, leaping energetically with his head thrown back and his tail touching his neck, save for two long streamers that trail behind him. Ostriches and bustards strut to win mates, and manakins hop about and clatter their wings.

Q: What birds use aerial acrobatics in their displays?

A: Aerodynamic exploits during courtship are exhibited by species ranging from tiny hummingbirds to mighty eagles.

Bald eagles perform stunning feats of aviation in their courtship flights, which not only match up birds but also maintain pair bonds. Two eagles will soar together, and then one (usually the male) suddenly dives at its partner, who flips upside down. The two birds then clasp each other's talons and tumble toward earth in spinning circles—a stunt known as the cartwheel display.

Other raptors perform in midair, too. Falcons fly high and fast and sometimes plunge earthward, as do harriers and accipiters. California condors play aerial games of follow-the-leader. On the ground, the male condor displays more somberly, turning in slow circles while rocking back and forth.

Among the most energetic displays are those of hummingbirds. Males describe arcs, swoops, and swirls as they dart up, down, back, and forth, both to warn away intruders and impress females. These flights are so distinctive that they can sometimes be used to identify species.

Woodcocks, skylarks, and snipe soar to great heights during breeding season. Songbirds also use flight displays. A male and female mockingbird chase through the male's territory, an activity that may allow the female to scope out its quality, as well as her potential mate.

During courtship, bald eagles engage in aerobatic displays, including cartwheels, roller-coaster swoops, and chases. The bonded pair will then build its nest near fresh or salt water in the tallest, widest tree in a forest stand.

Building a Relationship

Q: What birds create structures as part of courtship?

A: In some species, males build nests to win over females. A male frigatebird assembles an untidy nest of sticks and then sits in it, displaying his inflated throat sac to passing females. A male penduline tit expends much time and energy over a span of several weeks constructing a hanging nest made of grass and other fibers. A female inspects the male's work and indicates her acceptance of him by moving in and lining the nest with soft materials. Males of some wrens build several nests and then go "house hunting" with prospective mates to see if she will choose one.

The top architectural award of the avian world, however, goes to the weaver birds. Male African village weavers adorn thorny trees with dangling orbs woven from grass and other fibers. They then vie with each other to lure females to their nests, calling and flying near the entrance holes or clinging to them.

Bowerbirds also become busy construction workers during courtship, but they do not build nests. Instead, they build elaborate bowers and then carefully decorate them, making them their stages for displaying to females. Each species of bowerbird builds a specific type of bower. Different species also favor different colors for their decorations.

The most famous bowerbird is the satin bowerbird of Australia. The glossy blue male first builds the bower, a U-shaped avenue of sticks. He then paints it blue by pressing juice from berries with his beak or mixing saliva with charcoal. (In past decades, some enterprising birds swiped bags of bluing from laundry baskets for

Left: Male marsh wrens are polygnous, having two or more females in their territory at one time. The male builds many unfinished nests and then shows them to the female, who shows her approval by adding a lining to it.

Right: A male satin bowerbird builds a bower and decorates it with as many blue objects as he can scavenge, both natural and human-created. He then shows off these treasures to prospective mates.

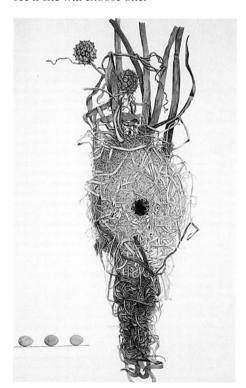

A male gentoo penguin offers a stone to its choice of mate as a symbolic nesting material. Pebbles are also occasionally exchanged as partners complete their turns incubating their eggs.

this task.) Often, he uses a leaf or twig as a paintbrush. Finally, he decorates the bower with an array of blue objects such as pebbles, shells, flowers, feathers, and iridescent beetle carcasses. He may also pilfer items from human dwellings: bits of glass, straws, paper, clothespins, toys, even pens and toothbrushes.

When his work is done, the male bowerbird perches on a limb and calls loudly. Any female that stops by to view his bower is promptly treated to a display of prancing and wing flashing. The male may also pick up and carry or toss items from his precious horde. If he wins her over, mating takes place inside the bower; the female then departs.

Q: What birds gather nesting materials as part of courtship?

A: Some male birds present nesting materials to their partners as "gifts" during courtship. These materials are not necessarily used in the actual construction of a future nest. Instead, the gathering and sharing of them serve as ritualized versions of behavior borrowed from actual nest building, recycled to help birds form pair bonds.

Male pinyon jays of the southwestern United States, for example, place sticks and grass in front of their mates. Great crested grebes include diving for water weeds and then exchanging them in their courtship routine. Male antarctic penguins such as the Adelie, chinstrap, and gentoo, which arrive on breeding grounds shortly before females, prepare for the latter's arrival by collecting nesting materials. In this stark habitat, the only handy materials are pebbles. These are assiduously gathered by the males. Two penguins pairing up for the first time mark the occasion by the male giving the female a pebble. The habit continues throughout incubation, with the penguin coming off duty sometimes being given a pebble by the returning parent.

Choosy Females

Q: Does courtship feeding influence a female's choice of mate?

A: Courtship feeding is practiced by many species of birds. Typically, it is the male who feeds the female. The term refers not only to feeding that occurs during courtship but also during incubation. Feeding also helps maintain the pair bond. Many females actively solicit such feeding by begging like baby birds.

Research shows that courtship feeding is more than just "lovebird" behavior; it also directly contributes to reproductive success. A female needs extra energy to form and lay eggs. In addition, she cannot forage as efficiently when incubating. The food a male provides is an important part of her nutrition. In some species, a male provides up to 50 percent of his mate's food intake. Thus, a male who feeds his mate can directly affect clutch size and the health of his offspring.

Small wonder, then, that courtship feeding signals to a female whether a male will be a good provider—not only for her, but for their hungry brood. Studies of common terns show that females whose mates feed them prodigiously when they are laying produce more eggs. They may also abandon males who are poor providers. As a result, male terns not only feed their mates but also flaunt food in their initial attempts to attract females by carrying fish in their beaks.

Q: What drives a female to choose mates based on songs, displays, and outward appearance?

A: A male bird with a loud song or riotous plumes, or one that engages in flamboyant courtship displays, would seem to be at greater risk of falling victim to a predator because he makes himself so noticeable. Scientists theorize that these attention-grabbers

A male common tern offers a tidbit of food to a female. Courtship feeding is a common behavior that cements the pair bond between mated birds.

have evolved as a result of female selection: Females chose males who displayed these features and often chose the most extreme versions, thus perpetuating them. But why do females select these features in the first place? Researchers have come up with several hypotheses to explain this behavior.

The "runaway selection" hypothesis states that over time males evolved special features in response to females choosing them for these features. The male offspring thus produced would likewise possess these features, and the female offspring would continue to select the most extreme versions. Over time, this "sensory bias" on the part of females would continually drive further development of male finery. By choosing such males, females ensure that their male offspring will be the sort that will be selected by females in the future.

The "good genes" hypothesis suggests that a male who has the energy to learn and sing a large repertoire, successfully defend a territory, display enthusiastically, or sport attention-getting, often cumbersome plumage must have an excellent

genetic profile. His genes endow him with vigor and good health, making him a good choice as a father.

This hypothesis ties in with the "parasite hypothesis," which proposes that a male's displays reveal his state of health. A poor display may signify that he is infected with illness or toting a load of energy-sapping parasites. Studies show that this may be a factor in mate choice by female barn swallows, which overwhelmingly favor males with long, symmetrical outer tail feathers. Researchers found that well-endowed males did indeed have fewer parasites, and that parasite resistance could be inherited. Similarly, the young of male peacocks with numerous eyespots on their tail feathers were observed to grow more quickly and exhibited better health.

In addition, a female also benefits directly by shunning males who are sick or infested with parasites. She is more likely to lay fertile eggs if she has a healthy mate, and at the same time avoids picking up parasites herself or passing them along to her young. Not surprisingly, this idea is known as the "direct benefits" hypothesis.

Above left: The male bobolink's ecstatic and gleeful song is a strong factor in the choice of mate for the female, who will choose the strongest and most flamboyant singer.

Above right: Great blue herons must battle predators, such as deadly bald eagles, to survive, especially during mating season. Therefore, females are drawn to males that exhibit signs of good health and vigor.

Mating for Life

Q: Are most birds monogamous?

A: Monogamy is the most common mating system among birds. More than 90 percent of all bird species are monogamous. Some species are monogamous for the duration of one breeding season. Others mate for life, pairing up again each breeding season or remaining with each other year-round.

Monogamy would appear to be counterproductive for males, since by mating with many females they could spread their genes far and wide. By sticking with one mate, however, a male's reproductive success may actually be greater because more young will survive thanks to his assistance in feeding them. Most songbirds, for example, must work very hard to catch insects to feed their babies' insatiable appetites, so maintaining a two-parent household is vital for reproductive success.

Devotion to one's mate and nest is also crucial for many colonially nesting birds. Among herring gulls, for example, raising a brood requires the efforts of two parents. One parent must always be at the nest while the other forages. If the nest is left unguarded, predators or other gulls will eat the eggs or chicks.

A monogamous and attentive male can also keep an eye on his mate and chase off any competing males that try to mate with her. A male mallard, for example, does not help his mate build a nest, incubate eggs, or rear ducklings. But there are more male mallards than females because females are more likely to be killed by predators while tending to eggs and young. Thus, a male who wants to ensure that his mate raises young that are his and his alone must keep other males away. By guarding her, he not only fends off competitors but also gives her a chance to feed quietly instead of constantly fleeing from amorous males.

In addition, monogamy simply saves time and energy. It

Below: A mallard drake sticks close to his mate before she begins to lay eggs in order to prevent other drakes from mating with her. The hen carries out the tasks of building the nest, incubating eggs, and raising the ducklings without the male's help.

Below right: Pairs of Adelie penguins are monogamous, keeping the same mates and nest-sites each year.

allows birds to get on with the business of rearing a family. Studies of kittiwakes show that pairs who reunite on breeding grounds pare down their courtship display, lay eggs earlier, and raise more young than newly formed pairs.

Q: What birds mate for life?

A: Many monogamous birds pair up with the same mate season after season. Species in groups as diverse as songbirds, seabirds, waterfowl, and raptors are known to mate for life, either by reuniting on the breeding ground each spring or staying together all year.

Penguins, most of which are monogamous, frequently seek out their partners of previous years when they arrive on their breeding grounds. Researchers have found that Adelie penguins typically reunite with their partners from the previous breeding season about 60 percent of the time, chinstrap penguins about 80 percent of the time, and gentoo penguins 90 percent.

Swans, geese, and cranes are among the best-known mates for life. These birds remain together year-round, even during migration. Species of tropical birds are typically monogamous and remain together all year, too, the male and female working as a team to protect their territories. Birds that mate for life often stay together until one dies. Sometimes, a pair may split up if their reproductive success is low, as might happen if eggs are infertile. Although infidelity is a frequent occurrence in monogamous species, researchers have found that many of these mates-for-life are often "genetically monogamous," too—that is, the rate of infidelity is low, as indicated by DNA testing of nestlings and parents.

Swans usually mate for life, remaining together throughout the year. If one of a pair dies, the survivor usually seeks out a new mate, and forms another strong pair bond.

Other Mating Systems

Q: **What is polygyny?**

A: In about 2 percent of the world's bird species, males do not form a pair bond with one female. Instead, they mate with two or more females, a system known as polygyny. Polygynous males provide little or no care for their young. Researchers divide polygynous males into those that defend resources and those that defend females.

A male red-winged blackbird, for example, defends resources. He stakes out a territory that provides nesting sites and ample food. He then defends this territory against other males while displaying to attract as many females as possible. He does not form a pair bond with one female. Instead, females stop by to look him over and evaluate his territory. If they approve of both, they mate with him and nest in his territory. The male provides no care for the young except for perhaps a bit of help with the babies of the primary female (the first female who pairs with him) or with youngsters that hatch late in the breeding season when mating opportunities wind down. But with a rich territory around them, females can usually cope with raising nestlings on their own.

A distant cousin of the blackbird, the oropendola, practices female-defense polygyny instead. Oropendolas live in tropical forests of Central and South America and nest in colonies. A tree may have as many as 100 hanging nests, woven by the females, dangling from its boughs. A dominant male does not defend a territory rich in the fruit favored by these birds. Instead, he defends the harem of females, chasing off lower-ranking males and preventing them from mating. Boat-tailed grackles of North America, which also nest colonially, also keep harems.

Q: **What is lekking?**

A: Some species of polygynous male birds gather in one area to perform courtship displays. This behavior is called lekking, and both the group of birds and the performance area are called a lek. Each bird in the lek defends only the little patch of ground where he stands to show off. Females visit to assay the males and select one to mate with. They usually choose the dominant males, who claim the best "stages" on the lek. After mating, the females leave to nest and raise young entirely on their own.

Female crested oropendolas weave spherical nests out of grass and palm fibers, draping them from high, isolated trees. A dominant male guards the females to prevent any other males from mating with them.

The five-month mating season of the Attwater's prairie-chicken begins in late December when males gather at leks to perform their competitive courtship rituals, which include the inflation of their vibrant orange-yellow esophageal sacs.

The well-known strutting, tail flaring, and pumping noises of North American prairie-chickens are all part of lekking behavior. Among other species that practice lekking are the sage-grouse and buff-breasted sandpiper, also of North America; cotingas and manakins of Central and South America; the ruff and black grouse of Europe; the long-tailed widow-bird of Africa; and the bowerbirds and birds-of-paradise of Australia and New Guinea.

Q: What is polyandry?

A: Polyandry, the mating of one female with several males, is a mating system used by a scant 1 percent of birds. Typically, a polyandrous female mates with a male, lays eggs in a nest, and then leaves them for the father to incubate while she pairs up with another male. He also raises the young. This mating system is

As do their American cousins, male African jacanas do most of the nest building. After the female has laid a clutch of eggs, the male takes over all parenting responsibilities, incubating the eggs and protecting them from danger.

practiced by the northern jacana, a long-toed shorebird found in southern Mexico, Central America, and the West Indies. The female pairs up with several males at one time. She defends a territory against other females and will also help repel predators. Her mates build the nests, incubate the eggs, and raise the young. Phalaropes and spotted sandpipers are also known to be polyandrous.

In some polyandrous species, such as the brown skua, a female mates with several males but lays all the eggs in one nest. She then assists in helping with incubation and raising young.

Outside the Pair Bond

Below: Evidence that birds "cheat" came from a study to assess vasectomy as a means of population control among red-winged blackbirds. When the females mated to vasectomized males, they still laid eggs that hatched.

Below right: Although fairy-wrens form solid, lifelong pairs, studies reveal that females often mate with other males.

Q: Do monogamous birds ever "cheat" on their mates?

A: Long-term studies and close observation of birds in recent years, combined with new scientific tools such as DNA fingerprinting, have revealed that "cheating" is common among many monogamous avian species. Scientists have labeled these trysts extra-pair copulations, or EPCs for short. In most cases, the EPC apparently does not shake up the pair bond. A male that has mated with a second female continues to shower attention on his mate and fulfill his parental duties; a female that has mated with a neighboring male likewise attends to her mate and offspring. This situation posed a puzzle to researchers. Males, they assumed, had much to gain and little to lose by seeking out EPCs. By mating with other females, they might sire extra offspring outside their pair bond, thus extending their genetic reach without having to invest time or energy in caring for these offspring. Sneaking in under a resident male's radar screen and mating with the female at just the right moment—before she lays her eggs—can enable an intruding male to fertilize one or more eggs in the clutch.

Why females might seek EPCs was not as clear to researchers. A primary reason for why it might behoove a monogamous female to "cheat" on her mate focuses on one of the imperatives that govern the

female's initial mate choice: The selection of a male with top-notch genes. By mating with a superior neighboring male that some other enterprising female snagged first, a bird can endow some of her offspring with his genes.

A study of the fascinating little superb fairy-wrens of Australia supported this idea. Why did fairy-wrens, which mate for life, also have the highest known frequency of EPCs of any bird species?

Most of the females that took part in these EPCs did so with one of four males, a quartet made up of a male, a pair of his sons, and one grandson. In addition, DNA fingerprinting revealed that up to three-quarters of the young the females produced had been fathered by males other than the ones caring for them.

Some researchers also hypothesize that EPCs may be a female bird's way of avoiding a nonproductive breeding season due to a mate's infertility or the offspring's failure to thrive. If she mates with a neighboring male, she will manage to lay a clutch even if her mate proves infertile. Similarly, the young that hatch may be more likely to thrive and survive if they are genetically diverse.

Today, researchers often acknowledge the possibility of EPCs by specifying what they mean when they describe a species as monogamous. A pair of birds that raises its young together is referred to as socially monogamous. This leaves open the question of whether all the young being raised are products of their union. If the nestlings are indeed the young of both parents, then the birds are said to be genetically monogamous as well. Even if a species is socially, but not always genetically, monogamous, the rate of EPC varies. It may be rampant in one species, such as superb fairy-wrens, but very low or extremely rare in others. To date, scientists have documented EPCs in varying proportions among more than 100 species, including birds of prey, starlings, geese, ducks, swallows, finches, penguins, and swallows.

Among female European starlings, the incidence of EPCs are slightly higher for first-year breeders than among older females.

The Evolution of Birds

Are birds feathered dinosaurs? How did feathers evolve? What is the origin of birds' flight? These are some of the questions engaging paleontologists and ornithologists as they study fossils of dinosaurs, early birds, and reptiles with avian traits.

A fossil known as the Berlin specimen is exhibit A in the study of birds' origins. It is a fossil of crow-sized *Archaeopteryx*, the earliest known bird, found in a limestone quarry in Germany in 1876. The 150-million-year-old creature looks like a reptile-bird hybrid. Its beaklike face has toothy jaws. Its arms and clawed fingers are surrounded by fans of feathery impressions. Its long, bony tail is likewise framed by feathers. Each foot has three toes pointing forward and one pointing backward, as does the foot of a modern perching bird.

Preserved forever in a slab of limestone, a fossil archaeopteryx appears to be a dramatic blend of reptilian and avian features.

The Berlin specimen, along with other fossils found later, provides a glimpse into how birds evolved. Archaeopteryxes are the oldest birds found to date, ancient cousins of modern birds but not their direct ancestors. Fossils of other species of early birds shed some light on bird evolution, too. A quarter of a million years after archaeopteryx's

time, there existed a species of ancient, toothless perching birds called *Confuciusornis*. There also existed a toothed perching bird called *Sinornis*, and various species of loonlike diving birds with teeth, among others. It is thought that birds achieved true flight at least 138 million years ago. Many bird species, however, died out when the dinosaurs did, 65 million years ago. Any birds that survived this cataclysm are the ancestors of today's birds.

BIRDS, REPTILES, AND DINOSAURS

The relationship between birds and dinosaurs ignites heated debate among researchers, with each new fossil find or analysis of an old one providing fuel for the flames. The debaters agree that birds descended from reptiles, just as dinosaurs did, but disagree on other points.

One view has it that the avian line of descent begins more than 230 million years ago. In this scenario, ancient reptiles gave rise to creatures

Feathers, such as the ones in this goose's ruffled plumage, appear to have evolved from scales and served as insulation.

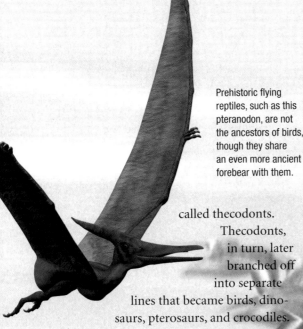

Prehistoric flying
reptiles, such as this
pteranodon, are not
the ancestors of birds,
though they share
an even more ancient
forebear with them.

called thecodonts.
Thecodonts,
in turn, later
branched off
into separate
lines that became birds, dinosaurs, pterosaurs, and crocodiles.
These early birds' scales may have evolved into
insulating feathers that later served to aid
them in gliding from tree to tree.

The other primary view traces birds'
lineage to dinosaurs. In this scenario,
thecodonts gave rise to just three main
lines of descent: dinosaurs, pterosaurs, and crocodiles. One line of dinosaurs eventually split off
to produce theropods, meat-eating, two-legged
creatures with shortened front legs. These theropods' scales evolved into feathers, which might
have helped lengthen their leaps and bounds and
balanced them while running, or served as both insulating material and as netting for catching insects.
These actions then led to flight from the ground up.

Crocodilians
descend from
thecodonts, as did
other ancient reptilians
such as the dinosaurs. Paleontologists have unearthed crocodil-
ian fossils dating back 230 million years.

THE FIRST FEATHERS

Researchers in either camp focus on such details as
tooth, hip, skull, digit, and limb structure as well
as breathing mechanisms, claw curvature, and the
timing of a fossil's appearance in the fossil record.
The existence of feathers in a fossil, however, does not
seem to guarantee that the creature was an early bird.

The first fossil feather was discovered in 1861 in
Germany. It was shaped like a flight feather, indicating that perhaps archaeopteryx could fly. In recent
years, scientists have also discovered feathering in
some dinosaurs and ancient reptiles. Some dinosaurs,
dating back about 128 million years, bear feathers
on backs, arms, and tails; one even had feather-lined
hind legs. A reptile fossil dating back 220 million
years likewise boasts what appear to be feathers or
feathery scales along its spine.

The structure of a therapod, a swift,
bipedal dinosaur with reduced forelimbs,
suggests that of a featherless ostrich.

Species and Subspecies

The ancestors of modern birds existed during the waning years of the age of dinosaurs. They shared their world with species of birds quite unlike modern ones. Many of these other species went extinct along with the dinosaurs 65 million years ago. The surviving birds gave rise to two major groups of birds: one that eventually produced the ratites (emus, kiwis, cassowaries, ostriches, and rheas, as well as the now-extinct moas and elephantbirds), the other evolving into all other kinds of birds.

When, why, and how species evolve is the subject of ongoing research. Scientists are still working to piece together the fossil record as well as to understand the development of species that occurred in the last two million years. This effort involves comparing and contrasting the anatomy of different birds and also analyzing their DNA to determine the relationships between different species.

The flightless ostriches and emus, above, evolved separately on different continents.

WHAT IS A SPECIES?

The basic definition of a species is a group of living things that not only look and act similarly but also breed only with others of their kind. This union produces viable young that can potentially reproduce. The songs, calls, plumage, and behaviors of birds help ensure that each species will mate only with others of its species. Should these characteristics fail to prevent mating, physical differences in the birds may prevent ovulation, cause the clutch to fail, or result in hybrid offspring that cannot reproduce. These preventive devices are known as "isolating mechanisms." Altogether, this approach to defining a species is known as the biological species concept.

An alternative definition of species is called the phylogenetic species concept. It focuses less on which birds could mate with each other (either in nature or just theoretically) and more on the evolutionary history, the phylogeny, of bird populations. Within

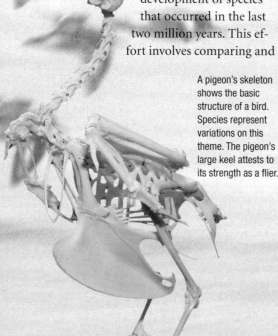

A pigeon's skeleton shows the basic structure of a bird. Species represent variations on this theme. The pigeon's large keel attests to its strength as a flier.

Birds of the same species, such as these Victoria crowned-pigeons, mate and produce fertile eggs. New data, however, sparks frequent revisions in species designations.

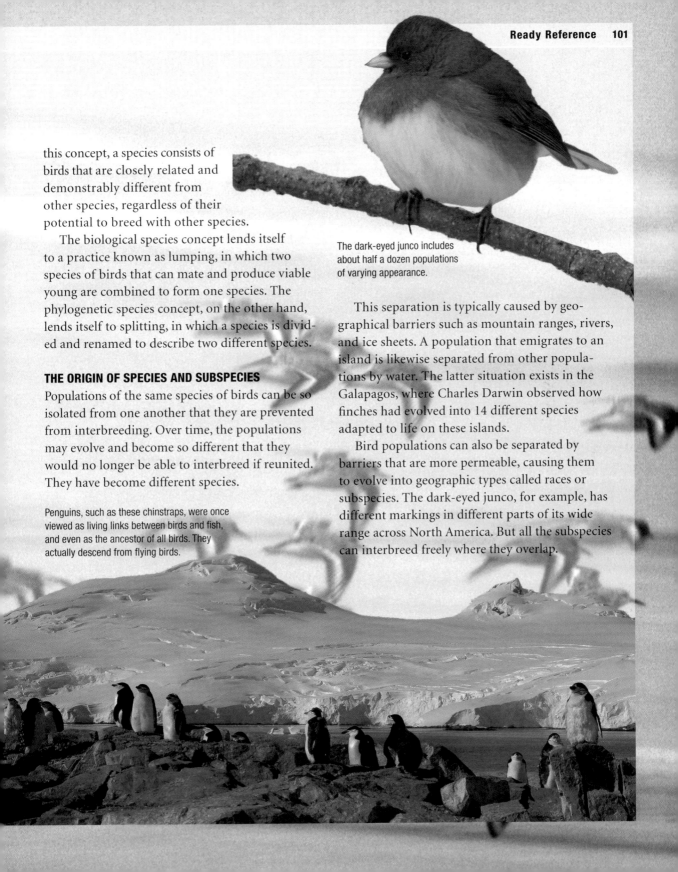

this concept, a species consists of birds that are closely related and demonstrably different from other species, regardless of their potential to breed with other species.

The biological species concept lends itself to a practice known as lumping, in which two species of birds that can mate and produce viable young are combined to form one species. The phylogenetic species concept, on the other hand, lends itself to splitting, in which a species is divided and renamed to describe two different species.

The dark-eyed junco includes about half a dozen populations of varying appearance.

THE ORIGIN OF SPECIES AND SUBSPECIES

Populations of the same species of birds can be so isolated from one another that they are prevented from interbreeding. Over time, the populations may evolve and become so different that they would no longer be able to interbreed if reunited. They have become different species.

Penguins, such as these chinstraps, were once viewed as living links between birds and fish, and even as the ancestor of all birds. They actually descend from flying birds.

This separation is typically caused by geographical barriers such as mountain ranges, rivers, and ice sheets. A population that emigrates to an island is likewise separated from other populations by water. The latter situation exists in the Galapagos, where Charles Darwin observed how finches had evolved into 14 different species adapted to life on these islands.

Bird populations can also be separated by barriers that are more permeable, causing them to evolve into geographic types called races or subspecies. The dark-eyed junco, for example, has different markings in different parts of its wide range across North America. But all the subspecies can interbreed freely where they overlap.

Grouping Birds

About 9,600 species of birds exist today. These species are divided among 31 larger groups known as orders. Scientists consider a species' appearance, behavior, and genetic makeup when placing it in an order.

But just as birds have common names as well as scientific names, so too are there catch-all terms for grouping birds. A bird's behavior and habitat, as well as appearance, often give rise to these broad terms. In this way, birds can be divided into two general categories—land birds and waterbirds—and then into groups within these categories. Land birds include ratites, gallinaceous birds, raptors, perching birds, and songbirds. Waterbirds include waterfowl, seabirds, shorebirds, wading birds, marsh birds, and divers. Species such as pigeons, parrots, and woodpeckers, however, evade these categories and are typically grouped by just these generic names.

Raptors, also known as birds of prey, share features such as forward-facing "eagle eyes," a hooked beak, and grasping talons.

LAND BIRDS

The land birds include all birds that do not lead a primarily aquatic-based life, though many certainly exploit waterways for feeding and nesting (a few, such as the dipper, are even more aquatic than some shorebirds).

Ratites

Ratites are birds that do not have a keel, the plowlike extension on the breastbone. This group includes most of the world's flightless birds: cassowaries, emus, kiwis, rheas, and ostriches. (Other flightless birds, such as penguins, do possess keeled sternums.) Even though the chunky, chickenlike tinamous

The Atlantic puffin is a seabird; its scientific name is *Fratercula arctica*, which denotes its genus and species. An ornithologist may also call it an alcid, referring to its family name, Alcidae.

The American kestrel is a raptor. It is North America's smallest falcon species.

of South America have a keel and can fly, they are considered distant relatives to the ratites and are sometimes placed into the same group.

Gallinaceous birds

Gallinaceous birds are all those that can be termed "chickenlike" in many ways. This group includes many species that are game birds: turkeys, grouse, quail, pheasants, partridges, ptarmigans, chukars, and prairie chickens. Other gallinaceous species include peafowl, megapodes, curassows, guineafowl, and the domestic chicken.

The dusky seaside sparrow, a songbird, went extinct in 1987.

Raptors

The raptors are birds of prey that have talons adapted for catching other animals. This group includes eagles, hawks, falcons, kites, owls, and ospreys. It also includes vultures, which scavenge rather than catch live prey.

Perching birds

The term perching birds sounds casual but is actually a formal scientific order known as Passeriformes (or passerines). It includes about three-fifths of all bird species, ranging from sparrows and crows to dippers and lyrebirds. Most land birds are perching birds. All perching birds have four toes, with three pointed forward and one pointing backward. These toes are never webbed, and the backward-pointing one is not reversible —that is, it cannot be swiveled to face forward. It is specially adapted to enable a bird to clasp a branch firmly, even while sleeping. All birds not in this group are termed nonpasserines.

Songbirds

Songbirds are a subgroup of perching birds. They are also known as oscines. Perching birds that are not songbirds are called suboscines. Songbirds are known for their often complex songs. A songbird's sound-producing organ, the syrinx, has more muscles in it than the syrinx of a suboscine.

The chaffinch is one of the most common songbirds in Europe. Its mobbing call is a loud *chink*, and the bird is known by this name in some dialects.

WATERBIRDS

Waterbirds are those that spend much or all of their lives in or around water. They nest near water and feed in or around it. Many swim or dive. As befits a watery medium, some birds' categorization is fluid. Bitterns, for example, are in the heron family and hence can be considered waders, but some conservation plans include them with marsh birds.

Waterfowl

The waterfowl category consists of ducks, geese, and swans. They are known as wildfowl in Great Britain.

The Arctic tern spends about three-quarters of the year at sea, the other two or three months in its breeding grounds circumpolar in the Arctic.

Seabirds

Seabirds are birds that feed in salt water and spend much or all of their lives swimming on or soaring above oceans and seas. They include such birds as albatrosses, boobies, cormorants, frigate birds, fulmars, gannets, gulls, jaegers, kittiwakes, pelicans, penguins, petrels, sea ducks, shearwaters, skimmers, skuas, storm petrels, terns, tropic birds, and members of the auk family (dovekies, guillemots, murres, puffins, and razorbills). Some of these seabirds, such as gulls and cormorants, may also be seen in freshwater habitats.

Shorebirds

Shorebirds are birds that typically feed on muddy or sandy shorelines at low tide, probing and poking in the ground for their food or skimming it from water and mud. Many are also found in grassy uplands and wet meadows. Included among the shorebirds are such birds as avocets, curlews, dunlins, dowitchers, godwits, knots, jacanas, oystercatchers, phalaropes, plovers (including killdeer and dotterels), ruffs, sanderlings, sandpipers, sheathbills, snipes, stilts, surfbirds, tattlers, turnstones, whimbrels, willets, woodcocks, and yellowlegs. Certain sandpipers are sometimes referred to as "peeps." In Great Britain, shorebirds are called waders.

Two kittiwakes perch side by side. One is a black-legged kittiwake, the other a red-legged kittiwake—different species, but both seabirds.

The great blue heron is an adaptable large wading bird with an extensive range. It patrols shorelines from North American city parks to the coast of the Galapagos Islands.

Wading birds

Wading birds typically have even longer legs in relation to their bodies than shorebirds do. They enable these birds to wade into water to search for food without getting their feathers wet. By wading, they can access foods such as fish that cannot be found on a beach or mudflat. Like shorebirds, however, many wading birds can also be seen stalking the edges of waterways and in fields while foraging. This group includes cranes, egrets, flamingoes, herons, ibises, and spoonbills.

Marsh birds

The term "marsh bird" is a fairly loose one used to refer to species that frequent marshes and swamps. These two habitats are dominated by different plants. A marsh is a wetland filled with grasses, rushes, cattails, and the like, but lacking trees. A swamp is a wetland where trees and shrubs hold sway. Although wading birds and waterfowl could be considered marsh birds, the term is most often employed to refer to rails (including coots, crakes, and gallinules) and limpkins.

Diving birds

Many waterbirds dive after prey, but the term "divers" is typically reserved for loons and grebes. In Europe, the term specifically refers to loons and is part of different species' common names. Divers have legs far back on their streamlined bodies and are graceful in water but extremely awkward on land.

Lakes in East Africa support huge nesting colonies of flamingoes. The greater and the lesser flamingo can be found in such colonies.

The Study of Birds

Aristotle perceived that birds migrated and that migration differed from species to species centuries before this idea was generally understood.

Many scientists, naturalists, artists, writers, photographers, filmmakers, and others have advanced our knowledge of and appreciation for birds. In ancient Greece, Aristotle (384–322 BCE) wrote about birds based on his firsthand observations and the accounts of others.

Compendiums of knowledge about birds were published periodically throughout the sixteenth and seventeenth centuries. Ornithology took off in the mid-1600s just before the Swedish botanist Carolus Linnaeus (1707–78) pioneered a system for classifying species that is still in use today. English naturalists John Ray (1627–1705) and Francis Willughby (1635–72), for example, traveled throughout Europe from 1662 to 1666 to study birds. Their studies are recounted in *Ornithologia libri tres*,

Swedish botanist Carolus Linnaeus devised a system of classifying animals and plants that is still in use today.

which was published in 1676 in Latin, and then two years later in English. The work is notable for its classification of birds by physical features rather than by habitat or mythological attributes, as was still common at the time.

Half a century later, another English naturalist, Mark Catesby (1679–1749), published an ornithological work. He spent about a dozen years exploring the southeastern United States. *The Natural History of Carolina, Florida, and the Bahama Islands* described the bird and plant life of

Mark Catesby's *Natural History*, featured colored plates of his paintings of birds and other wildlife.

these areas based on firsthand observation in a style reminiscent of modern works, and its illustrations depicted them realistically.

English naturalist Gilbert White (1720–95) stayed close to home in southern England but in 1789 nonetheless produced the enduring work, *The Natural History of Selborne*. His studies are marked by his scientific point of view, with an emphasis on measuring, observing, and meticulous record-keeping. He questioned patterns of bird migration in an era when people still believed that swallows hibernated underwater, deep in mud. His careful observations enabled him to tease apart three nearly identical warbler species based on their songs and behavior.

John James Audubon's work was praised by the eminent French naturalist Cuvier as "the most magnificent monument which has yet been raised to ornithology."

The fledging of ornithology continued in the next century with the publication of the nine-volume *American Ornithology* by Scottish naturalist Alexander Wilson (1766–1813). Wilson emigrated to the United States in 1794 and was a self-trained ornithologist and artist. His work was enhanced by copious notes and measurements taken during his travels. It was Wilson's work that inspired the most famous ornithologist of all, Audubon. John James Audubon (1785–1851) grew up in France and emigrated to the United States in 1803 at the age of 18. Like Wilson, he was self-taught. During the next two decades, he drew and studied birds, and then published *The Birds of America* as a multivolume work starting in 1827. A companion work, *Ornithological Biography*, was published simultaneously. His paintings are noted for their dynamic and accurate portrayals of birds. Another self-educated ornithologist, Frank Chapman (1864–1945), rose in the ranks to become curator of birds at the American Museum of Natural History in New York City in 1908, a position he held until 1942. Chapman wrote voluminously about birds, produced a guide to the birds of eastern North America, and founded *Bird-Lore* magazine, which later became *Audubon.* He also inaugurated the Christmas Bird Count in 1900, a tradition that continues today among birders and provides valuable information about bird populations and ranges. Field guides used by birders worldwide have been influenced by American ornithologist and artist Roger Tory Peterson (1908–96). His first guidebook, *A Field Guide to the Birds,* facilitated bird identification by presenting birds in a uniform stance throughout, with identification clues (known as field marks) indicated by arrows. English ornithologist David Lack (1910–73) likewise sparked popular interest in birds with his books, such as *The Life of the Robin*, published in 1943. Lack also studied animal populations and published several books about island-dwelling birds.

Audubon's painted buntings highlight, in his words, the "pugnacious habits of this species."

Birdwatching, or Birding

Birdwatching, or birding, is an activity that can be enjoyed in many ways. It can be done locally and casually, with or without binoculars, or it can be done more intensively, using spotting scopes and sketching or photographing one's discoveries.

According to U.S. Forest Service surveys, about 85 million Americans state that they go birding. Birding is also popular in other countries, and some travelers, when they vacation, book holidays devoted to birding. But even people who do not seek out birds frequently notice them and are apt to wonder what they are, and what they are doing.

IDENTIFYING BIRDS

The ability to identify birds develops gradually the more one watches birds. The difficulty in sorting out similar species is evinced in the birding term "little brown jobs," or LBJs, which refers to the many small, dusky birds that flit by and elude identification. By looking for certain clues, however, one can begin to sort the birds one sees and so train one's mind and eye to classify them. Consulting a field guide will confirm some observations; it can also lead to doubt, which encourages one to notice more the next time. The following clues are used by both beginning and experienced birders.

Shape

It is often useful to envision a bird as a silhouette rather than focus on details of its plumage at first glance. A bird's general body shape can help place it in a group. For example, an American robin has a "basic bird" shape, while a bobwhite has a plump, round shape.

Binoculars enable birders to get a closer look at their alert, often-elusive subjects.

The European robin is one of Great Britain's most familiar birds. Watching it closely can reveal many typical bird behaviors.

Posture

Different species of birds stand and perch in different ways, so taking note of a bird's posture can help in its identification. A finch perches at a relaxed angle, while a wren often tilts forward with its tail in the air.

The northern cardinal does birders the favor of sporting colorful plumage and a highly distinctive, crested shape.

A blue jay's coloration, harsh calls, and brazen behavior make it another instantly recognizable bird. Its size is useful as a basis for comparison in identifying other species.

Flight

Birds flap, glide, and soar in different ways. Flight patterns are valuable clues, especially when trying to identify a songbird zipping through a yard or a distant raptor soaring on thermals. A turkey vulture, for example, holds its wings in a slight V, but a bald eagle's wings are held flat.

Size

Comparing and contrasting new birds you see with birds you are familiar with can help identify them. A cardinal and a jay, for example, may look somewhat similar in silhouette, but the jay is bigger.

Listening to recordings of bird calls and songs is helpful for any birder but particularly one who wishes to identify nocturnal birds, such as the barred owl.

Behavior

Birds feed, sing, and walk or hop in different ways, so behavioral differences provide excellent clues. A mallard, for example, eats by dabbling on the water's surface and tipping up with its tail out of the water to grub for food, whereas a bufflehead dives. A nuthatch moves headfirst down a tree trunk while foraging, but a woodpecker props itself head-up.

Field marks

A bird's plumage, of course, provides both color and pattern for reference—but birds do not usually pose in the convenient stances shown in a field guide, and tricks of lighting can muddy or distort colors, especially at a distance. Colors may also not be easy to distinguish in a dim woodland. Hence, birders look for characteristics called "field marks"—markings that are readily visible at a glance. These marks include stripes on the head, rings around eyes, spots and stripes on the breast, stripes (called bars) and patches on the wings, the shape and length of the tail and bill, and the color and length of the legs.

Habitat, range, and season

After using the above clues to arrive at a tentative identification, one might find several birds that seem to fit the bill in a field guide's portraits. The guide's text and maps, however, offer information about a bird's habitat, range, and migratory behavior that can help narrow one's choices.

Bird Record Holders

THE OSTRICH'S MANY CLAIMS TO FAME

The ostrich of Africa's grasslands can almost fill a top-ten list on its own. Not only is it the heaviest living bird, it is also the tallest: It can weigh up to 345 pounds (156 kg) and stand as tall as 9 feet (2.7 m) high. Much of the ostrich's height is attributable to its neck, the longest in the bird world, as well as its legs, likewise the longest among birds. This height helps an ostrich watch out for predators with the largest eyes of any land animal. Each eyeball is almost 2 inches (5 cm) in diameter, nearly the size of a tennis ball. If an ostrich spies a prowling cheetah, it can sprint away at 40 miles per hour (64 km/h), a speed that makes it the fastest two-legged land animal.

A bird this size must hatch from a large egg, and indeed, the ostrich's egg is the world's biggest. It measures about 7 inches (18 cm) long and weighs about 3 pounds (1.4 kg).

ON THE WING:
AERIAL RECORD HOLDERS

The heaviest birds able to fly include wild turkeys, mute swans, white pelicans, California condors, and kori and great bustards. These birds average between 20 to 30 pounds (11–15 kg), though some individual bustards weigh up to

The long-legged, long-necked ostrich holds avian records right from the start, beginning with the size of its egg.

44 pounds (20 kg). Their weight makes taking off a strenuous effort. Great bustards and condors run to build up speed before taking off. Swans likewise run across water to gain momentum.

The longest wingspan belongs to a seabird: the aptly named wandering albatross. Wandering albatrosses crisscross the southern ocean in search of food. They soar on slim wings that stretch 11 feet, 11 inches (3.6 m). On land, the Andean condor of South America and the marabou stork of Africa both spread their wings to a span of 10 feet, 6 inches (3.2 m) as they soar in search of carrion.

Speed records, however, belong to smaller—and lighter— birds. The peregrine falcon holds the record for diving through the air. It has been clocked at speeds of up to 175 miles per hour (282 km/h). Honors for level flapping flight go to the spine-tailed swift of India, which reportedly zips along at more than 100 miles per hour (161 km/h).

A Rüppell's griffon—an African vulture— set an altitude record by flying at a height of 37,900 feet (11,290 m). Unfortunately, this feat ended with the unlucky bird being sucked into the engine of a passing jet. More typical but

A peregrine falcon, or "bullet hawk."

A wandering albatross may soar for hours without flapping its wings.

An onagadori rooster's extraordinarily long tail feathers are a product of selective breeding in captivity by humans.

equally impressive is the altitude achieved by migrating bar-headed geese, which fly over the Himalaya at 27,880 feet (8,503 m).

Other birds fly at lower altitudes but log mind-boggling hours. The sooty tern, for example, may spend years after fledging on the wing over the tropical oceans, never alighting. As an adult, it comes ashore only to breed.

The sooty tern's land-based counterpart is the common swift of Europe, Asia, and Africa. It, too, may be entirely airborne for the two to three years between fledging and first breeding. Common swifts can sleep, forage, and even mate on the wing. The world's champion long-distance migrant, however, is another tern: the Arctic tern. This hardy traveler makes an annual round trip of up to 25,000 miles (40,200 km) between its Arctic breeding grounds and its winter range over the Antarctic Ocean.

BIRD TAILS

The world's longest feathers grow on the rump of the male onagadori, a domestic breed of chicken. The tail coverts, which grow continuously and are never molted, can reach up to nearly 35 feet (10.6 m). In the wild, the tail of the crested argus pheasant of Southeast Asia can grow to be 5.7 feet (173 cm) long and 5 inches (13 cm) wide.

The long-distance champion of the bird world is the unexhaustable Arctic tern.

The Indian and green peacock trail just a tad behind for the longest tail coverts of a wild bird at 5 feet, 3 inches (160 cm).

AND THE SMALLEST . . .

The world's smallest bird is the tiny bee humming-bird of Cuba. Only 2.24 inches (5.7 cm) long and weighing a mere 0.056 ounces (1.6 g), its wingspan is a scant 2.6 inches (65 mm). The female of the species, which is slightly larger, lays pea-sized eggs in a nest about the size of a thimble.

The Cuban bee hummingbird is not much bigger than the eye of an ostrich.

NEST MAKING

In producing nurseries for their eggs and young, birds use skills that would be recognized by potters, weavers, and engineers. Nest building also requires much time and effort: A Baltimore oriole was once observed putting 40 hours of intensive labor into building its nest. The researcher estimated that the industrious bird had taken 10,000 stitches and tied a few thousand knots.

Nest forms seem to display evolutionary accretions of refinements in construction. Scrapes and mounds, so like those of reptiles such as alligators, are at one end of the continuum. Scrapes built up with material pulled in from nearby vegetation sit somewhere near the middle. At the other end is an array of increasingly complex structures, ranging from the familiar bowl-shaped nests of many garden birds to elaborately woven hanging nests complete with entrance tubes and decoy chambers. Many birds, however, get by without building any nest at all. Some birds, such as the Indian courser, lay eggs right on the ground. The white tern likewise simply lays her egg on a branch. The chick hatches with strong claws ready to cling for dear life.

Above: A female pigeon builds a well-hidden nest from sticks and twigs brought to her by her mate.

Left: The light-mantled sooty albatross nests on a low, grass-lined mound.

Where Birds Nest

Q: How are plants used as nest sites?

A: A nest site must provide shelter from the elements and protection from predators as well as access to a source of food for nestlings. Plants in a bird's habitat offer these amenities.

Trees are favorite nest sites. Tree holes provide homes for birds such as owls and woodpeckers. A nest on a branch likewise keeps eggs and young out of reach of ground predators. Leaves conceal the nest and protect it from rain and wind. A tree-nesting bird takes care to build its nest on the tree's lee side, away from the direct force of storms and winds. It secures its nest to the tree by cramming materials into a fork and wrapping fibers around twigs. The rest of the nest is built upon this base. The tailorbird of Southeast Asia uses a different technique: It pokes holes in leaves with its bill, stitches them together with threads of silk and plant fibers, and then builds its nest in the resulting pocket. But danger lurks even in trees in the form of monkeys, snakes, and other birds. Some birds foil these animals by building hanging nests at the very tips of slim, flexible boughs that cannot support a predator's weight.

Right: Weaver birds build their nests on the weaker ends of branches to thwart predators that would try to climb down to the nest to harm the mother and her chicks.

Below: A hollow in a tree offers the perfect home for a downy woodpecker, offering security from weather extremes and concealment from the sharp eyes of predators.

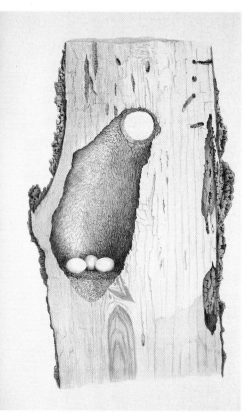

Birds also nest in shrubs, thickets, and grassy fields. Bobolinks of North America conceal their ground nests amid stems of grass and forbs. Among certain species of larks, the female evaluates the territories of potential mates, sizing them up to see if they offer a suitable shady spot for a nest.

Beds of reeds and cattails provide nesting sites, too. Red-winged blackbirds nest among plants at edges of lakes and ponds. Reed warblers bind the stems of reeds with strips of grass and leaves to build their nests. Ducks, geese, swans, and loons also build nests among plants along the water's edge.

Q: What birds use cliffs as nest sites?

A: Sheer cliffs and narrow ledges are tricky places to nest, but these remote sites are also inaccessible to most predators, making them ideal sites for many birds. Seabirds around the world nest on

Northern gannets breed in colonies on high, seaside cliffs that protect them from most predators. They return to the same nesting sites year after year.

cliffs. Certain raptors, such as peregrine falcons, also use cliffs. Bank swallows, cliff swallows, and crag martins are all named for their nest sites of choice. In the Pacific Northwest, black swifts fly right into waterfalls to reach the damp cliffs behind them. They then creep up the wall to find ledges where they can build their little mud nests. Even some parrots, such as Patagonian conures, nest in cliffs by burrowing into them.

Q: What birds nest in colonies?

A: From albatrosses to zebra finches, about one out of eight bird species breed in colonies. Among these colonial birds are many seabirds, such as terns, gulls, shearwaters, and gannets. Birds may nest colonially when sites close to their food source are in short supply; there is no choice but to squeeze together on shores and cliffs.

Colonial nesters may also benefit by watching the behavior of other birds to find out where they are getting their food. If a neighbor returns with a beakful of fish or insects, other birds will follow it when it flies off again. Group defense against predators is another benefit, as is the synchronization of egg laying. When the young hatch, their superabundance overwhelms predators, and each individual chick enjoys better odds of surviving.

There are drawbacks to colonial life, too. High levels of aggression keep a colony on the boil with squabbling, which requires frequent displaying to defuse it. Neighbors steal nesting materials from each other. In some species, neighbors kill and sometimes eat the eggs or young of other birds if the nest is left unguarded. The concentration of nests also raises the risk of disease and the spread of parasites. Each species, in effect, has drawn up a balance sheet to weigh the pros and cons of coloniality.

Kinds of Nests

Q: What is a scrape?

A: A scrape is a shallow bowl scratched by a bird in the ground. Plovers, terns, noddies, skimmers, and many other seabirds and shorebirds dig scrapes. Sometimes the scrapes are augmented with bits of shell, small stones, or plant material that the bird picks up and tosses in with a quick jerk of its head. An ostrich makes a simple scrape in sand or dirt. A cassowary fills its scrape with leaves and grass. Many penguins gather pebbles to place in the scrape to elevate the eggs enough to keep them from being soaked by runoff from melting snow.

The motions a bird uses to make a scrape—scratching with the feet, pressing down with the breast, spinning slowly to form a bowl—are the same as those used by a bird when it builds a cup-shaped nest of grass, twigs, and mud. A goose's nest is a good example of the link between a primitive scrape and a carefully woven cup nest. A nest-building goose first digs a scrape and then sits in it as she reaches out with her long neck to pluck plant material and tuck it around her body. Some ground-nesting birds will also use existing depressions. The water dikkop, for example, will happily lay its eggs in pats of hippopotamus excrement. The sandgrouse may lay its eggs in a large hoofprint.

Some birds do not even bother with a scrape and simply lay right on the ground. Whip-poor-wills and most other nightjars lay their eggs on the forest floor. Killdeer sometimes lay theirs on flat rooftops.

Q: What is a platform nest?

A: A platform nest is a heap of material with a shallow bowl in its top. Many pigeons and doves build platform nests by piling twigs on a branch and then lining the bowl with grass and leaves. A flamingo makes a round mud mound and lays

Right: In the sparse woodland of Eurasia and Africa, nightjars lay eggs directly on the ground, hidden among the bushes they hide in during the day.

Below: A mating pair of Adelie penguins scrape a shallow hollow into a rocky nest of small stones carried in the birds' beaks and dropped into place.

Storks are known for their massive platform nests, which are often set on rooftops or high in the boughs of sturdy trees. They will add and build on them year after year, even passing them down to succeeding generations.

her egg in the scooped-out top. Grebes construct rafts made of reeds, grasses, and other water plants and then moor them to plants rooted underwater. Jacanas, coots, and some terns also build floating platforms. The horned coot, however, carries stones to the Andean lakes in which it nests and piles them to form a small hill. It caps the hill with a heap of plant material.

The best-known platform nests are those of storks and eagles. The white stork of Eurasia builds a massive nest of sticks atop trees, houses, and other structures. These are added to each year. One nest in Germany was used by generations of storks for nearly 400 years. Bald eagles also pile more sticks onto their nests yearly. A nest in Florida measured 20 feet deep and 9 feet wide (6.1 by 2.7 m) and contained about two tons of material.

Q: What birds build gigantic mound nests on the ground?

A: Huge compost heaps work as incubators for many megapodes of Australia, New Guinea, and the many islands stretching across Micronesia. These turkeylike birds build enormous mounds of sticks, leaves, and bark. The male hollows out the top, and then buries the structure under a layer of loose sand and other material. He opens the top to let the female lay her eggs inside, and also carefully adjusts material to maintain a constant temperature inside the rotting heap. The nest is excavated and replenished each year. It may grow to a height of 15 feet (4.5 m) and sometimes even higher: One megapode nest is known to have reached 50 feet (15.2 m).

Q: What is a cup nest?

A: When most people think of a bird's nest, they picture a cup nest—a bowl of grass and twigs mixed with mud. Many birds build this kind of nest. A bird shapes a cup nest by leaning against the materials with its breast and scraping with its legs as it turns in circles, tucking in materials around its body. It also presses its tail and head along the edges to form the rim. Some birds, such as bobolinks and reed buntings, build cup nests on or near the ground. Swifts and swallows build cup nests of mud and saliva that they "glue" to vertical surfaces. Many birds, such as robins and warblers, build cup nests on sturdy tree limbs. These round, roofless bowls are known as open cup nests.

Open cup nests may also be found hanging from twigs by their rims. Such nests are made by vireos, kinglets, blackbirds, flycatchers, and many Australasian songbirds. Extra-deep hanging cup nests are fashioned by birds such as Baltimore orioles in North America, oropendolas in Central and South America, and weaver birds in Africa. This kind of nest is typically suspended from the end of a branch. Eggs are safely contained inside the saclike nest even as it sways and bounces in the wind. Predators find it difficult to climb across the branches to get at the nest because the flexible boughs bend beneath their weight. The planalto hermit, a hummingbird of South America, makes its tiny nest even more inaccessible: It hangs from a twig or even the tip of a leaf by a single, slender woven strand. Another strand dangles from the bottom as a counterbalance to stop the nest from tipping sideways.

Q: What is a domed nest?

A: A domed nest is a cup nest with a roof. Some birds that nest in temperate climates construct domed nests. Both the eastern and western meadowlark

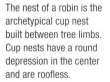

The nest of a robin is the archetypical cup nest built between tree limbs. Cup nests have a round depression in the center and are roofless.

Left: Swallows prefer to build their nests high on vertical structures, such as this nest under the overhang of a porch, and on cliffs sides.

Below: When natural materials are unavailable, Baltimore orioles will scavenge for man-made materials such as yarn, rags, and other fibers to build their nests.

build little grass huts in fields, knitting them into nearby stems. These cozy hideaways conceal both eggs and incubating parents and provide shade from sun and shelter from rain. Magpies build cup nests covered by a large dome of sticks. North American ovenbirds construct rounded nests directly on the forest floor. Marsh wrens, cactus wrens, sedge wrens, and verdins build round roofed nests known as globular nests.

Domed nests are the nurseries of choice for many perching birds living in tropical habitats, where hot, scorching sun and torrential rainfall are both common. A particularly sturdy version is built by the South American rufous hornero. The hornero uses a mixture of mud, cow manure, grass, and animal hair to build a globe the approximate size of a soccer ball. The entrance leads into a foyer, which in turn leads to an interior nest chamber. These round mud "ovens," which can weigh up to 11 pounds (5 kg), can be seen perched on branches, fence posts, and utility poles. They are sometimes even set one atop the other.

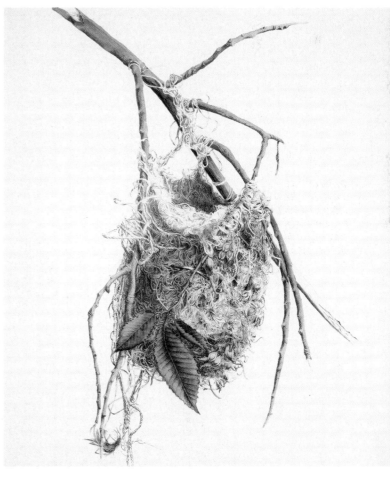

Defending the Nest

Q: How do some birds modify nests to deter predators?

A: Birds choose nest sites with an eye toward concealment and safety, even building them near stinging wasps, in thorny thickets, and amid the spines of cacti. Some species also incorporate security systems into the nest itself.

One technique is to put extra effort into camouflaging a nest. The varied sitella of Australia employs this trick. It builds a nest out of spiderwebs and insect cocoons in the fork of a branch. It then carefully covers the nest's exterior with materials that match the tree's bark. Naturalist David Attenborough observed one sitella applying bits of bark that matched the tree's texture, while another bird, nesting in a lichen-covered tree, attached lichen to its nest.

Another technique is the building of "dummy" nests. The yellow-rumped thornbill of Australia, for example, builds a dummy nest to prevent

Right: The penduline tit is named for the pendulous, hanging nests the males suspend from tree branches or reeds. The baglike nests are constructed of feathers and soft plant fibers.

Below: An ovenbird builds a ground nest in dense woods beside a log, at the foot of a bush or sapling, or among leaves and grasses, which afford it camouflage from predators.

omnivorous birds called currawongs from devouring its eggs. It weaves what looks like a typical open-cup nest. This nest, however, remains empty. The actual nesting chamber is hidden in a "cellar" built underneath it.

Winter, marsh, and sedge wrens take even more precautions against predators. The male wren builds extra nests in his territory. These dummy nests may lure predators and distract them from the real nest. Studies show, too, that males with many extra nests are preferred by females.

A third technique is simply to make the nest difficult to enter. Weaver birds of Africa achieve this goal by constructing long, thin entrance tubes.

The entrance tube of a lesser masked weaver's nest deters not only snakes, but also thwarts any cuckoo that tries to sneak in to lay her own eggs inside.

A cape penduline tit uses both tricks. The male builds a large, inviting dummy entrance on its pendulous nest. This entrance leads to empty space. The actual entrance is a thin slit lined with sticky webs above it, which the little tit can slip through and seal shut.

Although yellow-rumped caciques are gregarious and build conspicuous colonies, their nests are often protected from predators by their close proximity to wasps' nests.

Q: What birds nest among insects?

A: Stinging or biting insect neighbors are beneficial to a bird. Bees, wasps, and ants will swarm out of their nests to attack animals that venture too close. Many species exploit these social insects' nest-defending behavior by building their own nests next door.

This behavior is particularly widespread in tropical habitats. In South America, yellow-rumped caciques nest in colonies, hanging their long nests as close as three feet (0.9 m) away from a wasps' nest. Monkeys, hawks, toucans, and snakes that come to prey on the birds' eggs and chicks are likely to be repelled by the stinging wasps. Oropendolas likewise build hanging nests near wasps, which not only harass predators but also attack flies that lay eggs on their young—eggs that hatch into greedy, bloodsucking larvae. Elsewhere, raptors such as Mississippi kites and Aplomado falcons mingle with bees and wasps, which seem to repel botflies.

In Central America, rufous-naped wrens employ a triple defense: They nest in thorny acacia trees that are also home to wasps, as well as ants that attack intruders. Wrens nesting in acacias raise more young than wrens that do not.

Many species of birds utilize insects not for their fighting ability but for their architectural skills. Birds around the world peck their way into termite mounds and move in. The termites, which cannot bite, are outraged at first but soon give up trying to evict an intruder. Instead, they simply seal up their tunnels and chambers with new walls, leaving the bird in peace.

Homes in Holes

Q: What birds use tree holes as nests?

A: A hole in a tree is a hot property in the world of birds. A tree hole provides a nook safely enclosed against hungry predators and inclement weather. Birds vie with one another for this limited resource as if in a bidding war for a house, and are not above stealing a hole by evicting the current tenant and even tossing out its eggs or young.

Owls, hoopoes, bluebirds, starlings, and nuthatches are among the many species that nest in existing cavities. Surprisingly, a variety of waterfowl nests in tree holes, too. Black-bellied whistling ducks, buffleheads, goldeneyes, mandarin ducks, mergansers, Muscovy ducks, and wood ducks all share this preference. Nuthatches modify a tree hole by chinking its entrance with mud to make it too small for predators or cavity-usurping birds.

Many cavity nesters do not bother actually building a nest inside the hole.

To ensure protection from predator attacks, pairs of rhinoceros hornbills search for nest cavities in large trees with the smallest opening through which the female can squeeze.

Others, such as bluebirds, carefully line the hole with grasses, weeds, and other materials. Starlings also build nests in their tree holes and even add bits of fresh greenery periodically. The material selected produces chemicals that may help control populations of bird lice and other parasites that infest nests.

No amount of greenery, however, can freshen up the dank, messy interior of a hornbill's nest. Most hornbills in Asia and Africa nest in tree holes. The female sits inside the hole and helps her mate wall up the opening with mud, leaving just a tiny slit. She remains in her prison for up to four months to incubate the eggs and tend her brood, depending entirely on the male to bring her food. During this time, she also molts. When she finally breaks free, she helps her mate seal up the entrance again and joins him in feeding their offspring.

Many cavity nesters move into holes first made by woodpeckers, whose beaks are adapted for chiseling holes in wood. Woodpeckers then line the holes with the soft wood chips left from their labors. With the exception of the red-cockaded woodpecker, which may use the same nest hole for as many as twenty years, woodpeckers typically use a nest hole once. In the southwestern United States, Gila woodpeckers and gilded flickers peck holes in giant cacti called saguaros. A saguaro that has been drilled "heals" the wound by producing a liquid that hardens to form a firm-walled cavity that proves just right for a nest. When the Gila woodpecker is done with it, the cavity is quickly appropriated by an elf owl.

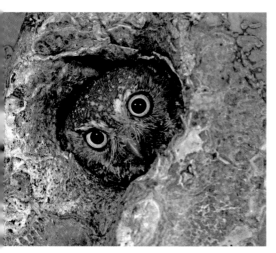

Far left: Elf owls of the American Southwest move into existing holes in cacti, elms, or other trees abandoned by Gila woodpeckers.

Left: To remain cool in scorching environments, the colonial-nesting carmine bee-eaters dig long, horizontal tunnels, often up to eight feet long, on sandy cliffs near riverbanks with their beaks.

Below: Many birds, such as shearwaters, dig burrows in the ground or on cliff walls to provide added protection for the nest from weather and predators.

Q: What birds nest in burrows?

A: Many species of birds are the feathered equivalents of prairie dogs, burrowing their way into the earth to raise their young. Frequently these burrowing birds carve into soft sandstone cliffs or dirt banks. Bee-eaters loosen soil with their sharp beaks and then scuff away the debris. Parrots such as Patagonian conures and maroon-fronted parrots dig with their strong, hooked beaks. A male bank swallow uses both feet and beak to dig a burrow, an activity that also serves to attract a mate who will later line the nesting chamber with feathers, grass, and other materials. Some fish-eating birds build burrows, too. Kingfishers dig tunnels that average about 3 feet long (0.9 m), kicking out dirt behind them as they scrape. The rhinoceros auklet's burrow may plunge more than 16 feet (5 m) into a slope or spruce-forest floor. A Manx shearwater digs a burrow that it visits only at night to avoid revealing its location to predators. The Atlantic puffin hacks at loose soil with its thick bill and digs with its webbed feet. Although they can dig their own burrows, they will also appropriate existing ones dug by rabbits or shearwaters. Pigeon guillemots, in turn, will dig burrows in clay banks but will also gladly move into an abandoned puffin burrow. Burrowing owls can also dig but usually opt to nest in existing tunnels drilled by desert tortoises.

> "A pair of starlings are renovating the knothole in the Balm o'Gilead on the front lawn, redecorating and trying to get everything done . . . before the arrival of the flickers, who walk right in regardless."
>
> —E. B. WHITE

Nesting Materials

A bird's choice of nesting materials depends largely on what is readily available. Most nests are constructed from local tree leaves and twigs, grass, and moss or lichen, and then lined with softer materials to cushion the eggs and the nestlings.

Q: What plant materials are used for nest making?

A: Grasses, weeds, twigs, leaves, reeds, lichen, and bark are commonly used as nesting materials. The inside of the nest may be lined with softer plant materials, such as moss, thistledown, and fluff from cottonwoods, dandelions, and milkweed. Seabirds and waterbirds often use water plants and even seaweed to line the inside of their nests. Birds as diverse as starlings and eagles are known to add fresh greenery to their nests regularly, perhaps to help control parasites.

Q: How is mud used in nest making?

A: Birds that build cup nests affixed to trees and shrubs often use mud as the foundation of a mix that includes grass and twigs. Other birds make nests entirely of mud. Magpie-larks in Australia build muddy cup nests on branches. Swallows scoop up mud from the edges of puddles, ponds, and streams and then construct rounded nests that adhere to walls. Hornbills seal the openings of their cavity nests with mud. South American horneros use mud to build round clay nests, collecting the material during the rainy season when it is still soft and pliable.

A long, thin gelatinous strand that the male black-nest swiftlet produces from salivary glands under its tongue is wound into a bracket-shaped nest. The saliva bonds like quick-drying cement to the inside of a cave wall.

Q: What birds use saliva to construct their nests?

A: Many birds add dabs of saliva when necessary while building nests and may even use it to moisten rotten wood to make a paste if mud is scarce. But the birds most noted for using saliva in nest construction are the swifts. These birds rely on their specially adapted, extra sticky and stretchy saliva to hold together their nests' materials. Their salivary glands even grow larger during breeding season in order to produce a copious supply. Some species of cave swiftlets are renowned for using saliva not merely as mortar but also as the primary building material for their nests. These are the edible nests in the Chinese dish called bird's nest soup.

Q: What other materials turn up in birds' nests?

A: Birds use a variety of materials in their nests in addition to vegetation. Pebbles and bones appear in the nests of penguins and other seabirds that make scrapes. Many birds use sticky spiderwebs to bind materials together and attach them to surfaces. These silken strands are particular favorites of hummingbirds. Ducks and geese pluck down from their breasts and line their nests with it. Many birds also eagerly collect the molted feathers of other birds to cushion their eggs. Animal hair, such as horsehair and wool, is also gathered. Most birds settle for picking up swatches of hair caught on fences and plants, although some bold ones will yank it right off the mammal growing it. Shed snakeskins are appropriated, too.

Manufactured materials also find their way into nests. The long list includes not-so-surprising items such as yarn, string, and dryer lint but also oddities such as barbed wire, dollar bills, eyeglass frames, and tissues. Osprey nests have turned up collections of fishnets, clothes, hats, boots, bottles, and toys. Author John Steinbeck once discovered his shirts and towels and even a rake in an osprey nest on his land. Items retrieved from a sunken ship have been found incorporated in a cormorants' nest. A pair of canyon wrens in California earned lasting fame by building a nest out of office supplies filched from a building and raising their young in a bed of shoelaces, rubber bands, paper clips, and thumbtacks.

The ruby-throated hummingbird builds its tiny nest from lichens and other materials "glued" together by spiderwebs.

Soft feathers line this Canada goose nest. A goose plucks down and some contour feathers from her breast to pad her nest shortly after beginning to lay.

Building a Nest

Q: Who builds the nest?

A: In most species with a monogamous mating system, male and female birds work together to build the nest, with each one contributing differently to the effort. The female typically builds the nest, with the male bringing her the necessary materials. In some species, both birds carry out the same tasks: A male and female kingfisher work side by side to dig a burrow, and male and female black woodpeckers take turns hollowing out a cavity in a tree.

Females take complete charge of nest building in polygynous species such as prairie-chickens, whose males do not participate in rearing young. In a few species, males take on the entire job of nest building. Male jacanas and phalaropes, who are responsible for raising young without the female's help, build the nests.

Males also build nests as part of courtship activities. Village weaver birds in Africa, for example, construct elaborate hanging nests to attract mates. A female indicates acceptance of the male by building a lining in the nest. If a first effort fails to win him a mate, a male will tear it apart and build another one.

Q: Are birds born knowing how to build a nest?

A: The construction of a nest involves both instinctive behavior and learning. A bird that builds a nest of mud, grass, and sticks in a tree uses many of the same motions as a bird that claws a simple scrape in the ground, such as scratching with its feet and slowly rotating its body—movements that are genetically rooted in the bird.

Birds also seem to possess instincts that compel them to seek out certain materials and use them in the proper order. A bird that builds an open cup nest in a tree "knows" that a base of mud, twigs, and grass must be constructed before it is lined with softer materials. A bird building a domed nest in the grass likewise

The social snowy egret usually nests in mixed colonies with other herons. Males and females work together to construct platformlike nests crafted primarily of sticks, and lined with fine twigs and rushes.

"knows" that the roof comes last. Each step in the nest-building process appears to stimulate the next step, as if the bird has put together part of a jigsaw puzzle and now knows what pieces to add.

An idea of what a finished nest should look like seems to be hardwired, too. Studies of male African weavers revealed that when part of a bird's nest was removed, the bird rebuilt only that part of the nest; he did not go on to construct an entirely new nest.

Hormones also play a role in kicking off this instinctive behavior: High levels of certain hormones in African collared doves propel males to bring their mates materials and the females to build nests.

Evidence for the role of learning, however, abounds. Young African weavers' first nests are often shoddy, but their weaving abilities improve as they gain experience. Birds must also learn where to find nesting materials, what to use if their traditional materials are unavailable, and how to adapt their nests to the environment. A common amakihi of Hawaii, for example, builds a thick, warm nest if its home is high up on a cold, dry mountain, but builds a looser nest that dries quickly in warm, moist rain forests lower down.

Q: Do birds reuse nests?

A: Many birds do not reuse nests because they tend to become infested with parasites after housing a brood. Some birds, however, will reuse a nest, despite the risk. Researchers have found that cliff swallows, for example, will reuse a nest for their second clutch. Eagles, ospreys, and storks, however, consistently reuse their nests and add to them each year. These nests may persist for decades and be taken over by successive generations.

A nest built by one species may be quickly acquired by another when the builder vacates the premises. Most wood-peckers, for example, chisel out new nest holes each year. Other cavity nesters, such as nuthatches, chickadees, titmice, and owls, move into the old holes. The round mud "ovens" of horneros are like-wise abandoned by their builders after one season and are quickly taken over by finches and martins.

Hawaii amakihis build nests of varying thickness and density according to the local environment.

Ospreys reuse their nests, adding new material each season. They nest near the water in large trees when they are available, but will settle for platforms if necessary.

CHAPTER 8

RAISING YOUNG

Birds' eggs are an age-old symbol of life, creation, and re-birth. A Chinese myth credits a hen's egg as the source of the sun, which sprang from the golden yolk, and of a deity. A black emu egg brought light to the world of Australian aborigines, and the islands of Oceania were said to issue from a celestial waterbird's egg. But even without a cosmic layer, an egg is a wondrous thing, a perfect capsule for nourishing and sheltering a growing life. By laying eggs a bird is able to reproduce without adding weight that would inhibit her ability to fly. The hatchlings vary by species in how much they depend on their parents, but they all start life weak and wet after struggling to escape their shells. The effort that most parent birds exert on behalf of their offspring is humbling. Raising young may involve thousands of sorties to collect insects, or risking life and limb to protect them from predators. Some birds, such as the emperor or chinstrap penguin, go without food in the bitter cold for many weeks, all for the sake of the life within an egg balanced atop its feet.

Above: Black swans nest in large colonies in Australia and New Zealand. Both parents incubate the eggs and care for the cygnets, which stay with their parents for up to a year.

Left: A chinstrap penguin prepares to settle down atop its egg. This species typically lays two eggs per breeding season. Both parents incubate the eggs.

Inside an Egg

Q: What are the parts of a bird's egg?

A: The hard shell of an egg is made up of minerals, mainly calcium carbonate. Gas exchange occurs through the shell; scattered pores let oxygen in and carbon dioxide and water vapor out. Inside the shell lie two membranes. The outer membrane adheres to the mineral shell to help hold it together. The inner shell membrane encloses the egg white, or albumen, which consists of protein and water. Like the outer shell, the albumin helps protect the inner part of the egg in addition to helping regulate the eggs temperature and moisture. An air space lies between the two membranes.

Floating in the albumen, surrounded by its own membrane, is the yolk, which is rich in fat for nourishing an embryo.

A spot of tissue (called the blastoderm) on the yolk develops into an embryo if it is fertilized. This spot, with the yolk, forms the true ovum, or egg cell, within the larger package we call an egg. Left to its own devices, the yolk would rise to the top of the egg, but instead it is attached to a pair of cross-ties, called chalazae, that keep it in place. The chalazae twist when an egg is rotated and allow the yolk to roll so that the embryo is always on top.

Q: How is an egg formed?

A: A female bird is born with all the egg cells, or ova, it will ever need for a lifetime of reproduction. During breeding season, some of the ova grow larger as the female's body wraps them in layers of yolk. This process can take up to two weeks. Then laying can begin.

Typically, one developed ovum migrates to the ovary's surface and erupts each day. The ovum is then ingested by the trumpet-shaped upper end of a tube called the oviduct. This part of the oviduct, called the infundibulum, is also where fertilization occurs, using sperm that have been stored in the wall of the oviduct.

Muscular contractions move the fertilized ovum through the oviduct. Along the way, different sections add materials such as membranes and albumen. The ovum then rests for up to 20 hours in a section called the shell gland, where the mineralized shell is added. In species that lay colored or patterned eggs, pigments are daubed on here, too. When the egg is ready for laying, it exits the oviduct, enters the cloaca, and is pushed from the bird's body.

A bird egg's hard shell is stippled with pores that allow gas exchange to occur. Membranes in the egg facilitate the exchange, supplying the embryo with oxygen. The yolk nourishes it, and fluids protect it. They carry out tasks akin to those of a mammal's placenta and amniotic fluid.

The Parts of an Egg

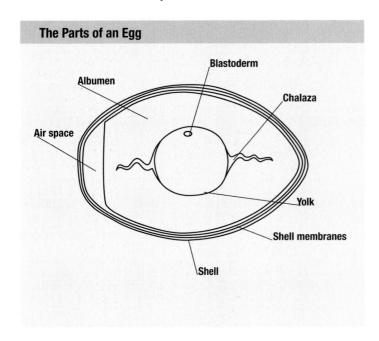

Blastoderm

Albumen

Chalaza

Air space

Yolk

Shell membranes

Shell

Q: **How does the egg change as the embryo inside it develops?**

A: The basic egg structure changes as an embryo grows. The embryo develops membranes and sacs to carry out different life functions. One sac, the amnion, is filled with fluid that bathes the embryo. This amniotic fluid keeps the embryo moist and also prevents its growing body parts from rubbing against each other or getting stuck together. Another sac, the allantois, is a receptacle for waste products. All these parts as well as the yolk are contained in a membrane called the chorion. Together, the chorion and the enclosed allantois form a structure called the chorioallantoic membrane, known as a CAM. The CAM is rich in blood vessels. It attaches to the eggshell and carries out the job of gas exchange, providing the embryo with oxygen and getting rid of carbon dioxide. As the embryo grows, the CAM does, too.

Meanwhile, the albumen and yolk shrink as the embryo uses them. This causes the air space at the egg's blunt end to grow larger. A day or two before hatching, the embryo jabs its beak into the pocket and takes its first breath, although its oxygen needs will continue to be provided by the CAM until the egg actually breaks.

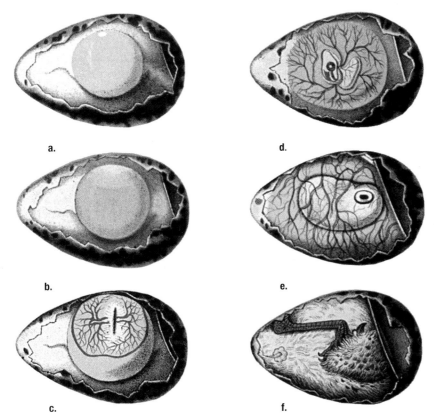

a.

b.

c.

d.

e.

f.

a. A freshly laid egg harbors a large, nutrient-rich yolk. The fertilized ovum began dividing before laying and has formed a white disk called the blastoderm. **b.** The blastoderm continues to grow, forming a three-layered structure. **c.** Blood vessels spread through the yolk as the embryo develops into a thin streak. One end becomes the head, the other the tail, with the spinal cord growing in between. **d.** As the embryo develops eyes and other organs, the network of vessels and membranes continues to grow. **e.** The air pocket at the egg's blunt end grows larger as yolk and albumen are consumed and water evaporates from the egg. **f.** The chick, nearly ready to hatch, is tightly curled up with its head tucked under its wing.

The Diversity of Eggs

Right: The highly pointed form typical of the common murre egg was long thought to prevent the egg from falling off cliffs, an assumption that is currently undergoing scrutiny.

Below: Eggs exhibit a wide range of colors and shapes, as shown by an array of eggs belonging to various falcons. Even eggs laid by the same species may exhibit diversity.

Q: What is the size range of birds' eggs?

A: The eggs of the smallest bird, the bee hummingbird of Cuba, are a mere 0.4 to 0.5 inches (10 to 13 mm) long. According to the Cornell Lab of Ornithology, about 5,500 of them could fit into the largest bird egg in existence: that of the largest bird, the ostrich. An ostrich egg measures up to 7 inches (18 cm) long and weighs almost 3 pounds (1.4 kg).

Q: Are all eggs "egg-shaped"?

A: Birds eggs range in shape from the nearly round eggs of owls to the long, narrow, pointed eggs of murres. These extremes bracket the basically oval eggs laid by most species of birds.

Birds lay eggs typical of their species, although eggs in a clutch may vary not only in coloration but also in shape. An egg's shape is determined partly by its journey through the muscular oviduct, the diameter of which varies from species to species. A wide-bodied bird such as a great horned owl, for example, lays nearly round eggs, while a missile-shaped bird such as a swallow lays more elliptical eggs.

Shorebirds, which most commonly produce four eggs per clutch, lay eggs tending toward the conical that fit snugly together in the nest when their pointed ends are touching in the middle. This is thought to be an adaptation that helps a shorebird incubate them efficiently. An incubating bird will even nudge its eggs back into this position if a researcher moves them.

A common murre's sharply pointed eggs roll in a circle with the pointed end toward the center, which has long been

American kestrel   Lesser kestrel   Lesser kestrel

Sparrowhawk   Kestrel   Goshawk   Merlin

Hobby   Hobby   Red-footed falcon

thought of as an adaptation for cliff nesting. A disturbed murre egg would pivot on a narrow ledge instead of dropping off the edge as an oval egg would do. Many ornithologists, however, question this assumption because many cliff-nesting species do not lay pointed eggs.

Q: Why do eggs exhibit such a variety of coloration and patterning?

A: Many birds lay unadorned white or off-white eggs, just as reptiles do. Ornithologists speculate that all birds once laid white eggs and that the various colors and patterns evolved later.

White eggs are typical of cavity-nesting birds such as owls and kingfishers. White eggs may be easier to see in the darkness of a hole or burrow, and their concealment makes it unnecessary to camouflage them. Some cavity nesters, however, lay colored or patterned eggs. Among these birds are chickadees, bluebirds, and wrens. It is thought that such birds once nested in the open and later "rediscovered" cavity nesting. White eggs are also laid by various ducks, geese, and grebes, which nest on the ground and cover eggs with plant material when they step off their nests. Birds that start incubating as soon as they have laid one egg, instead of waiting for the entire clutch to be produced, typically lay white eggs, too. This latter group includes such birds as hummingbirds, doves, and hawks.

Seabirds and shorebirds lay eggs that are speckled, spotted, splashed, streaked, scrawled, and scribbled with pigment. These markings camouflage the eggs on beaches strewn with pebbles and shells. Parent birds also appear to recognize their eggs by patterns; murres will reject eggs that don't look like the ones they laid. Many songbirds also lay colored or patterned eggs. Ornithologists are not quite sure why some birds, such as robins, lay blue eggs that do not seem to benefit from camouflage. Perhaps odd coloring helps birds distinguish their eggs from those of parasitical cowbirds.

Among the most curiously colored bird eggs are those of the emu, which are green when laid, but darken to a glossy black within days; the blue eggs of South America's guira cuckoo, which are blue covered with lacy white markings that can be washed off; and the eggs of the booted warbler of Russia, which are pink with spots in the western variety and white marked with black in the eastern variety.

The eggs of the Australian emu are dark green at first and become black over time. An egg exposed to sunlight, however, will gradually fade to white. The male incubates a nest full of eggs laid by several hens.

Incubating Eggs

Q: What is a brood patch?

A: A brood patch is a featherless area of skin on a bird's belly that is used to keep eggs warm. It is also called an incubation patch. Males and females may both develop brood patches if both sexes incubate the eggs. Nerves in the brood patch may help a bird gauge the temperature of its eggs and thereby regulate its incubating behavior.

A songbird has one brood patch. The patch starts forming a few days before laying begins. Down feathers on the patch fall out, and its skin thickens and swells. Blood vessels in the patch also grow larger. The brood patch becomes a heating pad that efficiently warms the eggs when the incubating bird settles on top of them.

Grebes, pigeons, and raptors also develop one brood patch. Geese and ducks

Right: The blue-footed booby lacks a brood patch, but by wrapping its webbed feet around the top and sides of the eggs as it crouches on them, it keeps them warm nonetheless. One study showed that an incubating booby has more fine blood vessels spreading across its webbing than a booby that is not incubating.

Below: The brood patch of a female yellow warbler is clearly revealed when her feathers are gently blown aside. The bare skin helps warm the eggs. Here, the tips of new feathers can be seen growing in.

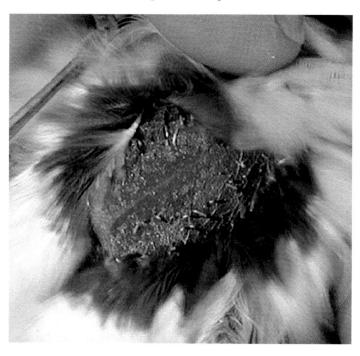

pluck down from their breasts to reveal their brood patches. Gulls have three brood patches. More than one brood patch may also be observed in different species of gamebirds and shorebirds. Penguins develop one brood patch, which in the emperor penguin is under a loose fold of belly skin. Most albatrosses have brood patches that are rather like pouches and partly surround the egg.

Pelicans and their relations, such as gannets and boobies, do not have brood patches. Some of these birds, however, warm their eggs by wrapping their big webbed feet around them.

Q: Do males and females share the job of incubation?

A: Both males and females of most species share the job of incubation. This is typical of species in which the sexes look mostly or completely alike. Shorebirds, grebes, gulls, albatrosses, boobies, cormorants, pigeons, doves, woodpeckers, toucans, penguins, and puffins and their relatives all share the responsibility of incubation. Great spotted kiwi pairs share incubation tasks, but males of two other kiwi species incubate with only occasional help from their mates.

Most songbirds relegate incubation duties to the female, although there are many exceptions. Starlings, Clark's nutcrackers, some finches and wrens, and rose-breasted grosbeaks are among the species in which both sexes incubate their eggs. African finches known as waxbills incubate their eggs with the male and female sitting side by side.

Female-only incubation is the rule among hummingbirds, ducks, swans, geese, most owls and other raptors, and species in which males have two or more mates. Females of most parrot species are also responsible for incubation.

Q: How do males that do not incubate assist females who do?

A: Males that do not equally share in incubation duties or that do not incubate at all often assist the female in other ways. A male swan, for example, may sit on the eggs briefly while his mate takes a break to eat. Bank swallow males also occasionally incubate eggs. Many males help feed their incubating mates. Male hawks and eagles carry food back to the nest and summon their mates with a feeding call. Hornbills are completely responsible for feeding the female, who is walled into

a tree cavity during incubation. Male songbirds also feed their mates. Males may also act as sentinels, perching near the nest to keep an eye out for predators.

Q: What male birds take full responsibility for incubation?

A: Male phalaropes and jacanas—not the females—develop brood patches, for it is the males that incubate the eggs and raise the young. Males of some shorebird species, such as spotted sandpipers, incubate one clutch while the female incubates another. Male emus, cassowaries, and rheas assume sole responsibility for incubating eggs and raising young. Male megapodes tend huge mounds of vegetation that serve as incubation chambers for eggs, using their tongues and beaks to take the mounds' temperature and removing or piling on debris to regulate it.

A male emu follows his young as they forage in the dry lands of Australia. He takes on full responsibility for both incubation and raising the chicks. Orphaned chicks that are younger than his own may also join his little flock.

Hatching

Q: How does a baby bird hatch?

A: A baby bird begins to get ready to hatch several days before it actually makes its debut into the world. It swallows the fluids in the amnion to supply its muscles with water. It also shifts its position so that it stretches from one end of the egg to the other, with its head toward the blunt end. It jabs its bill into the air pocket at this end and begins to breathe, although it still relies on internal membranes to supply sufficient oxygen.

The baby bird may begin calling at this time. This peeping may stimulate an incubating bird to change over to parenting behavior. In some species, such as terns and other colonial nesters, these prehatching calls serve to familiarize the parents with the sound of their chicks' voices so that they can find them in the crowd. At this point, the moment of hatching

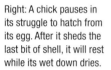

Right: A chick pauses in its struggle to hatch from its egg. After it sheds the last bit of shell, it will rest while its wet down dries.

Below: A chick peers from its egg after pipping an initial hole and then enlarging it. The chick pushes and scrapes as it turns in the shell, carving it open bit by bit.

is near. The baby bird's first job will be to peck a hole in its shell, a task called "pipping." In most species, the baby has a built-in tool for this job: a bump on its bill called an egg tooth. It also has a specialized muscle in the back of its head, called a hatching muscle, that helps it hammer. At some point after hatching, the egg tooth will fall off or be reabsorbed, and the hatching muscle will wither.

Meanwhile, other changes are taking place. The yolk sac is tugged into the baby bird's abdomen, where any yolk that is left will supply it with nourishment for several hours or days after hatching, depending on the species. By turning and wriggling and pecking, the baby bird finally pecks a line of holes to produce an exit hatch. It shoves and scrabbles with its feet and legs until it finally plops, exhausted, out of the shell. Most birds hatch headfirst in this way, although megapodes and some wading birds hatch out feetfirst. The time it takes to hatch depends on the species. The

chick of a domestic hen can pop out in just a few hours, while a sooty shearwater chick may struggle for four days.

Q: What is the difference between altricial and precocial young?

A: Altricial young are helpless upon hatching and depend on their parents for care and feeding. Most have their eyes sealed shut and are naked or covered scantily with down. They cannot produce enough body heat to survive on their own, nor can they walk. About all they can do is gape for food and huddle with their siblings. They are typically raised in nests. Songbirds, cormorants, penguins, kingfishers, boobies, pelicans, pigeons, doves, owls, raptors, parrots, toucans, hornbills, and woodpeckers are among the many species that hatch altricial young.

Precocial young, as their name suggests, are more developed upon hatching. Their eyes are open, bright and sparkling, and they are coated in down. With just a drying-off and a quick rest, they can walk and run soon after hatching. Precocial waterfowl can also swim. Many can feed themselves partly or entirely. Quail, grouse, chickens, turkeys, pheasants, shorebirds, ducks, geese, loons, grebes, gulls, and terns are among the species that have precocial young. The young of megapodes are the most precocial of all. After hatching, they crawl out of the mound of nesting material in which they were incubated and march off to fend for themselves without ever interacting with their parents.

Left: A chick that is highly developed at the time of hatching is said to be precocial. Precocial young can walk, run, and feed themselves, though nearly all stay with one or both parents for protection until they are grown.

Below: The naked, blind nestlings of the American robin are typical of altricial young. Altricial young are helpless upon hatching and require frequent feeding by their parents.

Caring for the Young

Right: The yellow-vented bulbul, a common garden bird in much of Southeast Asia, feeds its young berries and other fruit as well as insects and spiders.

Q: How do birds feed their young?

A: Young birds have voracious appetites. Many nestlings can easily eat their own weight in food each day. One scientist recorded the number of earthworms eaten by a fledgling American robin in one day and calculated that their total length added up to 14 feet (4.3 m).

Songbirds, hummingbirds, woodpeckers, and many others devote most of their waking hours to feeding their hungry nestlings. Research provides a steady flow of astonishing statistics: Hummingbirds have been clocked feeding nestlings once every 20 minutes. A pair of rose-breasted grosbeaks fed their young 426 times over the course of 11 hours. Tree swallows carry home about 8,000 insects each day. Pied flycatchers complete at least 6,000 feeding trips to raise their broods. Seabirds feed their young less often because they must range more widely to collect the food. A baby albatross, for example, may wait a day or more between meals.

Below: Nestlings gape and peep as they beg for food from a parent returning to the nest. Brightly colored mouth linings and flanges at the base of the beak help stimulate feeding.

Songbird nestlings beg for food from their parents by stretching upward and opening their beaks wide in a gesture called gaping. Many nestlings have brightly colored mouth linings to assist parents in aiming when they ram a beakful of food down a hungry throat. The fleshy edges, or flanges, of the nestling's beak may be brightly colored, too. A Gouldian finch nestling even has glow-in-the-dark spots in its mouth. A parent bird is stimulated to feed the most insistent gullet first. A sated youngster will stop gaping, while its hungry siblings continue to beg. Other signals used by nestlings to stimulate feeding include head bobbing and cheeping by flamingo chicks, nibbling the bill as in shearwaters, and tapping a spot on the parent's bill as in herring gulls. Young penguins, pelicans, and cormorants shove their beaks and even heads right into their parents' mouths.

Many birds, including waxwings, crossbills, albatrosses, petrels, pelicans, and hummingbirds, feed their young partly digested or regurgitated meals. Raptors carry prey back to the nest, where they tear it apart before doling it out to nestlings. Older nestlings are given prey to tear apart themselves. Pigeons and doves make "crop milk" for their young for a few days after hatching. Flamingoes' throats yield milk, too. A male emperor penguin likewise feeds its chick a milky substance from its throat until its mate returns from foraging at sea.

Q: How do birds keep nests clean?

A: Many birds keep nests sanitary for the sake of their nestlings' health. Eggshells are eaten or discarded so that they do not spoil the effect of camouflage or jab the nestlings. Rotten eggs and dead nestlings are likewise tossed. Raptors throw uneaten food overboard. Songbird and woodpecker nestlings' droppings are also removed or consumed by the parents so that nest and babies don't become a soggy mess. This job is facilitated by the youngsters' convenient adaptation of producing wastes tidily packaged in fecal sacs. The young of other species typically maneuver so that they excrete their wastes over the side of the nest. Still, the nests of many species—particularly those that do not reuse their nests—are revolting messes at the end of the breeding season.

Q: How do parents defend their young?

A: Adult birds are vigorous in defense of their young. Many species will raise their wings to ward off an intruder and do not hesitate to peck at one that comes near. Ostriches, rheas, and other large birds kick and slash with their clawed feet. Swans are famed for being able to break a human's arm with a whack from a wing.

Some species distract predators and lead them away from the nest. Killdeer and dotterels, for example, feign injury and lure predators with pathetic, "broken wing" displays. Other species simply pick up their young and flee. Loons carry young on their backs, jacanas tuck their babies under their wings and run away, rails carry theirs in their beaks, and sungrebes can even fly with their young tucked into pockets under the wings.

Below left: The greater flamingo produces a pinkish milky substance from glands in its throat and upper stomach. This is the chick's only food for its first two months of life.

Below right: The killdeer is famous for its "broken wing" display, in which the parent bird distracts predators by dragging its wing and peeping pathetically, thus luring it away from the nest.

> **Each bird learns first a single word, quite long for a beginner, but says it very plainly, 'Dinner Dinner Dinner.'**
>
> —*Anna Bird Stewart*

Collective Care

Q: What is a crèche?

A: A crèche is a group of young birds that have left their nests and banded together. Typically, the young birds are guarded by a few adults but fed only by their own parents. Forming crèches may benefit young birds in the same way that living in a herd protects mammals: There are more senses on the alert for predators, and each individual improves its odds of survival because there is safety in numbers. A crèche also helps young penguins and other birds in frigid environments to keep warm. This "babysitting cooperative" also benefits parents, giving them greater opportunity to forage.

Species whose young form crèches include flamingoes, many penguins and pelicans, ostriches, shelducks, some diving ducks, jays, and parrots.

Below left: King penguin chicks form a crèche on South Georgia Island. They huddle together for warmth while most adults leave to feed at sea. Each one may be fed only once every two or three weeks by a returning parent.

Below right: Young kookaburras may remain on their parents' territory to assist in incubating and feeding the next brood. They may supply up to two-thirds of the chicks' meals. Biding their time in terms of breeding is an investment in the future, for these helpers will one day inherit the territory.

Q: What is cooperative breeding?

A: Cooperative breeding describes a reproductive strategy in which birds that are not part of a mated pair assist in raising that pair's young. Often these helpers are related to the mated pair; typically they are young birds hatched during the previous breeding season or in an earlier brood of the current season. They may also be young, unrelated birds who have left home and do not yet have territories of their own, birds who have lost a mate, or a pair of birds whose nest has failed. Depending on the species, the helpers' duties may include assisting in nest building, incubation, territorial defense, and feeding incubating birds and nestlings. They often perform the lion's share of nestling feeding.

Cooperative breeding has been observed in about 300 species of birds, ranging from Florida scrub jays to kookaburras and moorhens. Most of these species live in the tropics or sub-tropics. The species differ widely but face a common dilemma—shortage of territory for new breeders to claim.

Smooth-billed anis build a communal nest from twigs broken off trees. Each female in the group lays from three to seven eggs. Early nesters' eggs may be removed or buried by later nesters. All or most of the adult birds, however, will care for the nestlings, as will young, nonbreeding birds.

Helpers are a boon to the parent birds. Researchers have found that when African bee-eaters have helpers, their babies grow faster and more of the clutch survives. But what is in it for the helpers? Since most helpers are siblings of the nestlings they help raise, they are benefiting by helping other birds that share their genes to survive. In addition, the helpers gain experience in raising nestlings. Sometimes, the young birds may be able to snag portions of the territory for themselves or "inherit" the territory if an older bird dies.

In some species, increasing the size of the flock by assisting in rearing another bird's young translates into increasing the size of the territory that can be defended, thus bettering the odds of eventually getting nesting space of one's own. White-winged choughs of Australia even lure the young of other choughs by displaying to them and leading them away,

effectively "kidnapping" them for their own group's use in territorial defense.

Anis, which are thick-billed cousins of cuckoos and roadrunners, put their own spin on communal breeding. As many as four pairs of anis may lay eggs in one communal nest. All the adults incubate, although a female groove-billed ani removes other females' eggs before starting to lay, while a female smooth-billed ani usually buries them in the nest instead. The female who lays first tends to incubate the most, and males take turns incubating by day, with one male (usually the mate of the last female to lay eggs) designated as the nighttime incubator.

White-winged choughs live in dry Australian woodlands. Foraging is time-consuming work in this habitat, so a breeding pair requires help from at least two and preferably as many as a dozen family members in order to raise a brood successfully.

Brood Parasites

Q: What birds leave the care of their young to other species?

A: Birds that lay eggs in other birds' nests and then abandon them to the nest owner's care are called brood parasites. The birds they parasitize are called hosts. About 80 species are known to be brood parasites. This group is made up of the black-headed duck and several tropical cuckoos, all of South America; honeyguides of Africa and Asia; whydahs, indigobirds, and the parasitic weaver, all of Africa; almost 50 species of cuckoo in Europe and Asia; and 6 species of cowbird in North and South America.

Each species parasitizes certain hosts. Its "hit list" may be restricted to a few species or expanded to include many. Each whydah species, for example, typically targets a particular species of waxbill, and the screaming cowbird parasitizes only the bay-winged cowbird. On the other hand, the notorious European or common cuckoo parasitizes more than 130 species, and the brown-headed cowbird parasitizes more than 200 species.

Female shiny cowbirds lay eggs in the nests of more than 200 other species. Some species detect the intruding eggs and remove them or abandon the nest, while others unwittingly raise the cowbird's young. Shiny cowbirds are native to Central and South America but have expanded their range northward into Florida in recent years.

Q: How do brood parasites manage to get away with their behavior?

A: The interplay between parasites and hosts has sparked the evolution of some fascinating behaviors and even physical adaptations. Brood parasites typically operate by stealthily keeping an eye on nesting birds of a target species and then darting in to lay quickly.

A common cuckoo, for example, can lay an egg in just five to ten seconds, whereas a host may take many minutes. The parasite may also eat or throw away one or more of the host's eggs to ensure that the clutch is not so large that it overwhelms the host's ability to feed the intruder. A female parasite's mate may assist by distracting the hosts while she commits the fly-by laying. The common koel, a cuckoo of Australasia, employs this technique most effectively. In India, koels parasitize crows. The male koel is black, and hosts mistake him for a crow intruder and chase after him. Meanwhile, the spotted female koel slips in to lay her egg.

Other adaptations of brood parasites extend to the eggs and young themselves. Some species, for example, lay eggs that mimic those of their hosts. Different races of common cuckoo parasitize different species, ones that are prevalent in their areas. Thus, cuckoos that parasitize garden warblers have evolved to lay speckled eggs, while cuckoos that parasitize reed warblers lay pale green eggs with blotches. Cuckoos that live in places where they parasitize many species, however, do not lay eggs that mimic the eggs of their hosts.

A meadow pipit fills the gaping mouth of a cuckoo chick. The chick, upon hatching, laboriously heaved its hosts' eggs out of the nest. The unsuspecting pipits feed the intruder with the same devotion they would lavish on their own young, seemingly unaware that their "offspring" is much bigger than they are.

The young of some brood parasites typically hatch earlier than their hosts' young, and then hog the food brought by the parents. Some young parasites even kill their nestmates. A honeyguide nestling is equipped with a hooked beak and nips other nestlings to death. A common cuckoo nestling hatches first and then cradles each of the other eggs in a hollow in its back and instinctively shuffles backward to the nest's edge and heaves it over. The young of indigobirds and whydahs have intricately patterned gapes that mimic those of their hosts' nestlings.

But hosts have evolved counter-measures. Weaver birds craft tunnels that are too small for cuckoos to enter easily. Cedar waxwings, Baltimore orioles, and warbling vireos smash cowbird eggs that they find in their nests; catbirds and robins throw them out. Yellow warblers build new nests on top of parasitized ones. Cardinals abandon them. Hosts who are duped will raise the parasite fledgling, even if it grows

Yellow warblers are often parasitized by brown-headed cowbirds, but they also frequently fend them off. The warblers cry alarm calls, sit in their nests and shield it with their wings, and even lurk near a spying cowbird, as if to let it know it is being watched in return. If the cowbird succeeds in laying, the warblers often build a new nest over the old nest and its contents.

to be several times their size. Recently, however, researchers have found that nearly one out of every two female superb fairy-wrens in Australia figures out that something is awry. A bronze-cuckoo nestling that hatches in a fairy-wren nest kills its nestmates within two days. Two days later, the female leaves the impostor to starve and goes off to start a new nest.

CHAPTER 9

THE MARVEL OF MIGRATION

The ancients noted the seasonal disappearance of certain birds, yet, where they went to was a mystery. Some astute observers noticed that birds headed in specific directions, and travelers ran into familiar species abroad. Still, folk beliefs lasted for centuries: People thought that redstarts turned into Eurasian robins; that kites, larks, and other species hibernated in holes; that swallows banded together to roll into balls and hibernate in the mud in ponds; and that swans flew to the moon.

With the advent of bird banding in the late 1900s, the secrets of migration were slowly revealed. The ability to track birds by radar and with transmitters further advanced our knowledge. Today, the study of migration focuses not only on where birds go but also on how they get there. Ecologists are also considering how migratory birds fit into ecosystems at either end of their journeys and how habitat change affects populations. Even as research dispels myths, it reveals facts that nonetheless challenge the imagination, particularly the astonishing endurance of birds. Tiny ruby-throated hummingbirds breeding in northern Canada, for example, fly to Central America for the winter, a journey that includes a 500-mile flight across the Gulf of Mexico.

Above: Flying geese sketch a V in the sky. Flying in this formation may enable birds to conserve energy.

Left: Sheer rock cliffs provide narrow ledges and sanctuary for many seabirds during nesting season. Increasing their odds of reproducing successfully propels many species to undertake grueling migratory journeys, sometimes of astonishing length.

The Reasons for Migration

The barn swallow exhibits remarkable site fidelity, usually returning to the nest site of the previous year. Barn swallows in Europe migrate to African wintering grounds. North American barn swallows migrate to Central and South America.

Q: Why do many birds migrate?

A: Each year, birds ranging in size from hawks to thumb-size hummingbirds fly hundreds, even thousands, of miles from breeding grounds to wintering grounds, and then back again, facing hardship and peril along the way—all to maximize their potential to survive another year and raise another brood. By migrating, these birds avoid severe winter weather and enjoy easier foraging for part of the year, and then exploit the extra-long days and abundance of food offered by their breeding grounds the other part of the year.

An insect-eating warbler, for example, cannot survive a cold northern winter because there are few insects to eat. It must fly south to mild climates in order to find food, so it leaves in late summer, even while insects are still available in the north. Arriving in the tropics, it finds warm weather and plenty of food. The same is true for birds that feed primarily on nectar and fruit, which are also seasonally abundant in temperate climates.

Patterns of migration among North America's populations of red-tailed hawks vary according to latitude and in response to weather conditions. Typically, the most northern birds migrate south to wintering grounds, which they share with red-tails that are year-round residents.

But why would a bird leave its wintering ground to raise young in the first place? Because to stay would mean competing with resident birds—those that live there year-round—for food and nesting sites, and also to miss out on a resource that the breeding grounds offer each year: a superabundance of insects. As spring warms the northern, temperate lands, insects that overwintered as eggs and cocoons hatch and become active. This feast comes at just the right time to feed birds that need to fuel their reproductive efforts, and subsequently to sate the furious appetites of their young.

Studies show that migratory birds experience greater reproductive success than birds that stay put in the tropics. About half of the migratory adults will die each year, with some of those deaths caused by the rigors of migration, but the survivors will raise a greater number of young on the breeding grounds as they exploit the profusion of insects. The tropical residents are more likely to survive from year to year, but they raise fewer young per nest because they do not have a sudden superabundance of food to exploit. They must also cope with a greater number of nest predators and parasites that harm nestlings.

These tradeoffs are also at work in bird populations that do not migrate. Birds such as chickadees, which typically spend winter in the temperate zone, benefit from the superabundance of insects in spring and raise the most young per nest. They are spared the effort of migrating and enjoy the advantage of possessing a territory right at the start of the breeding season; they can also start nesting sooner. This advantage, however, is offset by high mortality among adults due to starvation or freezing in winter.

Q: What is the origin of birds' migratory behavior?

A: Scientists theorize that migration behavior evolved as a result of tropical birds expanding their ranges during breeding seasons. This behavior came about as a result of competition for nest sites and foraging for food. Birds that were then inclined to return to the warmer tropics for the winter avoided becoming victims of winter weather. In this way, some migrants were able to produce more offspring than birds that stayed in the tropics because they could exploit seasonal insect abundance as well as the longer span of daylight provided by spring and summer in temperate zones. This, in turn, encouraged the evolution of migratory behavior because there was survival and reproductive value to being on the move in both seasons. Changes in climate have also affected the evolution of migration. The advance and retreat of glaciers during ice ages, for example, altered conditions and caused migrants to change their routes. Fortunately, migration, like other aspects of bird life, is adaptable. Changes in migratory behavior can even be measured in decades. In just the last quarter century, for example, some populations of blackcaps have evolved that migrate from central Europe in a northwestern direction to spend winter in England while other populations continue their traditional trek southward to Africa. This adaptation appears to have been spurred by the rise in winter feeding of birds in Great Britain and Ireland.

Blackcaps of northern Eurasia fly south to African wintering grounds, while those breeding in southwestern Europe may be either residents or migrants. Blackcaps bred in captivity have provided many insights into the evolution and heritability of migratory behavior.

Time to Go

Q: Why do birds fly "south" for the winter, or migrate?

A: Scientists have learned a great deal about why birds migrate, but just what signals them to get moving is still something of a mystery. Currently, much evidence points to a bird's built-in annual cycle as the trigger for migratory behavior. This annual cycle is called a circannual rhythm. Studies show that birds kept in constant light conditions year-round still exhibit an urge to migrate at the appropriate time. The captive birds indicate their desire with restless behavior and much whirring of wings, particularly after nightfall. This migratory restlessness is called zugunruhe. The birds even put on weight in preparation for their journey.

A bird's circannual rhythm is also thought to be influenced by external factors, such as light. The duration of daylight at different times of the year is thought to play an important role in stimulating the production of hormones that orchestrate a bird's seasonal activities. The length of daylight on a given day is known as a photoperiod. A bird's brain senses the changing length of the photoperiod throughout the year. The rhythm of waxing and waning photoperiods affects hormone production in the bird and may help orchestrate not only migration but also breeding and molting.

Although research has shown how birds kept in captivity under constant lighting still go through their repertoire of seasonal behaviors, studies have also

What sparks the onset of migration and compels birds to prepare and embark on their journeys? One important factor seems to be the length of daylight, at least in temperate zones.

shown that one aspect of the bird's internal clock goes awry if the bird is not exposed to natural lighting conditions. This biological clock is the one that influences a bird's cycle of typical daily behaviors, such as roosting and feeding. Deprived of external cues, a bird in captivity kept under constant lighting will have its clock drift out of sync with the 24-hour clock. It may, for example, experience a 25-hour-long "day." Likewise, its circannual rhythm will slowly become out of sync with the seasons.

Once the bird is exposed to natural lighting conditions, however, its internal clocks soon snap back into alignment, just as humans adapt to their new environment's time schedule after flying halfway around the world on a jet.

Some studies have also shown that altering light conditions dramatically can influence a captive bird's circannual rhythm. Researchers have managed to shorten a captive bird's "year" by changing the pace at which photoperiods lengthen. One study caused a starling to molt eight times in one year. It is thought that perhaps the effect of photoperiods is greater when birds are in temperate zones than it would be in the constant balance of day and night found in tropical zones.

A bird is not a clockwork mechanism, of course, and so it also must make some decisions about migrating. If the weather is unusually windy and rainy, for example, the bird puts its compelling drive to migrate on hold and sits out the storm. A bird can also determine wind direction and opt to fly when conditions are most favorable; flying with a tailwind, after all, saves energy, and bucking a headwind is hard work.

Food availability seems to play a role in the migration patterns of species that live in environments where food may be available more reliably all year, although there may be good years and bad years. In years of marginal food availability, some birds may migrate while others stay put. Even epic-journey migrants may tarry briefly in an area where food is plentiful and temperatures warm.

Birds regulate their overpowering urge to migrate in response to weather conditions. Rain and snow may cause them to delay departure or sit out the storm. Canada geese, shown here, may even turn around and go back to their departure site if the weather deteriorates.

Studies of captive and wild white-crowned sparrows over several decades have yielded much information about migratory restlessness, or zugunruhe, as well as how birds orient by the stars at night.

Gearing Up to Go

Q: What do birds do to prepare for migration?

A: Birds have molted and grown new feathers by the time of departure. They have finished raising their young. Now it is time for them to stockpile fuel in the form of fat. Their appetites increase, and they may switch from eating one food, such as insects, to gorging on seeds or fruit. This heightened intake of food is known as hyperphagia. A bird in this condition also experiences an uptick in its food-processing ability that quickly turns food into stored fat.

Birds that migrate long distances store up more fat than birds that migrate short distances. The fat accumulates in body cavities, internal organs, muscles, and under the skin. Flight muscles increase in size, too. Though the added weight may seem slight when measured, it is substantial for an animal in which nearly every feature is adapted for being lightweight. A British garden warbler, for example, that usually weighs about two-fifths of an ounce puts on about one-seventh of an ounce of fat prior to migration—an increase of about one-third of its body weight. A blackpoll warbler may nearly double its weight before migrating.

Q: Is knowledge of the migratory route inborn or learned?

A: Most migratory birds are born with the urge to migrate at the appropriate time of year in the appropriate direction for a certain amount of time. Researchers have found that young captive birds that have never migrated before will exhibit migratory restlessness and physically strive and leap in the direction of travel that would take them to their ancestral destination. This instinct combines with experience, which may include traveling with family groups or in large flocks.

To find out more, researchers have captured different species of birds in one place, taken them to distant locales, and then released them. Amazingly, the birds still manage to find their way to their breeding or wintering grounds. A Dutch scientist, for example, once caught European starlings migrating from the Baltic region to Great Britain and northern France in autumn. The birds flew in a southwesterly direction. He took the birds to Switzerland, which was 400 miles out of their way. He then released the adult

Migratory shorebirds, such as this lesser yellowlegs, feed heavily just before migrating and during stopovers. A study of lesser yellowlegs embarking on their fall migration from the Gulf of St. Lawrence to South America found that the average bird's fat level was substantial enough to fuel flight for a distance of about 1,300 miles.

The world's 40-plus species of gulls exhibit a variety of migratory patterns. Some species migrate from northern breeding grounds to southern wintering grounds. Species nesting inland typically migrate to coasts.

birds together, separately from the young of that year, who were undergoing their first migration. The results were fascinating, and showed that both inheritance and experience are involved in migration.

The adult birds realized that flying in a southwesterly direction would take them even farther off course, so they flew to the northwest instead to arrive at their traditional wintering ground. The young birds, however, obeyed their inborn orientation to the southwest and flew like arrows in that direction—straight into Spain. Moreover, birds from each group safely returned to their breeding grounds the next spring. During the next fall migration, however, some of the previous year's errant youngsters winged their way to Spain again. Clearly, it had been a good place to overwinter.

Certain species depend more heavily on experience. Many waterfowl, such as geese, travel with their parents on their first migration. They do not experience zugunruhe until they become adults in their second year. Tundra swans also migrate south from the Arctic tundra in family groups. The young swans learn not only how to get to the wintering grounds but also where to stop along the way to rest and feed. Young cranes also travel with their parents. Attempts to establish new whooping crane populations in the wild involve using aircraft to guide young birds on their first migratory journeys.

Tundra swans in North America and Eurasia migrate in family groups from their arctic breeding grounds to southern wintering grounds. There they may run into and reunite with young of previous years, forming an attachment and foraging together.

> " Be like the bird that, passing on her flight awhile on boughs too slight, feels them give way beneath her, and yet sings, knowing that she hath wings. "
>
> —*Victor Hugo*

The Rigors of Travel

Ruddy turnstones join flocks of other migratory shorebirds at Delaware Bay every May to feed on the eggs of horseshoe crabs. They lay down precious reserves of fat that will enable them to complete the final 1,500 to 2,000 miles of their northern journey.

Q: Where do birds feed and rest on their journeys?

A: Although a few migrating birds can fly astounding distances without stopping, most species must pause to rest and feed along the way. These birds may be seen in small groups scattered over a wide area, but sometimes many migrants are packed into one especially bountiful site. These sites are known as staging posts or stopover sites.

One of the most important staging posts in North America is the shoreline of Delaware Bay in Delaware and New Jersey. Every spring, horseshoe crabs creep out of the water to mate and lay eggs. Shorebirds migrating to northern breeding grounds stop to feast on the eggs and the juvenile crabs. The throng includes sanderlings, ruddy turnstones, and about 80 percent of North America's red knots. Likewise, waterfowl depend on seasonal bodies of water called prairie potholes. For migrating sandhill cranes, the Platte River Valley in Nebraska provides a stopover. Spring migrants arrive in late February and early March and stay until

early April. During their stay, the birds feed and put on about a pound apiece, enough fuel to sustain them as they push onward to western Alaska.

From Sandy Hook in the north to Cape May in the south, the New Jersey shore provides migratory birds with a number of welcome stopover sites.

Q: How does weather affect the timing of migration?

A: Birds take the weather into account during migration. They will sit tight if it is very rainy or windy, if the sky is extremely cloudy, or if they are socked in by fog. Birds also "analyze" temperature and wind direction so as to exploit favorable winds that will help them on their way. Fall migrants heading south from North America, for example, will wait out the headwinds and heavy rainfall brought by a cold front, and then fly with the benefit of a tailwind after the front passes. If a warm front brings winds from the south, the birds wait until conditions improve. Similarly, when these birds fly north in spring, the southerly winds of a warm front give them a boost after the front passes. A cold front bringing northerly winds, on the other hand, halts the migrants.

Sudden storms wreak havoc on migrating birds just as they can on ships at sea. At worst, storms fling flocks of birds into the ocean to their death. At best, exhausted birds plunge from the sky and find refuge wherever they can. "When a storm front hits, they grab for the first land they can find like castaways kissing the sand," writes ornithologist Scott Weidensaul in his book about bird migration, *Living on the Wind*. Flocks have even been known to land on container ships and aircraft carriers during storms. Such a precipitation of birds is known as a fallout.

Storms that do not force birds from the sky may still blow them off course. Shorebirds are sometimes blown far inland. Occasionally, lucky birds have expanded their range because their unexpected route took them to suitable habitat. Sometimes, however, it is just one bird that is knocked askew, to end up being a local celebrity for a few years—such as an ancient murrelet of northern Pacific waters who, in 1990, ended up on the Isle of Lundy between England and Wales after being whisked at least 7,000 miles off-course.

Q: What dangers do birds face as they migrate?

A: Birds face a number of perils while migrating, as well as at their destinations. It is estimated, for example, that only half of the five billion birds that migrate from Europe to Africa for the winter will return the next spring. Some dangers, such as storms or running out of energy, are ones that migrants have always endured. Today, however, many are a result of human activity. Development, agriculture, clearcutting, pollution, damming of rivers, and the like have reduced habitat for breeding, wintering, and stopovers. Collisions with power lines kill cranes. Millions of songbirds also die each year when they strike brightly lit high-rise buildings and towers, although programs are in effect to encourage shutting off lights during times of peak migration.

Storms have the power to blow migrating birds off course and even wring them from the sky, sending showers of them to the ground in a phenomenon known as a fallout. Texas's eastern coast receives such fallouts at times in spring, when birds migrating north across the Gulf of Mexico land wearily in shoreline habitats.

Birds as Orienteers

Q: **How do birds determine direction as they migrate?**

A: A little songbird is a handful of feathers, bone, and muscle weighing less than a few spare coins. Yet somehow this tiny creature, with a brain no bigger than a shelled walnut, can find its way to its winter habitat hundreds, perhaps thousands of miles away, usually flying in the dark of night—even if it is making the journey for the first time. How birds

How birds flying in flocks manage to coordinate their movements, and how they find their way to distant breeding and wintering grounds, has piqued the interest of ornithologists and birders for centuries. Technical advances such as satellite tracking are enabling researchers to get a bird's-eye view of these creatures' epic journeys.

manage this astonishing feat has been the subject of study for many decades.

Most birds inherit an inborn clock that signals them that it is time to migrate, as well as a sense of which way they should go and for how long they should fly in a given direction. In order to fulfill these inborn imperatives, however, the bird must also have the ability to determine direction and to find its way once it is headed in the proper direction. These two abilities are known respectively as orientation and navigation.

Orientation in birds appears to utilize a variety of environmental clues, with different species perhaps depending more on some than others. These clues come from the sun, the stars, and Earth's magnetic field. Using the sun as a compass requires a bird to be able to "read" the position of the sun in the sky. Its internal clock, synchronized to the natural world, enables the bird to recognize where the sun ought to be in the sky and in relation to the horizon at different times of the day. Thus, a bird can recognize that the sun rises in the east and sets in the west and occupies different positions in the arc of the sky in between. The sun operates as both a compass and a clock for a bird just as it does for a sailor. Even caged migratory birds can orient themselves properly if they can see the sun. Researchers who have used mirrors to alter the position of the sun in the captive birds' "sky" have found that the birds still orient correctly in relation to the perceived position of the sun, even if in actuality they are pointed in the wrong direction for migration.

Some birds use the sun compass even on overcast days. They can apparently perceive polarized light, which consists of light beams traveling uniformly at a 90-degree angle to the sun. If they can see part of this band of light, they will know where the sun is and orient themselves properly. Many birds, however, migrate at night. These birds appear to be guided by the position of stars in the sky. Although the original notion of birds hatching with internal star charts already inside them is an enchanting one, research has shown that what birds

Many birds appear to use the sun to orient themselves in the correct direction for migration. Some species even orient by the sun on overcast days, apparently detecting bands of light produced by polarization. Recognizing the location of the setting sun likewise orients a nighttime migrant.

actually use for orientation is the pole star and the apparent revolution of stars around it. This process involves learning: A young bird must be able to see the night sky in order to master this skill.

What the bird seems to possess at birth is the ability to recognize that the stars swirling above it in the night sky are circling around a fixed point. In the Northern Hemisphere, this point is the North Star. Over time, a bird learns where the center of rotation is located and orients toward it, rather than relating the positions of the constellations and other stars to a certain time of night.

Many birds may use both sun and star compasses to orient. A wheatear, for example, migrates nocturnally. It typically departs at dusk, orienting itself by the setting sun. Once darkness cloaks the sky, the bird looks to the stars for guidance. Nocturnal migrants that leave after the sun dips below the horizon may likewise use the polarized light that can still be detected for nearly an hour after sunset.

Birds are also sensitive to Earth's magnetic field and can align themselves in a north–south direction with it. Birds can also sense the angle at which the magnetic field intersects with the Earth, and whether those lines are dipping toward the Earth (as they do in the Northern Hemisphere) or angling away from it (as they do in the Southern Hemisphere). How a bird detects this information continues to be studied. When sun and stars are blotted out, however, this sensitivity is surely an important backup.

Stars in the night sky appear to travel in a circle, an illusion created by the rotation of the Earth. Young birds gazing at the night sky pinpoint the center of rotation and will use it as their pole star in future migrations.

Q: How do birds navigate as they migrate?

A: Navigation is to orientation as a map is to a compass. Being able to orient, or determine direction, is vital. But once a bird is pointed in the right direction, it must also be able to navigate to get to a particular place—and to be able to realize that it has arrived.

Just how birds navigate is still a mystery and an area of ongoing research. Studies focus on several possible explanations, including the use of landmarks, magnetic fields, smells, and sounds. Research into the famed abilities of homing pigeons to fly back to their roosts has shown that these birds can recognize landmarks, such as buildings. This suggests that other birds may be able to use landmarks, too, particularly while flying at a high altitude. Rivers, mountain ranges, island chains, and coastlines may speak as clearly to a migrating bird as a map does to a human. Seabirds may even be able to "read" ocean waves to determine where land is. These cues might be of less use at night, but sensing a magnetic map of the land below would compensate. Based again on studies of homing pigeons, scientists speculate that birds may be able to detect tiny gradations in the strength of Earth's magnetic field.

Homing pigeons have also supplied information for another leading hypothesis: that birds may use smell in navigation. Just as a salmon migrating from the sea swims toward the smell of its natal stream, so too might a bird familiarize itself with the smell of its birthplace and the area around it. It would also recognize a continuum of odors, from a high concentration of odor

The rock dove (known as a homing pigeon by fanciers) is renowned for its ability to orient and navigate. Studies involving this species have yielded a trove of information about how birds use their sensory abilities while migrating.

near the source and a lower concentration farther away, as well as the direction from which the odor comes. These odors would emanate from sources such as farms, pine forests, oceans and bays, cities, and the like.

Although birds are not considered to have a strong sense of smell, research has turned up evidence that this sense may not be as underutilized as once thought. Some seabirds, such as storm petrels, identify their nest burrows by smell. Albatrosses, petrels, oilbirds, and turkey vultures smell out their food, and crested auklets exude an aroma of tangerines that may attract mates. Indeed, scientists in Italy found that homing pigeons' navigation was severely affected when their sense of smell was blocked. Pigeons elsewhere did not seem to be affected in similar tests, but it is speculated that this may reflect the relative degree to which different

Storm-petrels, such as this white-vented storm-petrel, are known to use their sense of smell while foraging at sea. It is also thought that olfaction helps the birds identify their nesting burrows. Now scientists are exploring the possibility that other species may use smells to navigate.

populations may use the navigational tools at their disposal. One of these tools, some theorize, could be sound—specifically, the low-frequency waves known as infrasound. Infrasound can travel a great distance. Animals such as elephants and whales are known to use infrasound to communicate with far-off members of their species. Birds may be attuned to the infrasonic sounds of wind against mountains, waves crashing on beaches, and the rumblings of volcanoes and earthquakes.

Do topographical features come into play as a bird navigates? Studies show that some birds may be able to identify prominent landmarks, from mountains to buildings. Birds may also be able to detect subtle cues such as the sound of winds against mountains.

Patterns of Migration

Blue grouse spend the winter in dense coniferous forests. In spring, they migrate rapidly downhill to more open grounds for breeding. This altitudinal migration requires the birds to shift their diets as well as their locations.

Q: What is altitudinal migration?

A: Not all migrants fly great distances, nor do all migrants travel north–south or east–west. For a variety of birds, migration means traveling uphill or downhill. This is known as vertical or altitudinal migration. Mountain-dwelling species worldwide migrate in this way.

Altitudinal migrants typically leave the high mountaintops where they have foraged all summer and raised their young. They head downhill, where the weather is milder and temperatures are warmer. In Europe, most water pipits living in the Alps migrate downhill when snow and ice return to the peaks. Alpine chaffinches likewise slip downhill in winter. In North America, jays, juncos, bridled titmice, nuthatches, and northern pygmy owls are among the birds that breed at high altitudes and move downhill for the winter. In the Rocky Mountains, rosy-finches and pine grosbeaks migrating downhill may flutter past

another altitudinal migrant that trudges uphill or the winter: the blue grouse. Blue grouse living in the Rocky Mountains nest in woodlands during spring and summer, where they dine on insects and berries. In winter, they retreat uphill to the shelter of coniferous forests, where they feast on evergreen needles.

Altitudinal migrants are particularly abundant in the tropics. Their behavior has come to light as researchers have focused attention on the migration of tropical birds as a whole. These migrations are linked to seasonal food abundance. Quetzals, for example, eat avocados and the fruits of related trees. They breed in forests on the upper slopes of mountains, including cloud forests, when trees in these locations are producing abundantly. They migrate downhill when breeding season is over and their preferred diet becomes sparse on the breeding grounds. Dozens of other altitudinal migrants, including some parrots and hummingbirds, likewise migrate vertically,

After their young leave the nest, Clark's nutcrackers migrate to higher altitudes, where they feed on the seeds of coniferous trees. They also store these seeds for the winter. Wintertime itself brings migration back downhill.

with their breeding seasons occurring when fruit, nectar, seeds, and other foods are most abundant in the different zones.

Q: Do flightless birds migrate?

A: Many species of flightless birds migrate. Emperor penguins waddle for miles from the sea to their icy breeding grounds at the beginning of winter, and then the females return to sea to feed while the males huddle with the eggs tucked between feet and belly. King penguins also migrate from sea to colony and back again. Magellanic penguins swim north to Brazil from breeding grounds in Patagonia, a 3,000-mile round trip. Adelie penguins feed in areas of sea ice and then migrate to ice-free sections of Antarctica for their brief breeding season. Some flightless birds that do not swim also migrate: Ostriches and emus are kept on the move by rainy and dry seasons.

Common eiders leave their breeding grounds to migrate to areas where they can molt in relative safety from predators that would otherwise take advantage of the temporarily flightless birds. Males depart first; the females follow a month or two later. The eiders depart for wintering grounds once the molt is complete.

Some birds become flightless following migration. Such "molt migrations" are undertaken by waterfowl that migrate to traditional sites where they molt into "eclipse plumage" and are temporarily flightless. Male black scoters, for example, migrate from their inland breeding grounds to a coastal molting site, and then migrate to coastal wintering grounds once they can fly again. Canada's James and Hudson bays are home to thousands of black scoters during the molt. Surf scoters, Canada geese, Barrow's golden-eyes, eiders, shelducks, and many other species also undertake molt migrations.

The Pacific and Atlantic coastlines on the tip of South America harbor breeding colonies of Magellanic penguins. Populations on the Pacific coast migrate north to Peru, while Atlantic-based populations migrate up to Brazil.

Below: Carmine bee-eaters in South Africa migrate north to East Africa for the winter, while northern populations head south to parts of Kenya and Tanzania.

Above right: Some populations of vermilion flycatchers are resident in parts of North and South America. Populations breeding at the most northern latitudes, however, shift south, and those breeding at the most southern latitudes migrate north to Brazil and Colombia.

Right: Bronzed cowbirds living in the tropics migrate short distances up and down mountainsides, appearing at higher elevations during the breeding season. Most bronzed cowbirds that breed in the southwestern United States migrate to northern Mexico in fall.

Q: Do tropical species migrate?

A: Birds that breed in tropical regions are typically year-round residents. Researchers are finding, however, that many tropical species do migrate. Their migrations do not take them out of the tropical zone but from place to place within it. These migrations are linked to seasonal shifts in food availability and the cycle of wet and dry seasons. Carmine bee-eaters in tropical Africa, for example, move toward the equator in winter. Many hummingbirds in South America migrate up and down mountainsides, while others migrate up to 600 miles along an east–west line. Guatemala's tropical populations of bronzed cowbirds migrate vertically. Tropical migrants even put on fat reserves before migrating, with some of the accumulated fat preparing them for the breeding season.

Q: What is partial migration?

A: In many species, some birds in a population in a particular area migrate and others do not. This pattern of migration is known as partial migration. Partial migration may be the result of genetics: Resident birds of a particular species are ones that do not have genes for migration, while the migrants who join them for a season do. If it is not a result of genetics, it may be due to variables such as the amount of food available.

In southern Spain, for example, the breeding grounds of barn swallows are home to residents of this species, while migrants that live farther north come and go. In South America, vermilion

flycatchers living in Argentina and Uruguay fly north to Brazil and Colombia for the winter, adding to the area's resident population of flycatchers. Common poorwills in the southwestern United States go into a state of suspended animation called torpor during cold weather, while their northern kin migrate as far south as Mexico.

Partial migration is widespread among raptors, occurring in about 40 species. Northern populations of kestrels in North America migrate south into the southern United States and Central America, while kestrels living in southern states often stay put. Populations of peregrine falcons nesting in the Arctic spend winter in South America or Africa, while those in Australia are year-round residents of their breeding grounds. Northern prairie falcons fly south to wintering ground most years but will delay migrating if prey is plentiful; they may not migrate at all if winter proves to be mild.

Q: What is an irruption?

A: An irruption is a large, unpredictable migration of birds into areas outside their seasonal ranges. This migration is often linked to a shortage of food. Snowy owls, for example, feed on lemmings and other rodents in their Arctic range. If the population of prey drops, the owls leave to forage elsewhere. In irruptive years, snowy owls have traveled as far south as California and Louisiana and even Bermuda. Another predator of the far north, the rough-legged hawk, also irrupts when grouse and hares are scarce, popping up in such places as Florida and northern Africa.

Seed- and fruit-eating birds irrupt, too. Crossbills irrupt when crops of conifer

seeds fail. Severe winter weather and snow cover may make it impossible for pine grosbeaks, redpolls, waxwings, and other birds to find food, causing them to irrupt, too. Drought forces the Pallas's sandgrouse of central Asia and Russia to irrupt as far west as Ireland.

Red crossbills typically migrate nomadically in boreal forests as crops of seeds ripen in different places. They are among several species that make sudden, unexpected appearances outside their winter range in response to a shortage of food.

Q: Do all birds migrate?

A: From 50 to 60 percent of bird species migrate. Birds that are residents range from rain forest birds to the hardy species that reside year-round in the Arctic, such as ptarmigans. Many birds are also residents in zones between these extremes. Barred and great horned owls, as well as such familiar backyard birds as cardinals, chickadees, house sparrows, and house finches, are resident in much of North America. In Great Britain, the European robin remains on its territory in all seasons.

CHAPTER 10

HABITATS: WHERE BIRDS LIVE

Visit a hot, humid rain forest, and you will find birds. You will also find them in an arid desert seared by the sun, over the sea miles from shore, deep underwater in pursuit of fish, and high up on cold, rocky mountain slopes. Birds have made themselves at home in a wide array of habitats— and even manage to eke out places for themselves in city centers.

Every habitat actually harbors a variety of habitats within it. The Great Basin desert of the southwestern United States, for example, includes not only areas of prickly pear cacti but also piñon-juniper forests filled with pinyon jays and sage lands populated by sage-grouse, sage thrashers, and sage sparrows. Areas where habitats meet are particularly rich in species, a circumstance known as the edge effect. Here is where birds from each habitat may be spotted. The edge effect is also at work in environments altered by human activity: The hedgerows that once routinely separated farm fields offered abundant food and shelter for birds of fields as well as shrubby places.

Above: Various species of macaw live in the wild in forest habitats of Central and South America.

Left: The South Atlantic and Indian oceans are home to the macaroni penguin. This species' breeding range extends farther south than that of all other kinds of crested penguins.

Forests and Woods

Q: Where are the world's deciduous forests, and what birds typically live in them?

A: A deciduous tree is one that sheds all its leaves at the same time in response to the change of seasons. Broad-leaved trees such as maples and oaks are examples of deciduous trees. A forest is dominated by the canopies of such trees growing thickly together; a more spaced-out habitat of trees is usually called a woodland.

Deciduous forests and woodlands spread across the eastern United States, the British Isles and other parts of Europe, and areas of China, Japan, and eastern Asia. Mixed forests lie between these deciduous forests and northern coniferous forests. Different trees dominate in different places: In Scandinavia, many forests consist of birch trees, while maples, oaks, hickories, beeches, aspens, and birches rule in various North American forests. Beech forests prevail in parts of temperate South America and New Zealand, and tropical deciduous forests, populated mainly by species of eucalyptus, grow in Australia.

In the breeding season, North American forests and woods ring with the songs and calls of birds such as wood thrushes, wood-warblers, vireos, tanagers, chickadees, wrens, and jays. Ruffed grouse drum, and great horned owls hoot. Wild turkeys scratch in the leaf litter of mixed forests. In Europe, woodlands abound with chaffinches, bullfinches, thrushes, tits, jays, nuthatches, wrens, cuckoos, and warblers. Woodpeckers, owls, and nightjars dwell in woodlands, and small hawks hunt in them—sharp-shinned hawks in the United States, sparrowhawks in Europe.

Q: Where are the world's coniferous forests, and what birds live in them?

A: In North America, coniferous forests stretch in a broad band across Canada, north into Alaska, and south along the west coast to California and to New England on the east coast. They are also found on the upper slopes of mountains. In Eurasia, coniferous forests sprawl from Scandinavia across Russia. Coniferous forests offer

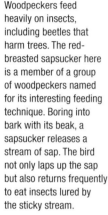

Woodpeckers feed heavily on insects, including beetles that harm trees. The red-breasted sapsucker here is a member of a group of woodpeckers named for its interesting feeding technique. Boring into bark with its beak, a sapsucker releases a stream of sap. The bird not only laps up the sap but also returns frequently to eat insects lured by the sticky stream.

Boreal birds consist of both migrant and resident species. Migrants include a variety of sparrows, thrushes, and wood-warblers. Among the residents are pine grosbeaks, spruce grouse, boreal chickadees, northern hawk owls, crossbills, and various finches.

Europe's coniferous forests are populated by birds such as crossbills, Siberian jays, long-eared and great gray owls, and gamebirds such as black grouse and capercaillie, which feed on conifer buds and needles. White-eyes and pheasants are typical of forests in Japan and China.

North American temperate rain forests are home to endangered species such as the marbled murrelet, which nests atop ancient trees, and the spotted owl. Pileated woodpeckers carve out nest holes in the forest, and Vaux's swifts lay their eggs in existing cavities.

Top left: Some European thrushes, such as the song thrush, redwing, and the fieldfare, visit gardens and feeders in parts of Great Britain after spending the breeding season in Eurasia's boreal forest.

Center left: Northern realms are home to a variety of grouse species, with different species favoring different habitats. Parts of Eurasia's belt of coniferous forest, for example, are home to capercaillie, while black grouse live in more open woodlands, fields, and moors.

The great gray owl is a denizen of thick, mature boreal forests in northern North America and also Eurasia. It frequently hunts by day and can even locate its prey beneath snow by virtue of its keen sense of hearing.

shelter and a bounty of seeds to many nesting birds as well as some hardy species that live in them year-round.

Like deciduous forests, coniferous forests are dominated by different species in different places, depending on the climate. In North America, for example, temperate rain forests thrive in the moist, mild climate of the Northwest and feature Sitka spruce, western hemlock, and Douglas firs. The taiga, or boreal forest, farther north consists largely of balsam firs and white spruce. Redwoods and sequoias reign supreme in various parts of California.

Tropical Rain Forests

Below left: Scarlet macaws nest in tree cavities. They feed on seeds and fruits. The macaw's powerful bill easily cracks open nuts that other birds' beaks cannot.

Below right: Rainbow lorikeets, which are divided into a number of differently patterned races, inhabit rain forests and eucalyptus forests in Australia and New Guinea as well as other habitats. This small parrot uses its brushlike tongue to sop up nectar and will also crush flowers in its bill to extract it.

Q: What is a tropical rain forest?

A: A tropical rain forest is made up of broad-leaved trees growing in the tropical zone along the Equator. Most rain forests receive abundant rainfall—typically more than 70 inches a year—which supports lush growth. Tropical rain forests grow in Africa, Southeast Asia, Australia, and Indonesia, as well as in Central and South America. The latter two areas' tropical zones are referred to as the neotropics. Some tropical rain forests have wet and dry seasons and receive less rainfall, and some trees may lose leaves seasonally; examples are found in Australia, New Guinea, Brazil, and a few other regions.

Rain forests provide birds with a year-round food supply and a layered environment that invites specialization. A rain forest's tall trees offer habitats ranging from the dense canopy to layers filled with vines and smaller trees, as well as the forest floor itself. Different species of birds live at all levels of the forest, just as different species of fish inhabit different layers of the ocean. Rain forests are highly valued for the diversity of life they shelter and support. Tropical rain forests are home to nearly one third of all bird species and also offer sanctuary for many migratory birds.

Q: What species of birds can be found in rain forests?

A: Each rain forest boasts its own unique variety of birds, many of them splendidly colored. Comparing and contrasting rain forest birdlife, however, reveals that many birds have evolved similar traits because they fill similar niches in their habitats. This is known as convergent evolution. Neotropical rain forests feature species of toucans, which use their large, colorful beaks to pluck fruit. The colors may also help potential mates recognize their species. Their counterparts in African and Asian rain forests are the big-billed hornbills, which also eat fruit as well as other foods and likewise nest in tree cavities.

Hummingbirds thrive in the neotropics, flitting from flower to flower in search of nectar and pollinating the plants as they feed. Some species have coevolved with certain plants so that the birds' bills and

the plants' tubular flowers are a perfect match. Sunbirds, the hummingbirds' equally iridescent counterparts in African rain forests, cannot hover with the same ease, but they also have long bills designed to fit perfectly into particular blooms.

The most famous rain forest dwellers are the colorful, raucous parrots. With their clinging feet and powerful bills, parrots are well adapted for an arboreal life spent feeding on nuts and fruit. Neotropical parrots include macaws, blue-headed parrots, and sun parakeets. New Guinea is home to eclectus parrots, which are unique in that the male is mostly green while the female is red and blue. In parts of Southeast Asia, blue-crowned hanging-parrots dangle from rain forest branches. Rainbow lorikeets display their vivid colors in rain forests throughout Australasia.

Other unique species include the spectacularly plumed birds of paradise of New Guinea, who share their rain forest home with ground-dwellers such as Victoria crowned-pigeons and cassowaries. Pittas and Congo peafowl feed on the floors of African rain forests. Neotropical rain forests are habitat for vivid green quetzals, bright orange cocks-of-the-rock, clamoring bellbirds, and the strangely reptilian hoatzin.

Not all rain forest dwellers, however, are colorful and noisy. Raptors such as South America's harpy eagle and the African long-tailed hawk stalk their prey more soberly. The eagle owl's plumage camouflages it in the African rain forest. West Africa's white-crested tiger-herons lurk inconspicuously near water.

The harpy eagle hunts for snakes, sloths, and monkeys in rain forests of Central and South America. Its strong legs, large feet, and massive talons are adaptations that enable it to tackle such large prey.

A forest bird never wants a cage.
—HENRIK IBSEN

Grasslands

Q: What sorts of birds are typically found on grasslands?

A: Plains, pampas, prairie, steppe, savanna, veldt—they are all names for the wide-open spaces known as grasslands. A grassland is a dry habitat dominated by grasses. Some grasslands support scattered patches of trees, such as the African savanna, while others are treeless. In many parts of the world, grasslands have been converted to pastures and croplands, and only remnants of the original habitat remain.

Grasslands abound with rodents, insects, and seeds from grasses and wildflowers and thus offer prime habitat for a wide variety of birds. Many of these birds have earth-toned, streaked, or stippled plumage that camouflages them. Because there are few elevations to use as singing posts, males of some species of grassland birds engage in aerial displays or dance conspicuously during breeding season. North America's grasslands are called prairies or plains. Songbirds such as bobolinks, meadowlarks, blackbirds, and a variety of finches and sparrows thrive in grassland. Male longspurs sing while in flight during breeding season. Greater prairie-chickens strut and boom on leks in northern prairies, ceding the stage to sharp-tailed grouse in Alaska and Canada. Shorebirds such as long-billed curlews and upland sandpipers nest in grasslands near water. Burrowing owls shelter underground. Raptors such as Swainson's hawks and ferruginous hawks soar and hunt over grasslands.

A look at birdlife in grasslands on other continents reveals a similar composition of species and some shared behaviors. On South America's pampas, for example, a birder might spy rheas sprinting or red-winged tinamous strolling. Songbirds include seedeaters such as lesser red-breasted meadowlarks and yellow finches, as well as the aptly named double-collared seedeater. Patagonian parrots nest underground. The savanna of Africa is home to birds such as ostriches, the snake-eating secretary bird, guineafowl, and finches, including the abundant quelea, and the paradise whydah, a species in which the male flaps above the grass displaying his spectacular tail in breeding season. Raptors include martial eagles and several kinds of vultures.

Australia's dry inland plains are stalked by large, flightless, insect-eating emus as well as long-legged bustards that are known locally as "plains turkeys." Huge

Populations of sandhill cranes frequently nest on prairies near seasonal bodies of water known as prairie potholes. They feed in meadows as well as pastures and fields, probing the soil in search of invertebrates.

Huge flocks of lime-green budgerigars scour Australia's dry grasslands in search of grasses and weeds with ripe seeds. When rainfall refreshes a swath of vegetation, budgies seize the opportunity to breed, colonizing a group of trees and nesting in cavities.

flocks of budgerigars and galahs feed on grass seeds. They share this feast with birds such as bronzewings, orange and crimson chats, doves, and quail-like birds called plains-wanderers. Raptors include falcons, kites, and harriers. Europe and Asia's vast steppes are home to a variety of larks. Males sing while flying and often exhibit special song flights such as those of the skylark, whose trilling song and high-altitude soaring has inspired many a poet. Whinchats, meadow pipits, and wheatears also sing in flight, sharing skies with raptors ranging from merlins to steppe eagles.

Q: Does fire affect grassland birds?

A: Dry grasslands are prone to fires. Birds that have specialized in living in grasslands benefit in the long run because fire renews the grassland and maintains the habitat by preventing shrubs and trees from gaining a foothold. Many species also benefit in the short term by deliberately seeking out fires to exploit the abundance of rodents and insects fleeing from the flames. On the African savanna, for example, kori bustards feast along the fringes of fires while carmine bee-eaters swoop through the smoke to snap up insects. Fork-tailed swifts in Australia likewise fly above fires to eat insects.

The whinchat is a bird of heath and grassland. A territorial male perches atop a low bush or an upright weed to sing or sings while in flight, both typical strategies of grassland birds seeking to draw attention. Nests, however, are carefully concealed amid clumps of grass.

Wetlands and Waterways

The common moorhen lives on several of the Hawaiian islands in freshwater marshes and wet fields as well as in irrigation ditches and reservoirs associated with farms. Its Hawaiian name, *'alae 'ula,* refers to its red frontal shield and its role in mythology as a bringer of fire.

Cormorants are most frequently observed perched with wings spread wide to dry them. Although the birds are clad in waterproof feathers close to the skin, their other plumage soaks up water to help them dive and stay submerged.

Q: What are wetlands, and which birds typically live in them?

A: A wetland is an ecosystem marked by water-soaked soil that, depending on the time of year, may be actually underwater. This body of water may be still or slowly moving. Marshes, bogs, swamps, fens, prairie potholes, and estuaries are all wetlands. The water in a wetland may be fresh, brackish, or salt. The plant life in wetlands varies and is used to describe them. A marsh, for example, is filled with water plants such as reeds and cattails but lacks trees. A swamp, on the other hand, has woody plants and trees.

Wetlands are vital habitats for many species of birds. Waterfowl, wading birds, shorebirds, rails, terns, and gulls feed and in some cases breed in them.

Songbirds nest in them, too, and certain migratory species use them as stopovers. Raptors such as osprey and northern harriers hunt in wetlands.

Florida's Everglades provide a ready example of the many bird species that thrive in a wetland. Wading birds include little blue and tricolored herons; great, snowy, and cattle egrets; white ibis; wood storks; and the pink-feathered roseate spoonbills. These species all nest in trees in this habitat. Smaller waders include least bitterns, king rails, and limpkins, all of which nest in the Everglades, too. Cormorants and anhingas dive after fish, and snail kites hunt for snails. Purple gallinules, common yellowthroats, common moorhens, and red-winged blackbirds nest among plants. Brown pelicans, swallow-tailed kites, eastern screech and barred owls, bald eagles, ospreys, and northern harriers also share this habitat, along with many migratory birds.

Q: Which birds typically inhabit ponds, lakes, streams, and rivers?

A: Ponds and lakes provide fish, frogs, plants, and insects for hungry birds as well as vegetation in which to nest. A pond tends to be shallow with many water plants, called emergents, rooted in it and poking above its surface. Lakes are typically larger, with plants just around the edges and more open space in the water. Waterfowl, grebes, coots, loons, kingfishers, and shorebirds frequent ponds and lakes. Songbirds such as red-winged blackbirds and marsh wrens nest on their edges. Swallows dip and dive over them, and ospreys fish in them.

Lake Nakuru in Kenya provides a spectacular example of a lake popular with birds. More than a million lesser flamingoes flock to feed in its alkaline waters in some years. White pelicans, yellow-billed storks, marabou storks, African spoonbills, sacred ibises, Egyptian geese, cormorants, herons, gulls, fish-eagles, and shorebirds join the throng. Altogether, the lake provides habitat for more than 50 species of waterbirds, including migratory species using it as wintering

Marabou storks live in African grasslands, marshes, and lakes. Its primary food is carrion, but fish, insects, and small rodents are also included in its diet. It also frequently invades colonies of flamingoes to feed on eggs and chicks.

grounds or as a stopover site. Another 350 species inhabit its surroundings. This avian spectacle resulted in Lake Nakuru's being selected as Africa's first national park in the 1960s.

The running waters of streams and rivers attract many of the same species as ponds and lakes. Many land birds also inhabit these shores, which are known as riparian zones. A few birds are specially adapted for stream or river life. The dipper, for example, is a songbird that dives into streams and runs along the bottom to feed on insects. Membranes over its nostrils shut when it submerges. It nests in a cup of moss tucked close to the water. Dippers in North America are gray birds that dwell in western streams. In Europe and Asia, dippers are brown and white birds of mountain streams and are sometimes called water ouzels.

White pelicans, such as the one shown left, mainly feed in freshwater and forage by scooping up fish with their pouched bills while swimming slowly. Brown pelicans typically plunge-dive after saltwater fish. The bump on this bird's bill is an adornment that appears during the breeding season.

Lands of Ice and Snow

The snow bunting, a species of sparrow, breeds on the tundra in North America and Eurasia. It winters farther south in open fields and along shores, forming large flocks with fellow snow buntings and other species.

Q: What is the Arctic tundra, and what birds typically live there?

A: The Arctic tundra is the area of land above the northern timberline that circles the globe, encompassing vast sweeps of North America, Greenland, Scandinavia, and Russia. It is devoid of trees; plants here tend to hug the ground, growing in the thin, heaving soil that rests atop a permanently frozen layer of earth. Sprawling shrubs and grasses interspersed with lichens and mosses form islands of vegetation among the shallow lakes and muddy bogs.

This golden-eyed gaze and white plumage is unmistakably that of the snowy owl. This large North American owl nests on the tundra. Adaptations to its snowy realm include insulating feathers that cloak legs and feet and even shield its nostrils.

Winter is long, dark, and cold on the tundra, and few bird species other than ravens and ptarmigans call it home year-round. A rich, speckled brown in summer, ptarmigans turn white in winter. Their feet and legs are clad in feathers that keep them warm and also help the birds walk on snow. Snow buntings, which breed along the Arctic Sea's edges, migrate south to wintering grounds that echo the tundra's wide-open spaces.

Spring and summer heralds the return of more than a hundred species of breeding birds, which come to take advantage of the abundance of insects and long daylight of the Arctic and subarctic summer. Among the summer visitors are various species of swans, loons, geese, ducks, gulls, larks, shorebirds, pipits, wagtails, yellowhammers, redwings, and wheatears.

Q: What birds live in the harsh environment of Antarctica?

A: Seabirds are the most obvious inhabitants of Antarctica's snowy, windswept mainland, its chilly islands, and the surrounding seas. The most prominent seabirds are penguins, who share the southern polar region with petrels, cormorants, gulls, skuas, and terns, as well as a few species of ducks and sheathbills.

Seabirds are ready-made to endure cold, since they have already adapted to chilly ocean temperatures. Like summer visitors to the Arctic, most of these birds visit Antarctica's shores only to feed on its abundant stocks of fish and plankton.

Penguins, however, are specially adapted for Antarctic life. A layer of fat and thick skin covers a penguin's body. Densely packed, tightly overlapping feathers and a layer of down form a waterproof, insulating coat. Active penguins can get so warm in their built-in parkas that they open their mouths and gape to cool off. Their wings, useless for flight, serve them well as flippers underwater, where they "fly" while feeding on plankton and fish. They also plunge in and out of the water in a fast swimming style known as "porpoising." On land, they flop onto their bellies and toboggan by pushing themselves with wings and feet.

Emperors are the largest penguins. They breed in colonies on the sea ice during the Antarctic winter, enduring the coldest, snowiest, windiest weather so that their young will be fully fledged by the time spring arrives and opens up the frozen seas again. After laying, the females leave to feed miles away at sea for about eight weeks. The males stay behind to incubate the eggs by balancing them on their feet and cuddling them within a warm flap of belly skin. When chicks hatch, males feed them crop milk until the females return to relieve them.

The king penguin breeds on the coastlines of subantarctic islands and the tip of South America. It can dive to a depth of 1,000 feet to catch squid, lanternfish, and other oceanic prey, which it swallows underwater.

The shores of western South America and adjacent islands harbor the breeding colonies of Humboldt penguins. These birds exploit the cold waters of the Humboldt current, which swirls north along the coast bearing abundant schools of anchovies and other fish.

Sea and Shore

Right: The common murre pursues fish beneath ocean waves circumpolar in North America and Eurasia. It nests on cliffs near open water. Murre chicks fledge when they are about three weeks old, leaping down to the sea below to join their parents on migration to wintering areas.

Below: Gannet nests are scrapes on shores, and colonies of gannets are often busily engaged in elaborate courtship rituals such as bill-fencing, shown here. Gannets make spectacular plunge-dives into the ocean in pursuit of fish, slicing into the water with their daggerlike beaks.

Q: **What birds are typically found on seashores?**

A: Beaches worldwide are home to shorebirds, which share these rich feeding grounds with gulls and terns and are also thronged during the breeding season with a variety of seabirds. Skuas prowl and make raids on nesting colonies, while gannets plunge-dive offshore. Eagles, crows, and other birds also visit.

A day at the beach on a rocky coastline of western North America may bring sightings of tufted puffins and common murres on cliffs. Black oystercatchers hammer at shells, while brown pelicans plunge into the sea for fish. Black turnstones pry under rocks. Wandering tattlers and rock sandpipers probe mud and wet sand in pursuit of worms, clams, and other invertebrates. Western gulls strut in the surf and squabble over food. In winter, flocks of surf scoters, red-breasted mergansers, and other waterbirds as well as western grebes can be seen.

A visit to a sandy beach on North America's eastern coast may yield sightings of black skimmers and brown pelicans flying low over the water. On the shore, several species of terns build their nests. Sanderlings skitter along the surf line. Other shorebirds here include willets, dunlins, semipalmated sandpipers, and various species of plover. They share this habitat with many gull species: herring, great black-backed, laughing, and ring-billed gulls, among others. European shores are likewise thronged by gulls, such as great and lesser black-backed gulls, black-headed gulls, and common gulls. Silver gulls frequent the shores of South Africa, Australia, and New Zealand.

Fairy penguins, also known as little blue penguins, pad along some southern shores in Australia. Silver gulls and crested terns frequent the coasts. Young Australian pelicans form crèches on their sands. Black noddies and black-faced shags both use seaweed to make their nests. Redshanks, sandpipers, and pied and sooty oystercatchers are among the many shorebirds.

Q: **What birds forage far out at sea?**

A: Breeding season brings many seabirds to shores, cliffs, tundra, and islands in order to nest; the rest of the year they spend at sea, seeking out schools of fish and shoals of plankton. Seabirds that live this pelagic lifestyle, however, do not wander randomly. Some species follow the movements of schools of tuna and other large fish. Other species' course is often set by ocean currents, which determine where minerals and nutrients on the seabed are lifted to the surface in a process known as upwelling. Upwelling nourishes the plankton layer, which is then fed upon by fish and certain seabirds; other seabirds, in turn, consume the plankton-eating fish. Upwellings typically occur where currents meet, flow over seabed canyons and mountains, or come near shore.

Tropical waters tend to be nutrient-poor because there is little upwelling. But there is much turnover in Arctic and Antarctic waters as cold upper layers sink and force deeper, nutrient-rich water to rise. As a result, pelagic seabirds such as albatrosses and petrels abound in these areas.

Seabirds divvy up the ocean's bounty just as insect-eating songbirds share a tree. Gull-like fulmars swim on the surface and duck their heads underwater to forage. Storm-petrels hover over the surface, pattering across the water with webbed feet and snapping up food with their beaks. Prions filter out planktonic crustaceans. Shearwaters dive and swim in pursuit of fish. Albatrosses and some petrels feed on squid, frequently at night. In tropical waters, frigatebirds pursue other seabirds and feed by harassing them into regurgitating their prey.

Waved albatrosses nest on the Galapagos Islands and forage in open waters, benefiting from a phenomenon known as the Peruvian upwelling. Nutrient-rich cold waters rising up from the seabed support an oceanic food web that also provides ample supplies of fish, squid, and crustaceans for these birds and other species.

Deserts

Q: What are deserts?

A: Deserts are parched lands that receive little rainfall. Only plants adapted to a dry environment can grow in them. The driest deserts may be nearly completely lacking in plants. Other deserts bloom profusely during a short rainy season.

Deserts are often associated with heat. Temperatures can reach more than 100 degrees Fahrenheit (38°C) in the Sahara Desert of Africa and the Mojave Desert of the southwestern United States. But cold rules deserts, too. Nighttime temperatures in the Sahara can drop well below freezing, and the Gobi Desert of China and Mongolia can reach minus 40°F (-40°C) in winter. This would be the equivalent of a summer day on the ice sheet of the world's coldest desert, Antarctica, which is considered a desert because its water is locked up in ice and snow and there is little annual precipitation.

Spotted sandgrouse dwell in deserts and arid mudflat regions of the Middle East and northern Africa. Like other species of sandgrouse, its plumage serves as camouflage in its dry surroundings, with feathers on the male's breast adapted for transporting water from waterholes to thirsty nestlings.

Q: How have birds adapted to life in hot, dry deserts?

A: Species of sandgrouse found in Africa and parts of Eurasia boast a remarkable physical adaptation to their hot, dry habitat. A male sandgrouse's belly is cloaked with absorbent feathers that work like sponges. At dawn, he flies to a waterhole and immerses his belly to soak up water with these feathers. Each feather can absorb eight times its weight in water. The male then flies back home, where he is greeted enthusiastically by his thirsty offspring.

Sandgrouse are unique among birds not only in this behavior but also because they have evolved a physical adaptation for life in a hot, arid habitat. Unlike mammals, birds have not evolved many physical adaptations for coping with desert extremes. Some birds, such as the Gambel's quail and the black-throated sparrow of the Chihuahuan Desert of Mexico and the inland dotterel and gibberbird of Australia, can survive two or three days without water if they are able to eat succulent plants or insects, but most birds must drink water each day. As a result, birds living in deserts have evolved behaviors for conserving water.

Many desert-dwelling birds simply avoid the heat of the day. They forage in the early morning and late evening, spending the day quietly in a shady spot. Larks and wheatears in the Sahara seek the shade offered by rocks and plants and entrances of burrows. Roadrunners in the Sonoran Desert shake off night's chill by basking in sunlight in the morn-

A gila woodpecker pecks out a cavity in a saguaro cactus in the Sonora Desert. Its diet consists primarily of insects but also includes saguaro fruit and pollen. Other birds, such as American kestrels, elf owls, crested flycatchers, and cactus wrens, nest in abandoned woodpecker holes.

ing, spreading feathers on their back to reveal dark skin that serves as a solar panel. When the Sun rises high, however, the roadrunners cease foraging and take shelter from its burning rays.

The breeding season itself is often timed to occur during a desert's rainy season. In Australia, flocks of pink galahs and lime-green budgerigars appear in rainy areas to feed and nest. The Indian bustard of the Thar Desert likewise migrates to rainy areas and breeds after the summer monsoon season begins. Birds take care to make their nests in cool spots. Wheatears build theirs in burrows or tucked among rocks. Gila woodpeckers and gilded flickers chisel nest holes in the cool interiors of saguaro cacti. Flocks of sociable weavers of the Kalahari construct giant thatched mounds in trees that may house up to 500 birds. Inside the mound are individual nests that belong to pairs. Because of its size, the mound keeps the nests cool during the day as it soaks up the Sun. In the cool of night, the warm mound helps keep the birds' nests warm. Eggs and young are particularly vulnerable to heat. Birds that breed in deserts, such as the sandgrouse, must go the extra mile to help their young survive. Desert-dwelling ravens carry water to their nests in their bills and throats and pour it into their gaping chicks' mouths. The Kittlitz's plover of South Africa covers its eggs with sand by day. Other birds shade their eggs or young by standing over them and spreading their wings.

Although the galah is adapted to life in Australia's vast grasslands, where it feeds on seeds, it flocks to the desert during the rainy season to feed and nest.

CHAPTER 11

THE ECOLOGY OF BIRDS

A bird is actually part of a complex ecosystem. It feeds on plants and animals, and other animals may eat it, its eggs, or its young. A bird uses materials in its environment to build a nest, or finds an appropriate cavity or other site in the habitat in which to lay its eggs. Its activities may open up feeding opportunities for other animals, or keep certain species at bay.

Just as canaries once aided coal miners by detecting dangerous gases, many birds today serve as clues to the health of ecosystems. They are known as indicator species. A drop in an indicator species' population, for example, may reveal that an invasive plant is taking over in an environment, or that pollutants have degraded a water source. The value of keeping tabs on such populations was dramatized in 1994, when researchers noticed Swainson's hawk populations were dropping. The trail led to the hawks' wintering grounds in Argentina, where the birds were dying after eating pesticide-laced grasshoppers. Since this discovery, the use of one of the most lethal insecticides has been restricted.

Above: Canada geese on the San Joaquin River National Wildlife Refuge. Wildlife preserves provide vital stopover sites for migratory birds as well as wintering grounds for many species, such as the Swainson's hawk.

Left: Found circumpolar in northern latitudes in summer, the common redpoll feeds on seeds.

What a Bird Needs

Roaming house cats are a menace to birds. The popular belief that belling a cat will adequately warn birds of an approaching predator offers false comfort: Birds do not instinctively link the tinkle of a bell to danger. Keeping cats indoors and placing feeders in the open, away from cat-concealing cover, are better solutions.

Q: **What essentials must a habitat provide for a bird?**

A: A habitat is the place in which a bird lives. It is made up of both nonliving and living things. A suitable habitat for a bird includes all the elements that a bird needs to survive, such as food and water. If it is the bird's breeding habitat, it must also supply nesting material and nest sites.

The nonliving, or abiotic, parts of a habitat include the nature of its soil, the presence or absence of water, and the climate. The climate is the range of weather, temperature, and rainfall experienced by an area over a long span of time. These abiotic elements, in turn, dictate what kinds of plants grow in an area. Habitats are typically described by the kind of vegetation they support. The living, or biotic, parts of a habitat include plants

Backyard feeders attract a variety of birds. A chunk of seed-speckled suet placed in a wire cage provides a welcome winter repast for this downy woodpecker.

and animals. These organisms furnish food for the birds in the habitat. Predators of birds form part of the biotic scene, too.

Suggestions offered to people who want to make their gardens more appealing to birds are based on birds' habitat needs. Aside from bird feeders, such needs could include a clean water source, preferably one that includes a dripping or splashing sound; shrubs and trees of varying heights to offer shelter, nest sites, and foraging opportunities; a brush pile for foraging and shelter; nest boxes for cavity nesters; flowers for hummingbirds; and protection from predators, such as careful location of feeders and birdbaths away from cover that might conceal cats. Avoiding the use of pesticides is also advised, so as not to poison the birds or eliminate their prey. Such a setup may provide good habitat for a variety of small, "backyard" birds.

Many species of birds, of course, have more particular habitat requirements. A pelican, for example, requires a large body of water and fish for eating. For breeding, it needs a site large enough for

Habitat needs vary from species to species. Craggy cliffs and narrow ledges, for example, constitute prime nesting sites for colonies of birds such as razorbills, murres, and guillemots. This forbidding habitat provides safety from land-based predators and ready access to open water for foraging.

a colony of its kind that is free of predators but not too far from its feeding site. Guillemots need cliffs and an ocean, while peregrine falcons require only cliffs. Pinyon jays reside in piñon forests, where they eat a variety of food but depend heavily on piñon seeds extracted from cones; the trees, in turn, depend on the jays to disperse their seeds.

Some species have very exacting requirements because of their specialized adaptations. The snail kite, for example, has evolved a long, curved bill specifically formed to fit into the shells of apple snails, its primary food. It hunts snails by hovering over fresh water and grabbing them with its long, curved toes. Its strict habitat requirements have contributed to its rarity. Habitat loss and degradation frequently force birds to accept less-than-ideal situations, but not all species are capable of doing so. Even if individuals survive, they may not reproduce

successfully enough to keep the species going. Other species, however, are known as "generalists." These birds can exploit a range of habitats. Crows, many jays, and starlings are familiar species that, as bird artist David Allen Sibley writes, have "specialized to be generalists." Pigeons even exploit urban habitats. A pigeon nesting in a neon letter of a store's sign and feeding on popcorn may not be in its ideal habitat, but it manages to find adequate replacements for its needs in a degraded one.

The omnivorous diet of the Steller's jay includes seeds, berries, nuts, insects, lizards, frogs, eggs, and even snakes. Reserved in its forest habitat, the Steller's jay becomes a raucous and bold extrovert in picnic areas and campgrounds, where it filches cookies and other tidbits.

Filling a Niche

Q: **How can different species of birds share the same habitat?**

A: A bird may protect a territory and resources against others of its kind, but it must also cope with other species heedless of its territorial claims. A closer look at the activities of birds sharing a habitat reveals that they typically utilize it in different ways so that they do not directly compete with each other. Each species is said to fill a different ecological niche.

A woodland in temperate North America shows how birds divvy up habitat by filling different niches. A woodpecker may be propped on a trunk, digging for insects, while a nuthatch is creeping head-first down the trunk, its posture enabling it to find insects the other bird would miss. Above them, a flycatcher zooms from a branch to catch a flying insect, while a nearby vireo gleans insects from the leaves. Meanwhile, in a small clearing,

a robin pulls a worm from the ground. Although all these birds eat invertebrates, competition between them is reduced because they forage in different ways. This phenomenon is readily observed in other habitats, too. The Pacific coast of North America, for example, is home to three species of cormorants. Each species looks for fish of a certain size at a particular depth. Likewise, a shoreline may be thronged with shorebirds of different species probing in sand and mud for prey. Different species, however, prefer different sections of the beach. A least sandpiper, for example, may restrict itself to drier sections, while dunlins tiptoe in soggy mud. Meanwhile, a ruddy turnstone busies itself flipping over stones to find food.

Physical differences between shore-birds also reveal how birds have evolved to share habitat while avoiding competition. A long-billed curlew can plunge its beak deep into sand, while a semi-palmated plover with a short bill just probes the surface. Several shorebirds with varying bill lengths range between them. In Hawaii, different species of

Left: Dunlins patrol mud flats and muddy beaches in search of food, probing with their long bills in search of sand fleas, worms, mollusks, and other invertebrates. Different bill lengths and feeding habits are key features of shorebirds, enabling them to share habitat while reducing competition for food.

Right: The spotted fly-catcher swoops from tree branches to snare insects. This feeding strategy allows the bird to exploit a resource not available to other insectivores in its habitat, such as vireos that glean insects from leaves, and minimizes competition between them.

The semipalmated plover runs along muddy beaches as it feeds, stopping suddenly to jab its short beak and snap up worms, mollusks, and crustaceans. It frequently forages in the company of semipalmated sand-pipers, which feed largely on water insects, and least sandpipers, which often probe for insect larvae and other prey with their longer bills.

honeycreepers have differently shaped and sized bills adapted to feeding from different flowers. In the Galapagos, finches have likewise evolved bills as well as behaviors that allow them to exploit their shared habitat in different ways.

Some species in the same habitat, however, are very similar to each other and not only eat the same food but also forage in much the same way. How, then, can an insect-eating bird share habitat with a similar insect-eating bird? Studies of five species of wood warblers living in coniferous forests in New England demonstrated how these small insect-eating birds coexist in the same habitat by filling different niches, too. Researchers found that one species fed primarily toward the top of a tree, another mainly around the middle, and a third frequently fed among the lower branches. Two fed in the upper half of the tree, but one

often foraged closer to the trunk than the other did. When one species was absent, another might extend its foraging area. The warblers also nested at different heights and at slightly different times, and used different foraging techniques. Altogether, these differences helped reduce competition between the species.

Birds can also minimize competition in a habitat by feeding at different times. Hawks and eagles, for example, hunt by day, while owls hunt by night.

In some species, males and females may have slightly different foraging techniques so that a mated pair can cut down on competition. Physical differences even occur. The extinct Huia of New Zealand most dramatically displayed this. The male had a short, straight bill; the female had a long, curved bill. He could tear bark off logs to find insects, while she could probe deeply for them.

Birds and Plants

Q: Do birds benefit plants?

A: Birds assist plants in two primary ways: by pollinating flowers and dispersing seeds. The most famous avian pollinator is the hummingbird. Hummingbirds dip their bills into flowers to collect nectar. As they do so, they are dusted with pollen. When the birds visit other flowers, the pollen adheres to sticky parts of these blooms. Other nectar-feeding birds that serve as pollinators are Africa's sunbirds, sugarbirds, and honeyeaters.

Plants that use birds as pollinators typically lure them with bright orange red, or pink, flowers such as those of heliconias, passionflowers, and fuchsias. Their flowers may be long, tubular structures designed to foil other animals. They may also have evolved sturdy stems to provide perches for birds that do not hover like hummingbirds. An Australian plant known as the kangaroo-paw hugs the ground but nonetheless manages to serve up meals for its pollinators: Its tubular flowers face downward and are angled so that a bird can stand on the ground while feeding.

Plants often rely on birds for pollination; they tempt them to perform this service by plying them with nectar. The African scarlet-chested sunbird is daubed with sticky pollen as it feeds on nectar with its long, curved bill.

Even birds without specialized bills help pollinate flowers. Parrots, warblers, and others often feed on pollen and nectar, sometimes shredding petals in the process, but they are painted with pollen in the process and will spread it to the next flower in which they wallow.

Plants likewise coerce birds into dispersing their seeds by luring them with meals. Rose hips, berries, and other fruits are all tasty packages containing seeds, and a wide variety of birds are eager to eat them. If seeds are small, such as berry seeds, they are swallowed and carried away to be deposited elsewhere in droppings. A large seed is typically covered with a thin, nutritious layer; the seed is swallowed whole and later regurgitated after the edible portion is digested. Birds that eat large fruits have evolved wide gapes to accommodate these seeds.

Birds spread the seeds of mistletoe, essentially turning into "farmers" planting future crops for their use.

Mistletoes, which grow as parasites on trees, have evolved sticky fruit that causes birds to wipe their bills on branches, thus depositing the seeds. In Australia, the mistletoebird eats almost nothing but mistletoe fruit, processing it quickly in its specially adapted digestive tract. The seeds stick to the bird's vent when it defecates, forcing the bird to rub off the irritating seeds.

Many plants, however, produce seeds that are actually eaten and digested by birds. Yet birds serve as dispersal agents for these plants, too. The copious seeds produced by conifers and oaks, for example, are carried away and frequently hoarded by birds. The birds will eat many of these seeds, but some forgotten seeds will grow.

A third service that benefits plants is pest removal. Many birds feed on insects, and included in their meals are many insects that feed on plants.

Q: Do plants adapt to form a partnership with specific bird species?

A: Some of the many plants that depend on birds to pollinate them and spread their seeds are species that appear to have evolved to partner with a particular bird. This process is called coevolution. Hummingbirds and flowers are often cited as examples of coevolution. The sword-billed hummingbird of the Andes, for example, has a bill nearly as long as its body that fits into the tubular blossom of a particular species of passionflower.

The extinct dodo is thought to have had coevolved with a tree called the tambalocoque. The tree was going extinct because its seeds would not grow. A scientist observed that the seeds were very thick-skinned and reasoned that dodos may have eaten them in the past. Perhaps the seed needed to be roughened, as it would have been in a dodo's crop, before it could grow. When the seeds were processed in this way—either by hand or in the gut of a turkey—they germinated.

The dodo, a large flightless bird, became extinct in 1681—about 175 years after European explorers first discovered it on the island of Mauritius. The seeds of a tree in its habitat appear to have required passage through its digestive tract in order to germinate.

Birds in the Food Chain

Q: Where do birds fit in the food chain?

A: Plants and various single-celled organisms form the basis of the food chain because they can turn energy from the sun into food in a process called photosynthesis. All animals, whether they eat plants, animals, or both plants and animals, are ultimately dependent on these primary producers.

Animals that eat primary producers are called primary consumers. Primary consumers in the bird world include species that eat seeds, fruits, leaves, buds, and the like. Many herbivorous birds, however, also eat insects and other small animals. When they do, they are part of the next level of feeders along with hawks, owls, penguins, and other flesh-eating birds—the secondary consumers.

A simple food chain, such as leaf-caterpillar–warbler–Cooper's hawk, links to other food chains in the habitat to form a food web. A food web shows the interrelationships among many organisms in a habitat and who preys on whom.

The Cape May warbler occupies more than one place in a food web, as do many species. It is primarily an insectivore, making it a secondary consumer when it eats plant-eating insects and a tertiary consumer when it snaps up insect-eating spiders. It also does stints as a primary consumer when it pierces grapes to drink their juice and feeds on sap oozing from trees.

Q: What animals prey on birds?

A: Animals of all kinds prey on birds—even some invertebrates. The Goliath bird-eating tarantula of South America can eat baby birds plucked from a nest, and an octopus was once recorded capturing a penguin.

Amphibians sometimes eat birds. Large bullfrogs swallow birds as big as a woodcock. In Australia, the gaping mouth of the introduced cane toad consumes small native birds as well as other animals. Fish eat birds as well. Waterbirds such as geese, cormorants, loons, and ducks are eaten by anglerfish. Seabirds are snagged by sharks. Bass and cod are also known to catch birds. Reptiles eat birds, too. Snapping turtles yank ducklings and other young birds underwater; larger ones can eat whole ducks. Alligators and crocodiles eat wading birds, such as egrets. Waterbirds are also consumed by water snakes, such as anacondas.

Snakes prey on birds and nestlings worldwide and also eat their eggs. Ground-nesting birds are especially vulnerable, but many snakes can climb trees to pursue birds and raid nests. The introduction of snakes onto islands has decimated some populations of indigenous birds. Brown tree snakes, for example, arrived in Guam in the 1950s, probably by accident, on cargo ships. Since first slithering onto the island, they have wiped out several bird species and threatened others.

Birds are also eaten by other birds. Jays and crows raid nests to eat nestlings. Skuas haunt the colonies of penguins and other seabirds to seize chicks. Falcons specialize in hunting other birds. Owls and other raptors also catch birds. Cuckoos may eat the eggs of a bird whose nest they are parasitizing. Egyptian vultures throw rocks at ostrich eggs to break them open and eat their contents. Some species do not hesitate to eat others of their own kind. Gulls, for example, will eat the unguarded nestlings of a neighbor.

Mammals, particularly rodents, are heavily preyed upon by birds such as hawks and owls. In turn, mammals feed abundantly on birds and their eggs. Squirrels take eggs and nestlings. Foxes, coyotes, raccoons, and weasels all eat birds and eggs. Bears eat eggs and young of cavity-nesting birds. Leopard seals prey on penguins. Monkeys raid the nests of tropical birds. Humans worldwide eat both domestic and wild birds.

Introduced mammals have taken a heavy toll on bird populations and have even caused extinctions. Mongooses

Birds are not averse to feeding on other birds, their chicks, or their eggs. The Diederik cuckoo of Africa shown here is a brood parasite, a bird that lays its eggs in other birds' nests. Various species of cuckoo also eat one or more of the host birds' eggs.

released in Hawaii and New Zealand have diminished those islands' native birds. Feral cats have halved the population of breeding seabirds on Christmas Island. Studies in England and the United States repeatedly show that domestic cats are responsible for the deaths of many birds and pose a significant threat to their populations. In England, at least 20 million birds are killed annually by a population of about 5 million house cats, at the time of the study. In the United States, it is estimated that house cats claim the lives of at least 100 million birds each year.

Adaptable omnivores, raccoons readily prey on eggs and nestlings. They will even raid a nest box, though they can be foiled by thickening the wall around the entrance hole so that they cannot bend their arms to reach the nest.

Q: What effect do birds have on populations of their prey?

A: Studies of birds' consumption of prey regularly yield some amazing figures. Analyses of stomach contents have revealed a flicker stuffed with 5,000 ants, a nighthawk replete with 500 mosquitoes, a bobwhite packed with 5,000 aphids, a cuckoo sated with 150 cotton worms, and an emu filled with 3,000 caterpillars. A study in the mid-twentieth century showed that sparrows and goldfinches in a 100-acre plot consumed a million grain aphids daily; another estimated that birds ate about 250 billion insects a year in Illinois alone. An African secretary bird was found to have three two-foot-long snakes along with locusts, lizards, and beetles in its gullet.

Clearly, the phrase "eating like a bird" should not be mistakenly taken as an indication of a delicate appetite. But what do these figures mean in terms of birds' impact on populations of insects, frogs, fish, mice, and other animals? Scientists are currently studying a variety of food webs to better understand the relationship between predators, prey, and their habitat. The bottommost strands of the web—the producers and the nonliving parts of the habitat that influence their growth—are thought to have the greatest influence on the populations of the consumers and predators above them. New studies are looking to see what kind of top-down effects exist— for example, if birds eat enough insects to actually affect plant growth.

Some recent studies have shown that birds had a significant effect on populations of caterpillars and other insects that ate leaves of hardwood trees during times when caterpillar populations were typical—that is, not experiencing a boom. They found twice as many leaf-eating insects on oak saplings that were enclosed in cages to keep out birds as they did on trees that were not enclosed. A study focusing on tropical trees yielded similar results. A third study involving conifers and the larvae of spruce budworms showed that trees without birds hosted six times as many hungry caterpillars as did trees visited by juncos, chickadees, and other species.

Other studies in recent years have found that gulls and skuas controlled populations of algae-eating limpets on the shore. Researchers are also studying other seabirds and raptors to learn more about how their feeding habits affect populations of prey. In the past, many raptors were considered pests and shot

Striding across Africa's grasslands on long legs, the secretary bird stalks in search of insects, frogs, lizards, small birds, and rodents to eat. Though these animals are its primary prey, the secretary bird is best known for eating snakes. The bird kills a snake with powerful stamping of its feet, aiming its short hind toe at the skull and spearing it with a sharp talon.

Smaller birds are revealing their role in predator-prey relations. Dark-eyed juncos and other insectivores, for example, have been found to significantly reduce populations of spruce budworm larvae.

on sight because they ate game birds sought by hunters, but studies showed that game birds were only seasonally abundant in their diets and that the birds consumed large quantities of rodents that are destructive to crops. This conflict echoes today in debates over double-crested cormorants and their effects on populations of sport fish.

Although scientists are just now teasing out the details of predator-prey inter-actions, humanity in general has long appreciated birds as custodians of animal populations. Ancient Greeks, Romans, and Egyptians honored birds as diverse as jackdaws, larks, and ibises for their role in controlling locust populations. In times

past, farmers in England included a win-dow for barn owls in the structure of their barns so that the owls could keep down populations of mice. In 1848, California gulls swooped into Utah and devoured hordes of grasshoppers that were ruining Mormon farmers' crops. This event is recalled as the "miracle of the seagulls," and a monument to the birds stands in Salt Lake City.

Corvids such as this Eurasian jackdaw were highly regarded in Europe in past centuries because they fed on carrion, providing a valuable street-cleaning service. They were also valued as food for falcons and as consumers of crop-eating insects. Their appetite for eggs, chicks, and grain, combined with their attendance on battle-fields, later branded them as vermin, caus-ing them to be persecuted.

The early bird catches the worm.

—*Proverb*

Birds and Their Neighbors

White-breasted nut-hatches frequently forage in mixed flocks outside the breeding season. They typically move headfirst down trunks, snapping up insects missed by woodpeckers moving up trunks. Experiments with woodlots artificially stocked with seeds in winter showed that birds abandoned mixed flocking when food was plentiful.

Q: **How do birds interact with other animals?**

A: Birds share their habitat with a variety of other animals that are not predators, prey, or others of their own species. Their interactions range from squabbling over a resource (such as carrion, a birdfeeder, or a suitable nest cavity) or merely being aware of the other animals' presence to actively exploiting the other, sometimes in an exchange of services that benefits both.

Birds of different species, for example, may form mixed flocks. In winter, a mixed flock in North America's temperate zone consisting of Carolina chickadees, tufted titmice, downy woodpeckers, brown creepers, and white-breasted nuthatches may forage together in the woods. By foraging together, the birds maximize their feeding efficiency and benefit by having more senses on the alert for predators. Migratory birds may also join mixed flocks on their wintering grounds.

Many birds tag after birds of other species because the latter serve as "beaters" for them, flushing prey or dropping edible tidbits as they go about their business. American coots, for example, hang around swans and ducks to eat food stirred up by the larger birds. Bluebirds tag after woodpeckers to eat any insects they overlook. Yellow robins in Australia

In winter, the tufted titmouse joins mixed flocks of insectivorous birds. Birds in a mixed flock are forced to share prime feeding sites, but foraging as a group cuts down on the time and energy involved in finding them. The titmice feed on insects revealed by downy woodpeckers' probing in bark; the woodpeckers, in turn, rely on the alert titmice as sentinels.

follow brushturkeys, which flush insects as they scratch in leaves; sparrows in Africa follow guineafowl for the same reason. Carmine bee-eaters ride on the backs of Arabian bustards. Emerald doves in New Guinea attend starlings that eat fruits and then regurgitate the hard-shelled pits, which the doves consume because their systems can digest them.

Other kinds of animals also serve as beaters for birds. Mixed flocks of resident and migrant birds follow battalions of army ants surging through tropical forests; the birds aim to eat insects escaping from the ants' path. Egrets follow herds of cattle, snapping up insects disturbed by their hooves. African drongos follow elephants and herds of antelope.

Wild pigs in Europe are trailed by robins, and dwarf mongooses in Africa by hornbills. Even seabirds employ this tactic: Some follow dolphins or tuna to catch fish that flee before them, while others eat prey stirred up by whales.

Some birds feed directly from their large animal partners. Oxpeckers ride on the backs of zebras, gazelles, wildebeest, rhinos, and other large African mammals to pick ticks off their hides. "Cleaner birds" of various species forage nonchalantly in the mouths of crocodiles and hippos for pests and food scraps.

African honeyguides go one step further: They actually lead badgerlike animals called ratels to bees' nests. The ratel breaks open the nest to feed on the honey; the bird then eats the wax. Honeyguides will also lead humans to these nests.

Nesting near other species is another way in which birds exploit their neighbors. Some species dare to reside in the base of an eagle's nest, benefiting from the unwitting protection of their large, fierce neighbor. Canada geese on the tundra will risk nesting near a snowy owl's nest; the vigilant owls keep foxes away, and the geese need only take care to slip away with their downy young after hatching before the goslings themselves attract the owls' attention. Oropendolas in the neotropics set up home near wasps' nests to gain protection from the insects' defensive behavior toward predators such as monkeys. Other birds, such as kingfishers and trogons, excavate cavities in termite and wasps' nests for their own use.

Some species use humans in their environment as they would any other animal. Gulls flock behind tractors, which stir up insects just as well as cattle do. Crows know that picnickers leave tasty scraps behind. House sparrows, house finches, and house wrens are named for their frequent proximity to human abodes.

Left: Oxpeckers perch on the back of a Cape buffalo in Africa. These birds eat ticks and insects found on the hides of buffalo and other large grazing mammals, such as giraffes and zebras. Their feet are adapted for clinging to the animals' hides. The birds deftly scramble all over a host, even creeping across its face to peck insects from its nostrils.

Right: The Cuban trogon typically nests in old woodpecker holes. Many species of trogons also chisel cavities in termite mounds. The disgruntled insects then seal off their tunnels from the intrusive cavity, leaving the birds with a cozy, strong-walled nesting chamber.

CHAPTER 12

BIRDS AND PEOPLE

For thousands of years, birds have fed not only the human appetite but also the human imagination. Birds sing in our poems and in our music. We freeze their flight in our sculptures and in paintings. Nations and states emblazon them on flags and emblems. Enthralled by their beauty, we seek to possess them by capturing their essence in our own creations. Our fondness and admiration for birds, however, is tragically contradicted by the death and destruction we have often inflicted on their kind. Whole species have gone extinct at the hands of humans through wholesale slaughter for food and feathers and the destruction of habitat. Yet, as we altered habitat to suit our needs, we created landscapes that suited birds often considered pests: millet-eating quelea in Africa, grain-eating starlings in Eurasia, red-winged blackbirds in North America. "For one species to mourn the death of another is a new thing under the sun," wrote naturalist Aldo Leopold in an essay about the demise of the passenger pigeon. As our love of birds and a better understanding of their importance in the natural world combine to impel us to work on their behalf, it is to be hoped that such epitaphs will no longer need to be written.

Above: Huge flocks of red-billed quelea roam African grasslands, feeding on seeds. Their incursions into croplands to feed on grain incurs large-scale campaigns against them.

Left: Passenger pigeons once numbered in the billions. Their range extended across eastern North America from the Gulf of Mexico into Canada.

Birds in Myth and Mystery

Thailand's national emblem features the Garuda, a mythical half-eagle, half-human being who is king of the birds. His powers include the strength to bear Vishnu on his back and the ability to devour evil creatures.

Q: What roles have birds played in mythology around the world?

A: Birds have long held a central place in myths and legends the world over. In some cultures, birds were associated with gods. Ancient Egyptians venerated Thoth, god of wisdom and inventor of writing, who was often depicted with the head of a sacred ibis. The god Horus was symbolized by a falcon. Both falcons and vultures were frequently shown flying near the king in artwork depicting battles, protecting him from harm.

In Hindu mythology, the god Vishnu rides on the back of Garuda, king of the birds; the wife of another god, Brahma, rides on a swan. Across the world in North America, the thunderbird soars through the mythology of many Native American cultures. A flap of its mighty wings produced thunder; lightning blazed from its eyes when it blinked. In South America, the Aztec god of war and the sun wore headgear bedizened with hummingbird feathers. A dove symbolizes the Holy Spirit in Christian teachings.

Many creation myths credit birds with giving form to the Earth, sky, and all other life. Loons and ducks dive into oceans to retrieve soil for making Earth in several Native American myths. Among peoples of the Pacific Northwest, Raven uses his cunning to steal the sun and plant it in the sky. A Finnish story relates how an eagle laid eggs in a goddess's lap; the eggs later hatched out the stars, the sun, the earth, and the sky. All creation burst from an egg in Chinese mythology, and an emu's egg likewise yielded the

cosmos in Aboriginal lore. The eagle became the sun in Aztec mythology. In the Amazon, however, a bird king greedily withholds the sun from Earth and must be overcome. The Maya twin gods conquered a monstrous bird called Vucub Caquix ("Seven Macaws") that falsely claimed to be the sun and the moon; later, these two heroes assumed those heavenly roles themselves.

Other mythical birds who vie with humans are the roc, a creature big enough to carry away ships and elephants; harpies, human-faced birds that feasted on humans; and Wuchowsen, a huge bird of the far north that pummeled the Pasamaquoddy Indians of New England with winds and storms whenever it moved. Amazonian peoples believed that after death, their spirits would battle with birds, and those who lost would be carried off by an eagle.

Perhaps the best-known mythical bird is the phoenix. Every 500 years, this glorious bird dies in a burst of flame, only to be reborn. The phoenix arises in different forms in many cultures around the globe and continues to emerge from its ashes in the best-selling Harry Potter books.

Q: What avian stereotypes inherited from fables still exist today?

A: Birds may be lightweight, but they carry a heavy load of symbolism. Worldwide, different species represent human vices and virtues and serve as omens. Raptors such as eagles, for example, frequently symbolize strength and power. Owls in many cultures convey knowledge and wisdom. In Japan, cranes stand for longevity. Doves symbolize peace.

Other birds symbolize human frailties. A cowardly person is called a chicken. The ostrich is also accused of cowardice based on the false belief that it hides its head in the sand in the face of danger. Turkeys symbolize stupidity, while geese are silly and parrots are mindless chatterboxes. To be "proud as a peacock" hints at vanity.

Many birds are branded as evil omens. Ravens, crows, and magpies frequently portend ill luck. Storm petrels are said to foretell storms at sea, and an albatross around one's neck is a terrible burden to bear. Nocturnal birds have been particularly associated with misfortune. The cries of nightjars, corn crakes, whip-poor-wills, owls, and even mockingbirds have been linked to lost souls and impending death.

Left: Thief, chatterbox, omen, insect-eating helpmate, grain-stealer: The various species of magpies, like many birds, are labeled with both positive and negative traits, often standing in for humans in folktales.

Below: Chickens, domesticated at least 4,000 years ago, appear frequently in mythology and folklore. Roosters, hens, and eggs appear variously as symbols of fertility, fidelity, maternal devotion, cowardice, caddishness, and foolishness.

Birds as Inspiration

Q: How have birds inspired artists and poets?

A: Birds have long inspired painters, sculptors, and other visual artists. Early humans depicted birds in cave drawings many thousands of years ago. Herons, ducks, doves, and other birds march and fly across the walls of ancient Egyptian tombs and the sides of Greek pottery. Statues of ibises and other birds also exist from ancient times. Inuit peoples carved birds from bone and ivory. Chinese artists painted delicate, lifelike birds on silk and paper. Bibles and other manuscripts crafted by medieval artists feature birds in their pages. Birds also appear in paintings and sculpture in Western art, with the ornithological works by such artists as John James Audubon among the best known.

Right: Birds frequently appear in Asian artwork. In China, the graceful depiction of birds and plants in paintings dates back hundreds of years.

Below: Native American cultures of the Pacific Northwest have long erected monumental sculptures from great trees. Believed to have been originally carved to recount familiar legends, clan lineages, or notable events, totem poles, such as this Tlingit pole in Ketchikan, Alaska, often depict eagles and ravens.

Birds have also been celebrated in literature. They are frequently used as symbols, drawing on their age-old associations with virtues and vices: wise old owls, innocent doves. Aesop's fables emphasized these roles for birds, and Shakespeare often drew on the power of this imagery in his works.

Poetry in particular abounds with birds. Famous poems that feature them include Shelley's "To a Skylark," Keats's "Ode to a Nightingale," Tennyson's "The Eagle," Frost's "Dust of Snow," and Poe's "The Raven." Wordsworth and Whitman also devoted lines of verse to birds.

Some of the most beloved literary birds exist in the realm of children's literature. This flock of feathered friends includes Hans Christian Andersen's ugly duckling that transforms into a swan; Beatrix Potter's hapless duck in *Jemima Puddle-Duck*; the performing seabirds in Richard Atwater's *Mr. Popper's Penguins*; the mallards of Robert McCloskey's *Make*

Way for Ducklings; Roger Duvoisin's Petunia the goose; the duckling in Marjorie Flack's *The Story about Ping*; and Mo Willem's feisty character, Pigeon.

Q: How have birds inspired musicians and dancers?

A: The warbling of songbirds and the acrobatic mating displays of cranes and other birds are echoed in the music and dance of many cultures.

The birds most often emulated in human dancing are those that engage in vigorous courtship displays. In North America, legend has it that Coyote gave the prairie-chicken the ability to dance, and the bird's motions subsequently inspired the prairie-chicken dance of various Plains Indians. Blackfeet Indians were similarly inspired by the sage grouse. Farther north, Inuit peoples invoked the ruffed grouse in their dances. The ruff likewise served as inspiration in Siberia, the black grouse and capercaillie in parts of Europe. Cocks-of-the-rock take over this role in neotropical regions, as do birds-of-paradise in New Guinea. Aboriginal men in Australia emulated the dancing of brolga cranes.

Other birds that have inspired native dances include eagles, owls, and night-hawks in North America, hummingbirds and turkeys in Central America, emus in Australia, and cranes in Siberia.

Tchaikovsky's ballet *Swan Lake* draws on many sources, including ancient legends about women who turn into swans and then back into humans. Swan-maidens appear in stories of many cultures including those of the Middle East, Russia, Germany, and Ireland.

Western music associated with birds include Ravel's *"Le paon"* ("The Peacock") in *Histoires Naturelles*; "The Swan," as well as pieces about hens and roosters, the cuckoo, and an aviary, in Camille Saint-Saens's *Carnival of the Animals*; Prokofiev's *Peter and the Wolf*, featuring a songbird and a duck; Stravinsky's *Nightingale*; Vaughan Williams's *The Lark Ascending*; Zoltán Kodály's *Peacock Variations*, based on a Hungarian folk song; Tchaikovsky's ballet *Swan Lake*; and Mozart's *The Magic Flute*. Mozart, it is believed by some, had a pet starling that whistled part of a movement from his Piano Concerto in G Major and may have even inspired its initial creation. French composer Olivier Messiaen was a serious student of birdsong and even wrote music for the flute that was based on the song of a blackbird. Birds also resonate in popular and folk music.

> **"No bird soars too high if he soars with his own wings."**
> —*WILLIAM BLAKE*

Domesticated Birds

Q: **When were birds first domesticated for use as food?**

A: The rock dove—the familiar pigeon of parks and cities—was one of the first bird species to be domesticated. The ancient Greeks, Romans, and Egyptians all kept domestic pigeons or built artificial clifflike structures for them to nest in so that the young could be harvested for food.

The pigeon's domestication may have coincided with that of the Asian red junglefowl, the ancestor of today's chicken. Domestic fowl were kept in India at least 5,200 years ago. The ancient Egyptians tended chickens, too, and the ancient Chinese even incubated chicken eggs artificially. Selective breeding has produced a stunning variety of modern chickens.

Greylag geese were domesticated across their Eurasian range at least 4,000 years ago. Again, selective breeding produced different varieties. The ancient Greeks cultivated at least nine breeds, and the ancient Romans favored white geese, including the legendary Capitoline geese that saved Rome from invasion of the Gauls. Several hundred years later, the mallard joined the ranks of the domesticated, most likely in China. Meanwhile, turkeys and Muscovy ducks were being raised in Mexico and other parts of Central America.

Other domesticated species used for food include helmeted guinea fowl, which were bred by the ancient Greeks, and pheasants, domesticated in China at least 2,000 years ago. Peafowl were also domesticated in India and exported to the ancient world, mainly for feathers but also as food. Mute swans were domesticated in England about 1,100 years ago. Today, large birds such as ostriches are farmed for their meat, hides, and feathers.

Domestic ducks include the Muscovy duck, shown here, and the white Peking duck. Muscovy ducks were first domesticated in South America by Indian peoples. The white Peking duck descends from mallards domesticated in ancient China.

Q: **What birds have been domesticated primarily as cage birds?**

A: Most small bird species with pretty plumage or pleasant songs have been caught and caged at some point in history. Some went on to be domesticated and bred as cage birds.

Historical evidence shows that at least 2,500 years ago, starlings, sparrows, nightingales, and magpies were kept as pets in ancient China and India and throughout the Middle East. Asian parrots were kept as pets in India and reached Greece and Egypt by about the third century BCE. By medieval times, parrots were chattering away throughout Europe. They were

cormorant are taken from it, but it is fed tidbits or allowed to catch and keep some fish for itself. In Japan, cormorants are caught for this purpose. In China, fishers typically buy their birds from breeders.

Using raptors to hunt is an older and more widespread technique. The ancient Chinese and Persians practiced falconry about 3,700 years ago. The sport later spread throughout Europe. Goshawks, sparrowhawks, and peregrine falcons are among the birds used by falconers. Depending on the species, the birds capture rabbits, hares, pheasants, and flying birds. Domestically bred birds are increasingly in use as prey for these raptors, although wild birds are allowed to be taken according to strict regulations in some countries.

joined by neotropical parrots, long kept as pets by rain forest peoples, after European explorers arrived in the Americas. Canaries, most likely first domesticated by native peoples, became popular after Spanish explorers encountered them in the late 1400s. Budgerigars joined the cage-bird ranks in Europe in 1840.

Q: How have birds been used as hunting animals?

A: Cormorants were used to catch fish in Japan about 1,500 years ago and for nearly as long ago in China. The practice continues on a small scale in a few places. A fishing cormorant wears a ring or band around its neck to prevent it from swallowing its catch. It is often leashed to the boat by one foot. Fish caught by the

Budgerigars are the world's most popular pet birds. Their ancestors are the wild, green-and-yellow budgerigars of Australia's grasslands. Domestic "budgies" have been selectively bred to produce colors such as blue and white.

Falconers, who call their birds "hawks" regardless of species, use raptors to pursue pheasants, hares, and other game. The hood is used to keep a bird calm or shield it from spotting prey while not hunting.

Birds as Resources

Deposits of guano, the accumulated excrement of animals, including bats, seals, and a variety of seabirds, are harvested to use as fertilizer. Guanay cormorants are even named for their famous by-product.

Q: In what ways have humans used birds as food?

A: When it comes to birds, the human menu has included everything from tiny larks' tongues to the haunches of giant elephantbirds and moas.

Today, domestic birds supply much of the meat and eggs eaten by humans. But wild birds of all kinds were consumed in times past and continue to be hunted in parts of the world today. Seabirds in particular have been heavily preyed upon by humans because they nest in colonies, offering abundant eggs and chicks as well as adults all in one place. As humans spread around the globe by sea, they took a heavy toll on seabirds and other island-dwelling birds. The great auk died out, as did the dodo. Although hunting is regulated in many nations today, wild birds and their eggs and young are still subject to over-hunting in parts of the world.

In many cases, regulated harvesting of wild birds and eggs—and, in the case of edible-nest swiftlets, nests—has successfully enabled local people to meet their needs without harming bird populations. The managing of wild areas to support healthy populations of waterfowl and game birds, such as pheasants and grouse, has also benefited other wildlife.

Q: What is guano?

A: Guano is the excrement of certain birds, primarily seabirds, that is rich in phosphate and nitrate and highly sought after for use as fertilizer. Bat and seal guano is also valued for this purpose, but it contains less of these substances than bird guano does.

In dry parts of the world on coasts where seabirds abound, guano carpets their nesting grounds. In the past, these layers of guano could be measured in tens and even hundreds of feet. The most famous source of guano lies off Peru's coast, where millions of seabirds gather on

In the wild, the golden pheasant lives in mountainous woodlands in China. Its beautiful plumage makes it one of the most popular ornamental birds bred in captivity.

islands to breed. This area's "guano birds" include brown pelicans, Guanay cormorants, and Peruvian boobies. Other Pacific islands as well as regions along the coasts of Africa and Arabia yield guano, too.

The mining of old guano deposits threatened birds on some islands, as its removal destroyed habitat. Currently, the biggest threat to guano birds and the industry they make possible is overfishing. Guano birds settle in Peruvian waters because this area experiences upwellings of nutrients, which feed schools of their primary prey, anchovies. A combination of heavy fishing by humans and fluctuations caused by natural climate changes have caused the birds' populations to drop.

Q: How else do humans exploit birds?

A: Birds have been hunted not only for their meat but also for their fat. In the neotropics, cave-dwelling oilbirds feed their young copious amounts of fruit, and the fat nestlings have been collected by native peoples to use as fuel. Penguins and the now-extinct great auk have likewise been used as fuel sources. The hides of some birds, such as ostriches, are used as leather. Native peoples in Arctic lands have long used waterfowl skins to make blankets and coats. In times past, people examined birds' bones to predict the weather and divine the future.

But it is feathers, a bird's crowning glory, that have long been coveted by humans. From New Guinea to Polynesia, from the South American rain forest to the streets of Victorian London, people have adorned themselves with plumes. Surprisingly, one of the most sumptuous feathery garments—the feather cloaks of Hawaiian chiefs—were created while treating some species as renewable resources: A few feathers were plucked from each bird, which was then released.

Less beautiful but undeniably warmer, the down of birds has also been collected for stuffing comforters, beds, pillows, and parkas. Today, domestic birds supply most of the down, and the collection of wild birds' down from nests is strictly controlled.

The greater rhea, a flightless bird of the South American pampas, has long been hunted for food. Rheas are also raised in captivity for their meat, hides, feathers, and eggs.

Bird Conservation

Q: What birds have become extinct as a result of hunting?

A: More than 150 species and subspecies of birds have gone extinct in the past 400 years. Some of these species were wiped out by hunting. One of the best-known extinct birds gave rise to the phrase "dead as a dodo." The dodo was a large, flightless bird that lived on the island of Mauritius. Sailors on long journeys stopped by to kill the birds for food; by the late seventeenth century the dodo was extinct. The same fate claimed the great auk, which once lived along the Newfoundland coast.

Native peoples are believed to have hunted the moa of New Zealand and the elephantbird of Madagascar to extinction when they colonized these islands. Likewise, European settlers in North America aimed their guns at vast flocks of passenger pigeons that contained millions of birds. Relentless hunting of the birds for the market and the table was one of several factors that led to the species' extinction in the wild by 1900. The last captive pigeon died in 1914. Once the passenger pigeons declined, gunners turned their sights on the Eskimo curlew.

This bird still teeters on the edge of extinction, if it is not already gone. Since one was shot on Barbados in 1963, no live specimen has been sighted. In the late 1800s, the plume trade came close to wiping out species of herons and egrets. Today, seabirds nesting colonially on remote islands are still menaced by unregulated hunting.

Q: What are the biggest threats facing birds today?

A: Pollution, pesticides, the pet trade, and market hunting have all taken their toll on birds. In modern times, however, habitat loss and degradation as well as the introduction of invasive species pose the biggest threats to birds.

Agriculture and development have claimed large areas of habitat. In North America, most of the eastern forests have been cut down; prairies have been converted to cropland; wetlands have been filled; and western grasslands have been damaged by ranching. Of the habitat that remains, much is fragmented —broken up into sections that are as remote from each other as scattered islands. These smaller habitats may not be large enough to sustain a breeding population of birds. Fragmented forests, for example, are too small to contain a "deep forest" area that is largely off-limits to nest predators, such as raccoons, and brood parasites,

Right: The fragmentation of forest habitat by cutting allows the brown-headed cowbird, a brood parasite, to lay its eggs in the nests of birds accustomed to the protection of deep forest. Among its many hosts are endangered species.

Below: The great auk was a large, flightless seabird that bred on islands near Iceland, Greenland, and eastern Canada. Vast numbers were killed for food and fish bait by early European explorers; later, they were slaughtered for their feathers. The last pair died in 1844.

such as cowbirds. As a result, these animals have easy access to the nests of songbirds. Many songbirds face habitat destruction at the other end of their migratory journeys, too. Rain forests continue to be felled at astonishing rates, partly for lumber and partly to create more ranch land. Coffee plantations, which once featured shade-loving coffee plants and supported many birds, are rapidly being replaced by plantations filled with sun-loving shrubs that must be intensively cultivated with pesticides and fertilizer.

People have also introduced nonnative species into many habitats. Snakes, rats, mongooses, and cats introduced onto oceanic islands have killed native birds, while feral goats and pigs have ruined habitat. The Hawaiian Islands, for example, have lost nearly a third of their native birds due to invasive species, including disease carried by introduced mosquitoes. In North America, introduced European starlings compete with native birds for nesting sites, and roaming house cats kill millions of birds each year.

Q: What efforts are being made to protect birds and their habitats?

A: Bird conservation is a many-pronged effort. National and international legislation—to control hunting, regulate the pet trade, and protect migration routes and stopovers—has helped to create awareness of the threats to birds and begin the process of mitigating them. Removing introduced species that harm native birds and habitat, and preventing

their arrival, is also being attempted. Key to the survival of many endangered species, however, is habitat protection and the creation of wildlife corridors: swaths of habitat that link the existing fragments of a former contiguous habitat.

Some endangered species, such as the whooping crane and the California condor, are being raised in captivity and released in order to resurrect them in the wild. A similar effort in the 1970s helped save the peregrine falcon after it had nearly disappeared from much of its North American range because of the effects of pesticides.

A combination of a slow maturation rate, habitat loss, shooting by hunters, and poisoning brought the California condor to the brink of extinction by 1987, when only a few zoo specimens remained. Captive breeding and releases are currently underway in an attempt to return this species to the wild.

Glossary

ALTRICIAL. A term that describes baby birds that are helpless and highly dependent on a parent or parents after hatching.

ANTARCTIC. Portion of the earth located below the Antarctic Circle that includes Antarctica, the South Pole, and surrounding ocean waters.

ARCTIC. Portion of the earth located above the Arctic Circle that includes the North Pole and surrounding ocean waters.

BOREAL FOREST. The coniferous forest that encircles much of the earth in northern regions in between the treeless tundra and deciduous forests farther south.

BROOD. A family of nestlings that hatched from the same clutch of eggs.

BROOD PARASITE. A bird, such as the common cuckoo or brown-headed cowbird, that lays its eggs in other birds' nests and leaves them to be incubated by the hosts, which also raise the young that hatch.

BROOD PATCH. A patch of skin rich in blood vessels on a bird's belly that is bared by molting or plucking and is used to keep eggs warm; also called an incubation patch.

CALL. A short, simple sound used by a bird to convey information or make contact with another bird and is not a song.

CAVITY NESTING. Using holes, such as tree holes, as nest sites.

CLUTCH. A group of eggs that constitute a single nesting endeavor (some birds lay more than one clutch per breeding season).

COLONY. A group of birds of the same species nesting closely together in the same place.

COOPERATIVE BREEDING. A breeding system in which helper birds assist in raising young that are not their own.

COURTSHIP. Behavior in which birds attract mates and indicate acceptance of mates via ritualistic displays, interactions, and vocal communications.

CRÈCHE. A group of fledglings of the same species from different nests in a colony that cluster together for warmth and protection.

CROP. A part of the esophagus that is used to store food in order to carry it and, in some birds, to begin the process of digestion.

CROP MILK. A thick liquid produced in a portion of the digestive tract in a few species that is used to nourish young.

DOWN. Fluffy feathers close to the skin that insulate a bird.

EXTRAPAIR COPULATION. Mating by a male or female bird outside of its pair bond.

FLEDGLING. A young bird that is ready to leave the nest.

GIZZARD. A portion of a bird's stomach that in some species is very muscular and tough and used to process difficult foods, such as seeds.

GUANO. Deposits of fecal droppings that have built up over time. Seabird guano is commonly mined for use as fertilizer.

HABITAT. The type of environment in which a species lives, e.g. a desert or a rain forest.

INCUBATION. The process of keeping eggs warm and cared for until they hatch, typically by crouching on them.

IRRUPTION. An irregular migration of a species into areas where it is not normally seen in response to weather conditions or a lack of prey in the species' usual range.

LEK. A group of males displaying to attract females on a communal patch of ground, which is often called a lekking ground.

MIGRATION. The seasonal movement of a species from one area to another.

MOLTING. Shedding feathers in order to grow new plumage.

NEOTROPICS. Tropical areas of Central and South America and islands in their tropical waters.

NEST. A place or structure used as a site for laying eggs.

NICHE. The ecological role filled by a species in its habitat.

OSCINES. Perching birds that are true songbirds.

PERCHING BIRD. A bird that is of a species in the order Passeriformes, also called a passerine.

POLYANDRY. A mating system in which a female has more than one mate.

POLYGAMY. A mating system in which a bird has more than one mate.

POLYGYNY. A mating system in which a male has more than one mate.

POPULATION. A group of birds of the same species that all live in a particular area.

PRECOCIAL. A term that describes a highly developed baby bird that is capable of walking, running, and, in some species,

swimming shortly after hatching and can partly or completely feed itself.

PREDATOR. An animal that hunts and feeds upon other animals.

PREENING. The grooming of feathers.

RAPTOR. A bird that catches its prey with its feet; also known as a bird of prey.

SCAVENGER. An animal that eats the remains of dead animals.

SEABIRD. A bird that frequents open ocean waters.

SHOREBIRD. A bird that feeds by probing with its bill, typically on shorelines but also in grasslands, fields, and meadows.

SONG. A vocalization produced typically by male birds that is used in attracting mates and defending territory.

SONGBIRD. A perching bird with a syrinx that is capable of producing a complex song.

SPECIES. A type of animal that shares particular traits with others of its kind and can mate with them to produce viable young.

SUBOSCINES. Perching birds that are not songbirds.

SYRINX. A bird's "voice box."

TROPICS. The region along the equator that is bordered by the Tropic of Cancer and Tropic of Capricorn.

WATERFOWL. A goose, swan, or duck.

Further Reading

Books

Brooke, Michael, and Tim Birkhead. *The Cambridge Encyclopedia of Ornithology*. Cambridge, England: Cambridge University Press, 1991.

Cramp, Stanley, and others, eds. *Handbook of the Birds of Europe, the Middle East and North Africa*. Oxford: Oxford University Press, 1979.

Elphick, Jonathan, ed. *The Atlas of Bird Migration*. New York: Random House, 1995.

Handbook of the Birds of the World (multivolume series) Barcelona: Lynx Edicions, 1992 (vol. 1)–ongoing.

Kroodsma, Donald. *The Singing Life of Birds*. Boston: Houghton Mifflin Company, 2005.

Podulka, Sandy, Ronald W. Rohrbaugh, Jr., and Rick Bonney, eds. *Handbook of Bird Biology*. Ithaca, NY: Cornell Lab of Ornithology, 2004.

Sibley, David Allen. *The Sibley Guide to Bird Life and Behavior*. New York: Alfred A. Knopf, 2001.

————. *The Sibley Guide to Birds*. New York: Alfred A. Knopf, 2000.

Stap, Don. *Birdsong: A Natural History*. New York: Scribner, 2005.

Terres, John K. *The Audubon Society Encyclopedia of North American Birds*. New York: Alfred A. Knopf, 1980.

Weidensaul, Scott. *Living on the Wind: Across the Hemisphere with Migratory Birds*. New York: North Point Press, 1999.

Magazines

The Auk (published quarterly by the American Ornithologists' Union), www.aou.org

Birder's World, www.birdersworld.com

Birding, www.americanbirding.org

Bird Watcher's Digest, www.birdwatchersdigest.com

Bird Watching, www.birdwatching.co.uk

Living Bird, www.birds.cornell.edu

WildBird Magazine, www.wildbirdmagazine.com

Organizations
African Bird Club, www.africanbirdclub.org

American Birding Association, www.americanbirding.org

The American Ornithologists' Union, www.aou.org

Bird Life International, www.birdlife.org

Cornell Lab of Ornithology, www.birds.cornell.edu

National Audubon Society, www.audubon.org

Neotropical Bird Club, www.neotropicalbirdclub.org

Oriental Bird Club, www.orientalbirdclub.org

Pacific Seabird Group, www.pacificseabirdgroup.org

Royal Society for the Protection of Birds, www.rspb.org.uk

Web sites
Birding on the Net, www.birdingonthe.net
Information, news updates, and bird-related links.

The Birds of North America Online, www.bna.birds.cornell.edu/BNA
In-depth profiles of North American birds.

www.birder.com, World checklists, links, and products
related to birding.

International Bird Collection, www.hbw.com/ibc
Photographs, videos, and information about birds worldwide.

www.ornithology.com, Information about birds and bird-related links.

At the Smithsonian

The Smithsonian Institution is a cornucopia of information and other resources for bird enthusiasts of all sorts—from backyard birders to the world's leading ornithologists.

Research projects focusing on birds are conducted and supported by the Smithsonian Institution itself. These projects include the study of avian biodiversity, conservation, systematics (phylogentic relationships), paleontology (fossils), evolution, ecology, behavior, reproduction, genetics, veterinary medicine, epidemiology, and the like. Current research projects include studies of the effect of climate change on bird populations; research into population declines among rusty blackbirds in North America; and tracking the spread of West Nile Virus along eastern seaboard of the United States and in the Caribbean.

The National Museum of Natural History is a rich resource for bird enthusiasts. The Division of Birds houses one of the world's largest collection of bird specimens.

In aiding scientists in their work, the Smithsonian Institution provides the third largest collection of bird specimens in the world. This stunning collection is maintained by the Division of Birds of the National Museum of Natural History (www.nmnh. si.edu/vert/birds/birds.html). It includes more than 600,000 specimens, ranging from skins and feathers to skeletons and organs as well as eggs and nests. The Division of Birds is also home to nearly 4,000 specimens, called type specimens, that have been used to arrive at the official description of avian species.

Live birds can also be viewed at Smithsonian Institution facilities. The National Zoo is home to an impressive collection of birds from around the world. Tropical species flutter and call in the Indoor Flight Room, a jungle habitat within the zoo's Bird House. This exhibit also offers a resource center where visitors can examine bones, feathers, and other artifacts. Outdoors, cranes stride majestically in the Crane Line exhibit, while other large species stalk the South American Run. Birds are also featured in the zoo's Amazonia exhibit, among others. Wild birds frequent the outdoor wetland exhibit and the zoo grounds.

Watching young animals learning to adjust to their new environment and interacting with their mothers can be a life-affirming experience for zoo visitors. Located outside of the National Zoo's Bird House, the Crane Line features long-legged wading birds. Shown here are a white-naped crane and her curious chick.

The brilliant-colored and slender-billed scarlet ibis is one of the denizens of the National Zoo's Amazonia exhibit, which recreates a tropical rain forest environment. Here visitors can catch a glimpse of Amazon River Basin natives such as the giant arapaima, piranhas, scarlet macaws, two-toed sloths, titi monkeys, and dart-poison frogs.

Among the zoo's breeding successes are North Island brown kiwis, which rarely hatch outside of their native New Zealand. The National Zoo became the first institution outside of New Zealand ever to hatch a kiwi in 1975. The zoo also maintains birds at its Conservation and Research Center in Front Royal, Virginia.

Zoo birds can also be viewed via WebCam by visiting the zoo's Web site (nationalzoo.si.edu). This site is also a portal to the Migratory Bird Center (nationalzoo.si.edu/ ConservationAndScience/MigratoryBirds), which conducts research on migratory birds and provides information to educators. The center is also involved in the promotion of shade-grown coffee through its Bird Friendly® coffee program, which helps protect vital habitat for migratory birds.

Bird-related items can also be found in many of the Smithsonian's art and history museums. The American Art Museum houses paintings, sculptures, and photographs that include birds; several works by Audubon are held within its collection. Images of birds from other cultures also abound, ranging from copper birds in the National Museum of African Art to the graceful birds painted by Chinese artists on silk in the Freer and Sackler Galleries.

For those too far away to drop in for a visit, the Smithsonian Institution's main Web site (www.si.edu) provides links to a multitude of bird-related items in its vast collection. Articles about birds are also available at www.smithsonianmag.com.

A Peacock by Mori Sosen. The Smithsonian's Freer and Sackler Galleries house an extensive repository of Asian art. Birds as subjects provide some of the collections' most spectacular pieces, such as this late-eighteenth-century hanging silk scroll featuring a peacock.

Index

Acknowledgments & Picture Credits

The author offers thanks to Bob Budliger for sharing his knowledge and experience and to Lisa Purcell and Aaron Murray for their thoughtful editorial guidance and expertise.

The author and publisher also offer thanks to those closely involved in the creation of this volume: Marcy Heacker, National Museum of Natural History; consultant Robert Budliger; Ellen Nanney, Senior Brand Manager, and Katie Mann, with Smithsonian Business Ventures; Collins Reference executive editor Donna Sanzone, editor Lisa Hacken, and editorial assistant Stephanie Meyers; Hydra Publishing president Sean Moore, publishing director Karen Prince, senior editor Lisa Purcell, editorial director Aaron Murray, art director Edwin Kuo, designers Rachel Maloney, Greg Lum, Shamona Stokes, Mariel Morris, La Tricia Watford, Gus Yoo, Erika Lubowicki, Brian MacMullen, editors Marcel Brousseau, Emily Beekman, Suzanne Lander, Franchesca Ho Sang, Brad Plummer, Kristin Maffei, copyeditor Glenn Novak, picture researcher Ben DeWalt, production manager Sarah Reilly, production director Wayne Ellis, and indexer Jessie Shiers; Joan Mathys of MJM Picture and Film Research.

PICTURE CREDITS

The following abbreviations are used: JI—© 2006 Jupiterimages Corporation; PR—Photo Researchers, Inc.; SPL—Science Photo Library; SI—Smithsonian Institute; SIL— Smithsonian Institution Libraries; iSP—©iStockphoto.com; SS—ShutterStock; IO—Index Open; BS—Big Stock Photo; USFWS—U.S. Fish and Wildlife Service; LoC—Library of Congress; VIREO—Visual Resources for Ornithology

(t=top; b=bottom; l=left; r=right; c=center)

The Wonder and Diversity of Birds
IIIcl JI **III**cr PR/Anthony Mercieca **IV**tr SI **IV**br ©2006 Stockbyte **IV-V**background JI **V**tr PR/Cary Meszaros **V**br iSP/Chad Reischl **VI** JI **1**br iSP/Martin Kawalski **2**bl iSP/Jeremy Edwards **2**tr iSP/Gert Very **3**br SS/Ruta Saulyte-Laurinaviciene

Chapter 1: The Bird's Body
4 IO/photos.com Select **5**background The Complete Encyclopedia of Illustration **5**cr ©Doug Wechsler/VIREO **6**bl SPL/Eye of Science **7**tr iSP/Chad Reishl **7**bl Hylas Publishing **8**bc Illustration by Hylas Publishing/Data Source: John Kimball **9**tc FWS/Gary Kramer **10** ©K. Schafer/VIREO **11**tl FWS/Gary M. Stolz **11**br iSP/Geoff Whiting **12**bl ©S. Bahrt/VIREO **13**cr FWS/Gary Kramer **14**bl FWS/Beth Jackson **15**cl ©I. Visser/VIREO **15**br iSP/Tony Campbell **16**bl FWS/Gary Kramer **16**tr JI **17**tl IO/Ralph Reinhold **17**br FWS/John Foster **18**bc JI **19**tl JI **19**br JI **20**lc iSP/Peter Llewellyn **21**c iSP/Joe Stone **21**tr iSP/Paul Wolfe

Chapter 2: Feathers: Form and Function
22 SI/National Zoological Park/Jessie Cohen **23**cr FWS/Scott Nikon **24**bl Illustration by Hylas Publishing/Data Source: Merry Lea Environmental Learning Center, Goshen College **24**cr PR/Andrew Syred **25**bl FWS **26**bc Hylas Publishing **27**tl iSP/Peter Llewellyn **28**cf iSP/Stefan Ekernas **28**bl JI **29**tr SS/National Zoological Park/Jessie Cohen **30**bl IO/Keith Levit **31**tl FWS/Dave Menke **31**br SI/National Zoological Park/Jessie Cohen **32**br JI **33**tr FWS/Dave Menke **33**cl SI/National Zoological Park/Jessie Cohen **34**bl JI **35**tl SI/National Zoological Park **35**cr IO/Edward Slater

Chapter 3: Birds in Motion
36 SS/Brad Whitsitt **37**cr SS/Fred Kamphues **38**bl PR/Sheila Terry **39**cf PR/Stephen Dalton **39**br JI **40**bl Laurie O'Keefe **40**tr IO/LLC, FogStock **41**c JI **41**br Stephen Dalton **42**br SS/Matthew Gough **43**tl ©K. Schafer/VIREO **43**tr JI **44**bl JI **44**cf JI **45**tr iSP/Steffan Foerster **45**br iSP/Mike Tolstoy **46**bl ©P. Robles Gil/VIREO **46**br ©G. Lasley/VIREO **47**tl LoC **47**tr IO/Hot Ideas **48**bl IO/LLC. Vstock **48**tr SS/Jan Martin Will **49**tr SS/Javier Sanchez **50**cl BS/Maarigard **50**bc iSP/Feng Yu **51**tl ©K. Smith/VIREO **51**bc BS/Vaida

Chapter 4: Finding Food
52 iSP/Rob Sylvan **53**cr PR/Nigel Cattlin **54**bl SS/Kris Mercer **54**tr JI **55**bc SI/National Zoological Park/Jessie Cohen **56**bl SS/EcoPrint **57**tl SS/Kirk Peart **57**bl FWS Dave Menke **58**bl FWS/Dave Menke **59**tl SS/Alan Heartfield **59**br SS/John Arnold **60**bc IO/Charles Canialosi **61**tl JI **61**br IO/LLC, FogStock **62**bl IO/photos.com Select **62**tr IO/LLC, FogStock **63**tc VIREO/B.K. Wheeler **63**br BS/Ffion **64**bl ©T.J. Ulrich/VIREO **64**tr SS/Bruce MacQueen **65**bl JI

Chapter 5: How Birds Communicate
66 PR/Jim Zipp **67**cr National Oceanic & Atomspheric Administration/Mr. Sean Linehan **68**br Illustration by Hylas Publishing/Data Source: Dr. David Swanson, University of South Dakota **69**tl FWS **69**br SS/Jason Kasumovic **70**bl BS/Olivia **70**tr PR/Jim Zipp **71**bl SS/Hazeelin Hassan **72**bl ©J. Schumacher/VIREO **72**tr BS/philw **72**br SS/Eml **73**br PR/Ken Thomas **74**c SS/Bryan Eastham **74**br ©A. Morris/VIREO **75**tl FWS **76**bc PS/Alan Williams **77**tl SS/Rui Vale de Sousa **77**br SS/Diane N. Ennis **78**tl National Oceanic & Atomspheric Administration **78**br PR/Jim Zipp **79**tc SS/Frank B. Yuwono **80**bc FWS/Tim Bowman **80**tr SS/Kwerry **81**br ©Sam Fried/VIREO **81**cl PS/Michael Patrick O'Neill

Chapter 6: Seeking a Mate
82 SS/Andrea Nilsson **83**cr PR/E.R. Degginger **84**bl FWS/Bob Hines **84**c FWS/Steve Maslowski **85**tl JI **85**br FWS/E. Kirdler **86**bc ©J. Sierra/VIREO **86**cr ©Sam Fried/VIREO **87**tr BS/simspix **88**bc SI **88**br ©R. BrownVIREO **89**tl PR/Gregory G. Dimijian **90**bc ©Dr. M. Stubblefield/VIREO **91**tl FWS/S. Maslowski **91**tr iSP/Wayne Stadler **92**bl iSP/James Metcalf **92**br iSP/Phil Sigin-Lavdanski **93**tc JI **94**bl ©A. & J. Binns/VIREO **95**tl FWS/George Lavendowski **95**c JI **96**bl FWS/Donna Dewhurst **96**br Wikipedia **97**br BS/uweo

Ready Reference
Background 92bl SS/Bob Ainsworth **98**br SS/Christopher Hall **99**tl SS/Ralf Juergen Kraft **99**bl BS/Definitivelabs **99**br SS/John Kirinic **100**t SS/N. Joy Neish **100**bl SS/Thomas Mounsey **100**br SS/J_S **101**tr SS/Tony Campbell **101**b SS/Silense **102**tr SS/Andrey Zyk **102**bl JI **102**br BS/TopShots **103**t USFWS/P.W. Sykes **103**b SS/Uwe Ohse **104**tr BS/Impala Stock **104**bl USFWS/Dean Kildaw/Alaska Maritime **105**tl USFWS/Lee Karney **105**br SS/Shakif Hussain **106**tl Beloit College **106**r SIL **106**bl SIL/Dibner Portrait Library **107**tl LoC **107**b LoC **108**l SS/Pam Burley **108**r SS/Joe Gough **109**tl JI **109**tr SS/Wendy Sue Gilman **109**bl JI **110**l JI **110**c ©B.K. Wheeler/VIREO **110**tr ©R.L. Pitman/VIREO **111**tr W. Mark King **111**bl ©A. Morris/VIREO **111**br ©R. Behrstock/VIREO

Chapter 7: Nest Making
112© Ingrid N. Visser/VIREO **113** SS/Carlos Gi **114**bl SIL **114**tr JI **115** SS/SF Photography **116**bl JI **116**tr PR/Sheila Terry **117** SS/David Kay **118** IO/LLC, FogStock **119**t BS/Chuew **119**b SS/Loy **120**bl SIL **120**tr SS/Lushnikova Olga Anatol'evna **121**©Sam Fried/VIREO **122** ©T. Laman/VIREO **123**tl ©R. & N. Bowers/VIREO **123**tr JI **123**br SS/Alexey Lebedinsky **124**t BS/Mbgadon **124**b ©Doug Wechsler/VIREO **125**tl SIL **125**br JI **126** JI **127**t ©R. & N. Bowers/VIREO **127**b BS/Joe32780

Chapter 8: Raising Young
128 PR/Art Wolfe **129** SS/Lee Torrens **130** Illustration by Hylas Publishing/Data Source: ©The Open Door Web Site **131** NOAA **132**tr Public Domain **132**bl *Birds of the British Isles*, by Henry Seebohm, 1896 **133** SS/Stuart Elfett **134**tr SS/Rebecca Picard **134**bl Powder Mill Nature Reserve **135** SS/Gary Unwin **136**tr SS/Jack Scrivener **136**bl SS/WizData, Inc. **137**t SS/Ursula **137**b PR/Millard H. Sharp **138**t SS/Loong Kok Wei **138**b BS/WizData **139**l PR/Helen Williams **139**r PR/Kenneth H. Highfill **140**l PR/Art Wolfe **140**r SS/Sharyn Young **141**t ©E. Endrigo/VIREO **141**b ©R. Brown/VIREO **142** SS/Luis Cesar Tejo **143**t PR/Roger Wilmshurst **143**b USFWS

Chapter 9: The Marvel of Migration
144 JI **145**cr IO/LLC, FogStock **146**bc SS/Brad Thompson **146**tr SS/Hway Kiong Lim **147**br ©R. Tipper/VIREO **148**bc SS/Hans F. Meier **149**tl iSP/Mark Hammon **149**br iSP/Bryan Eastham **150**bl FWS **151**tc SS/LLC, FogStock **151**bl FWS **152**tr SS/Lori Skelon **152**bc SS/Andrew F. Kamierski **153**tr SS/Emily H. Locklear **154**cl IO/LLC, FogStock **155**tl IO/photolibrary.com pty. Ltd. **155**br IO/Amy and Chuck Wiley/Wales **156**br SS/Lori Martin **157**tc ©G. Armistead/VIREO **157**bc SS/Matthew Apps **158**bl JI **158**tr SS/Muriel Lasure **159**bl SS/Luis Cesar Tejo **159**tc BS/Paul Edwards **160**tl JI **160**tr ©R. & N. Bowers/VIREO **160**bc ©R. Shantz/VIREO **161**tr SS/Richard C. Bennett

Chapter 10: Habitats: Where Birds Live
162 JI **163** JI **164** SS/James Doss **165**t iSP/Steve McWilliam **165**c BS/Zastavkin **165**b SS/Zastavkin **166**t SS/Gary Saliba **166**r SS/Tijmen **167** SS/Barbara Brands **168** USFWS/Gary Zahm **169**t BS/Ozflash **169**b ©R. Nussbaumer/VIREO **170**t JI **170**b SS/Joanne and Daniel **171**t SS/Willem Bosman **171**b SS/Fred Sgrosso **172**tr ©D. Tipling/VIREO **172**b SS/Neil Porter **173**t BS/Gfadel **173**b JI **174**bl JI **174**r JI **175** SS/Clara Natoli **176** ©H. & J. Eriksen/VIREO **177**t SS/Ferenc Cegledi **177**b SS/Sherrianne Talon

Chapter 11: The Ecology of Birds
178 ©R. Crossley/VIREO **179** USFWS/Gary Zahm **180**t BS/Sarent **180**b SS/Tony Campbell **181**t Alamy/Steve Austin **181**b iSP/Peter Llewellyn **182**l ©R. Crossley/VIREO **182**r SS/AJT **183** USFWS/Donna Dewhurst **184**l ©A. Morris/VIREO **184**r USFWS/Jane M. Rohling **185** JI **186** USFWS/Steve Maslowski **187**t SS/Jan Erasmus **187**b SS/Ferenc Cegledi **188** iSP/Nigel Ormond **189**t SS/Cheryl Paquin **189**b iSP/WinterWitch **190**l BS/Mark Hargrove **190**r iSP/Jason Cheever **191**l JI **191**r ©R. Behrstock/VIREO

Chapter 12: Birds and People
192 SPL/George Bernard **193**cr ©W. Tarboton/VIREO **194**tr SS/Vladimir Pomortzeff **195**tr JI **195**br SS/Raymond Neil **196**bl iSP/Michael Braun **196**tr iSP/Jin Young Lee **197**tr iSP/Jon Patton **198**bl iSP/Andrew Littledale **199**tl SS/Peder Digre **199**br SS/Leon Forado **200**bl BS/bprawl **200**tr BS/N Joy Neish **201**br SS/Grigory Kubatyan **202**bl SPL/George Bernard **202**cr iSP **203**br FWS

At the Smithsonian
208 Smithsonian Photographic Services/Dane A. Penland [80-12932] **209** SI/National Zoological Park/Josie Lohn **210** SI/National Zoological Park/Josie Lohn **211** Freer Gallery of Art and Arthur M. Sackler Gallery/SI